Writers and Politics in Modern Britain, France, and Germany

Writers and Politics in Modern Britain, France, and Germany

J. E. Flower
J. A. Morris
C. E. Williams

Holmes & Meier Publishers, Inc.
New York and London

First published in the United States of America
1977 by

Holmes & Meier Publishers, Inc.
101 Fifth Avenue
New York, New York 10003

LIBRARY OF CONGRESS CATALOGING IN
PUBLICATION DATA
PRINTED IN GREAT BRITAIN
Flower, John Ernest.
    Writers and politics in modern Britain, France,
and Germany.
    Bibliography. p.
    1. Politics and literature. 2. English litera-
ture—20th century—History and criticism.
3. French literature—20th century—History
and criticism. 4. German literature—20th century—History and criticism.
I. Morris, J. A., joint author. II. Williams,
Cedric E., joint author. III. Title.

PN51.F55   809'.933'1   77-7595
ISBN 0-8419-0320-4

Publisher's Note

This volume contains three essays reprinted from a
series of pamphlets on modern political literature. The
Table of Contents for each essay will be found
immediately preceding the essay. The pages of each essay
are numbered separately.

WRITERS AND POLITICS
IN MODERN BRITAIN

Foreword

The term 'political literature' like 'committed literature' with which it is frequently associated has become an accepted part of the language of literary history. Yet however convenient, it is, on examination, surprisingly imprecise and misleading. The whole area of the interaction between politics and literature is a vast and complex one which has yet, especially on a European scale, to be fully and comprehensively charted. Certainly invaluable contributions do already exist: Jean-Paul Sartre's *Qu'est-ce que la littérature?* (1947), George Woodcock's *The Writer and Politics* (1948), Jürgen Rühle's *Literatur und Revolution* (1960), Irving Howe's *Politics and the Novel* (1961), John Mander's *The Writer and Commitment* (1961) for example. There are, too, as the bibliographical information contained in the individual essays in this series will reveal, a number of equally important books which deal with the issue in purely national terms. With few exceptions, however, these, like many of the more general studies, suffer from the same defects resulting in the main from a failure to distinguish adequately between 'political literature' and what might be termed 'social literature', and from an incomplete assessment of changes both in political climates and in the writer's relationship to society as a whole. Yet, even when the area of investigation and terminology has been more carefully ascertained, we often find that these books are principally concerned either with an examination of the political ideas *per se* contained in various works of literature, or with an assessment of the ways in which parties and movements have controlled and used to best advantage writers and intellectuals who claim political allegiance. More recently Roland Barthes in *Le Degré Zéro de l'écriture* (1967), George Steiner in *Language and Silence* (1967) and David Caute in *Illusion* (1971) have suggested a wider perspective, outlining some of the problems of style and form which an imaginative writer has to face when he offers his pen to a political (or social) cause. On the whole, however, it is fair to say that the majority of critics have concentrated more on *what* ideas are expressed than on *how* they have been. In addition therefore to attempting to define the concept of political literature more precisely and to exploring such issues as the suitability of imaginative literature as a vehicle for political ideas or the effect such literature

v

can have on the public for example, one of the principal concerns of these essays is to attempt to examine ways in which an author's political sympathy or affiliation can be seen to affect or even dictate the way in which he writes. In some countries—in Russia, France or Spain, for example—direct influence of this kind is more apparent than in others. Elsewhere, notably in Britain, where political directives concerning art and literature have not been the rule, the problem is in some ways more difficult to assess. Indeed national variation of this kind is one of the principal contributory factors to the complex nature of the whole question. Thus while the subject is best illustrated and examined in the literature of France and Germany during the interwar years, it is after the Second World War that it fully emerges in the works of Italian and Scandinavian writers. Furthermore literary experiment seen and approved in some countries as an expression of a progressive, even revolutionary, political position is considered in others to be characteristic of subversion and decadence.

Given such problems as these and given too the amount of space available, these seven small volumes can do little more than hope to encourage a new approach to political literature. While free to explore the subject in the way they believe to be most useful within the context of the literary history of their particular countries, contributors have been encouraged to balance general comment with examination of specific examples. Inevitably therefore the essays appear arbitrarily selective. But like the literature which they choose to examine it is hoped that they will be judged not only for what they contain but also for the ways in which they deal with it.

John Flower

General Bibliography

The following are a selection of those books which discuss some of the general problems associated with this subject. Suggestions for further reading are contained in the notes to individual essays.

BARTHES, Roland, *Le Degré Zéro de l'écriture*, Editions du Seuil, Paris, 1953 (Translated: *Writing Degree Zero*, Cape, London, 1967).

CAUTE, David, *Illusion: An Essay on Politics, Theatre and the Novel*, Deutsch, London, 1971.

CROSSMAN, Richard, *The God that Failed: Six Studies in Communism*, Hamish Hamilton, London, 1950.

HOWE, Irving, *Politics and the Novel*, Horizon Press, New York, 1955.

MANDER, John, *The Writer and Commitment*, Secker & Warburg, London, 1961.

MUIR, Edwin, *Essays on Literature and Society*, Hogarth Press, London, 1965.

PANICHAS, George, A. (ed.), *The Politics of Twentieth-Century Novelists*, Crowell, New York, 1974.

RÜHLE, Jürgen, *Literatur und Revolution*, Kiepenheuer & Witsch, 1960 (Translated: *Literature and Revolution*, Pall Mall, London, 1969).

SARTRE, Jean-Paul, *Qu'est-ce que la littérature?* Gallimard, Paris, 1948 (Translated: *What is Literature?* Methuen, London, 1951).

STEINER, George, *Language and Silence: Essays and Notes, 1958–66*, Faber, London, 1967.

TROTSKY, Leon, *Literature and Revolution*, University of Michigan Press, Ann Arbor, 1960.

WINEGARTEN, Renee, *Writers and Revolution: the fatal lure of action*, Franklin Watts, New York, 1974.

WOODCOCK, George, *The Writer and Politics*, The Porcupine Press, London, 1948.

Contents

Introduction

Poetry was born from magic: it grew up with religion:
it lived through the age of reason: is it to die in the century of
propaganda?

C. Day Lewis, *A Hope for Poetry*

1. The Nature of Political Literature

Perhaps it would be a good idea to start with a fundamental question:
are literature and politics incompatible? Do they make an oil-and-water
mixture? When looked at more closely it soon appears that we are really
asking whether literature may have the premise that it should deal with
politics, make political points or even attempt to influence the political
persuasions of the reader. As with religious literature or social literature,
is there not a danger of the writing becoming didactic or propagandist?
Was English poetry of the eighteenth century, for example, over-
affected by the writers' concern with a neo-classical ideal which seemed
to dictate the restrictions and controls found in verse-form, rhythm,
imagery? But literature has to be about *something*—even if it is only
about how to write literature. Surely very little has been written that
is not about society, and if that is true, then such writing is inevitably
close to politics. Indeed it could be argued that politics (or society, or
economics, or whatever), by giving a writer a subject, also give him a
purpose. That is to say that it avoids dangers inherent in the 'art for
art's sake' kind of writing: the preciousness and self-indulgence which
some critics have detected in literature at once aesthetic and esoteric.
(The whole debate both stated and implied in Virginia Woolf's famous
essay, 'Mr Bennett and Mrs Brown' (1924) is relevant here.) Yet would
it not be more sensible to suggest that these two views are not mutually
exclusive? Didactic or satirical literature involving political discussion,
even to the point of revealing or expounding commitment, need not
necessarily exhibit a lesser kind of literary art, as *Gulliver's Travels*,
Absalom and Achitophel or, to use a foreign example, *Fathers and Sons*

3

readily shows. On the other hand there is no reason to suppose that political literature is necessarily of greater purpose or less self-indulgence than any other kind of writing: Nazi Germany would be a landmark in any history of bad art, its 'literature' characterized by the rambling aimlessness and uncontrolled hysteria which Hitler patented in *Mein Kampf*.

Having said the above, we are no closer to being sure what we mean by 'political literature': a term of peculiar difficulty, as I shall be arguing, for the British people and the English language. For there are those who will claim that *all* literature is political, which, if true, would, apart from anything else, instantly invalidate any reason for writing this essay. If we start by assuming that literary writers who deal with politics, in the defined sense of 'affairs of state', are writers of 'political literature', we can also assume that their works will vary as to commitment and purpose just as they will also vary as to form and style. A greater difficulty could arise in telling where political literature ends and social literature begins. A comparison between two quite different works, a play by Galsworthy and a novel by Koestler, will illustrate what I mean:

> HORNBLOWER. I must have those cottages for my workmen. I've got important works, ye know.
> HILLCRIST. (*Getting heated*) The Jackmans have their importance too, sir. Their heart's in that cottage.
> HORNBLOWER. Have a sense of proportion, man. My works supply thousands of people, and *my* heart's in *them*. What's more, they make my fortune. I've got ambitions—I'm a serious man. Suppose I were to consider this and that, and every little potty objection—where should I get to?—nowhere!
> HILLCRIST. All the same, this sort of thing isn't done, you know.
> HORNBLOWER. Not by you because ye've got no need to do it . . .
> (*The Skin Game*, 1920)

> Gletkin looked at Rubashov with his usual expressionless gaze, and asked him, in his usual expressionless voice:
> 'Were you given a watch as a boy?'
> Rubashov looked at him in astonishment. The most conspicuous trait of the Neanderthal character was its absolute humourlessness or, more exactly, its lack of frivolity.
> 'Don't you want to answer my question?' asked Gletkin.

'Certainly,' said Rubashov, more and more astonished.

'How old were you when the watch was given you?'

'I don't quite know,' said Rubashov; 'eight or nine probably.'

'I,' said Gletkin in his usual correct voice, 'was sixteen years old when I learnt that the hour was divided into minutes. In my village, when the peasants had to travel to town, they would go to the waiting-room until the train came, which was usually about midday; sometimes it only came in the evening or next morning. These are the peasants who now work in our factories. For example, in my village is now the biggest steel-rail factory in the world. In the first year, the foremen would lie down to sleep between two emptyings of the blast furnace, until they were shot. In all other countries, the peasants had one or two hundred years to develop the habit of industrial precision and of the handling of machines. Here they only had ten years. If we didn't sack them and shoot them for every trifle, the whole country would come to a standstill, and the peasants would lie down to sleep in the factory yards until grass grew out of the chimneys and everything became as it was before.

(Darkness at Noon, 1940)[1]

Both passages contain arguments for an expediency which is justified in terms of industrial and technological progress. Of course the social atmosphere of each differs greatly: in the first, an English gentleman is arguing with a *nouveau riche* industrialist who is planning to pull down a tied cottage which he had verbally agreed to leave standing. The whole question of English class prejudice lurks behind every word. In the second passage, Rubashov, an old Bolshevik, is being told why brutality is 'necessary' if the new Russia is to be realized. Yet it seems to me that what these passages share is more significant. For the justifications voiced by the new men, Hornblower and Gletkin, are the same justifications, albeit in a different environment (though Gletkin later refers to the Industrial Revolution in the North of England). In other words the crisis being dramatized or portrayed contains in each case the same forces, as well as its local elements. Yet one work is a socially realistic play and the other undoubtedly a political novel—also, incidentally, realistic.

Now certain facts emerge from this comparison. Clearly no special form is demanded to treat politics in distinction to society. Secondly, political literature and social literature can deal with the same subjects, in the same way, only the direction of approach and the reason for the approach may differ. Thus *The Skin Game*, in portraying a society, might indicate why a certain kind of political activity has reason to occur, and *Darkness at Noon*, while showing political activists at work, creates a picture of a society which stands condemned or justified in terms which political theorists may or may not accept. A further problem arises when we think of a fable such as George Orwell's *Animal Farm* (1945) or an allegorical novel like Rex Warner's *The Aerodrome* (1941). Both are political, or are generally regarded as political, since the authors were portraying indirectly the essence of political systems which they disliked. But how would a social fable or a social allegory differ from these? Each would seem to differ only in its applicability to political systems actual or imaginary. Indeed it is perfectly possible to think of a fable or an allegory which could be read as either political or social, or both, or neither. Aesop and La Fontaine wrote in this way, as did Swift in 'A Voyage to Lilliput'. The American publisher who rejected *Animal Farm* because there was no market for animal stories was not being entirely ludicrous: ambiguity in literature has its disadvantages.

Yet another difficulty in classing literature as political arises when a writer makes direct or overt political statements outside his literary publications and then produces poems or novels or plays which perhaps only in tone or implication reflect or suggest political affiliations. The writers whom John Harrison has called 'the reactionaries'[2] represent a good example of what I mean: Yeats, Eliot, Pound, Wyndham Lewis, D. H. Lawrence. For instance:

> Let us have done with this foolish form of government, and this idea of democratic control. Let us submit to the knowledge that there are aristocrats and plebeians born, not made. Some amongst us are born fit to govern, and some are born only fit to be governed. Some are born to be artisans and labourers, some to be lords and governors.

Here D. H. Lawrence is writing a letter to Lady Cynthia Asquith, in August 1915, and some critics would certainly argue that the views expressed are not outside literature. Dickens and Pope have been much admired for their letters, partly because they aided an appreciation of their literary creations but mainly because they were often masterpieces in their own right. (Indeed Pope rewrote his for publication.) I imagine Lawrence did not have any thoughts that the letter quoted above would be preserved for posterity—but there it is with many others of like sentiment collected in Aldous Huxley's edition. Now when we read a poem such as 'Mountain Lion' are we to detect overtones which can be described as political?

> And I think in this empty world there was room for me and a
> mountain lion,
> And I think in the world beyond, how easily we might spare a
> million or two of humans
> And never miss them.
> Yet what a gap in the world, the missing white frost face of that
> slim yellow mountain lion!

Although the style may not differ notably from other animal poems by Lawrence, may it not be argued that the admiration of the lion (similar, of course, to the admiration in 'Snake' where the animal is called 'a King') has implications outside love of nature. The animal is idealized in contrast to a vision of mankind which for an elitist might be typified by the word *'canaille'*. Is there not a Nietzschean contempt of the masses here—that 'dread, almost a horror of democratic society, the mob', as Lawrence put it in his novel *Kangaroo* (1923)? Thus even an animal poem could be taken, and possibly already has been taken, as fuel by those who would argue that Lawrence had Fascist sympathies. And would such an argument make 'Mountain Lion' political literature? Indeed even *The Plumed Serpent* (1926), in which critics have found primitive religious organizations anticipatory of Nazi Germany, or *Kangaroo*, which contains for Harrison 'a consistent and powerful attack on democracy',[3] might for other critics (F. R. Leavis for example) be almost totally apolitical novels which exhibit only the art of a great novelist.

  T. S. Eliot is another writer who tended to express himself with direct reference to politics in essays, articles and in prose works like *After Strange Gods* (1934), where his pronouncements placed him very much on the political right: 'the struggle of our time [is] to renew our association with traditional wisdom; to re-establish a vital connection between the individual and the race; the struggle in a word against Liberalism'.[4] For Eliot, of course, politics, if they are to mean anything, were inseparable from culture. Does, therefore, a poem such as 'A Cooking Egg' have political significance and, if so, is it a political poem in any meaningful sense?

> But where is the penny world I bought
> To eat with Pipit behind the screen?
> The red-eyed scavengers are creeping
> From Kentish Town and Golder's Green;
>
> Where are the eagles and the trumpets?
>
> Buried beneath some snow-deep Alps.
> Over buttered scones and crumpets
> Weeping, weeping multitudes
> Droop in a hundred A.B.C.'s.

You could argue that these lines lament the passing of lost classical grandeur now superseded by an unspeakable liberal-democratic mediocrity. You could also argue that these lines provide a wittily ironical conclusion to a poem about the naïve illusions of youth and that what the poem as a whole most clearly illustrates is a clever epigrammatic juxtapositioning of ideas and images, taken from history and the arts, which the poet has brilliantly yoked together in a 'metaphysical' fashion. Much depends on what you are looking for. In fact, it could be argued that a writer's political views can be detected just by examining the style of his work—in the way that, more obviously, his psychology would show itself. George Orwell said, in his essay on Yeats, 'One knows . . . that a Socialist would not write like Chesterton or a Tory imperialist like Bernard Shaw, though *how* one knows it is not easy to say.' And he claimed that Yeats's political beliefs were reflected in his verse by the 'wayward, even tortured style of writing'.[5]

A way out of the problem of what constitutes political literature, and how to deal with it when you feel you have found it, is perhaps suggested by Harrison:

> The question whether or not Yeats, Eliot and Lawrence, for example, were fascists seems to me unimportant. People who write letters to the *Times Literary Supplement* saying that Eliot said such and such a thing, *therefore* he is a bad man, are wasting their time. What is important is to find out why they held such views. This leads one to examine not only their social and political principles but their artistic principles. In the very close connection between those two sets of principles, and their very deep concern for the arts, lies the answer to this question.[6]

It is in ascertaining the connection, between apparently held political views and the ways they are expressed in literature, that we can find a way forward. Thus T. S. Eliot's apparent antisemitism can be shown to be no more (nor less) indicative of a political or social attitude than it is of an artistic one: that the references to 'Jews' were not unfortunate lapses inseparable from his verse but, on the contrary, intimately bound up at the time with his creative process—as an analysis of his use of animal imagery can readily show.[7]

In fact any consideration of the shaping effect on literature of political attitudes in the 1920s and 1930s should stress not so much that Auden, Spender and Day Lewis revealed near-Communist sympathies in their verse (while Yeats, Eliot, Lawrence, Pound and Wyndham Lewis revealed strongly right-wing sympathies) but that, whatever their politics, writers solved similar technical and stylistic problems in similar ways. Because these writers had inevitably to try to communicate their reactions to unprecedented realities and problems of twentieth-century mass society they, equally inevitably, felt the need to involve themselves to suffer, to appreciate, the same social and thus political questions of the time, however much their political sympathies might vary. It therefore follows that the difficulty of distinguishing between 'political literature' and that which is not really political is, if you will excuse the colour, a red herring—at least in the period between the Wars. If we follow the development of literary forms from about 1910 we find a growing involvement in political ideas which by about 1935 had become almost universal, for, by then, the expression of political views, tacitly or implicitly, had become itself stylistic rather than ideological. What I am saying here may be illustrated by reference to the interesting discussion between C. Day Lewis and L. A. G. Strong which introduced *Modern Verse 1920–1940: A New Anthology*:

> STRONG. . . . why do you think that the poets of today are likely to offer special difficulty to their contemporaries?
> DAY LEWIS. It's a question of subject matter, and of tradition. Many of us believe that there is nothing in the world which is not potential subject matter for poetry. The world we live in has increased in complexity more rapidly than the world at any other time of history. As a result, both the sense data which are presented to us, and the scientific or philosophical theories which have been evolved to explain modern developments, have reached a bewildering profusion and variety.
>
> Consider, for example, the rapid changes that have taken place during the last hundred years in what the eye sees. A landscape

which for centuries had been developing and changing gradually, almost imperceptibly, the contours of a countryside, the architecture of a village, showing so little alteration for centuries—have suddenly been changed out of all recognition. The village has become a town. Or there is a railway line or a line of pylons running through the field, there are aeroplanes flying overhead, there is a public telephone booth beside the village green. All this happened in what, compared with the rate of progress of previous centuries, is the twinkling of an eye. All this the poet must try to absorb into his work, if—as often happens—it appeals passionately to his imagination.[8]

Day Lewis is close to saying that in 1945 current events *should* be the stuff of poetry. In this situation how could politics escape the attention of the poet's eye, not as a separate specialized interest but as part of the total, fascinatingly changing phenomenon? And could not politics be seen as the most fascinating part since they tended, or were intended, to direct the change? By stating that the unprecedented contemporary scene had a profoundly influential effect upon the nature of poetry, Day Lewis is putting social and political phenomena in terms of literary form, style, technique, etc. Moreover, in the twentieth century the phenomena, which the creative artist has always used both as the material and the shaping power of his art form, were uniquely analysable —especially since *nothing* was sacred or prosaic. The following from the same 'interview' shows how, for a poet like Day Lewis, politics and poetics seemed scarcely separable, and the spectrum of revolution touch both:

DAY LEWIS. . . . I still think Eliot's influence on younger poets was a revolutionary one; it was through him chiefly that the technique of the French Symbolist poets was communicated to them.
STRONG. Certainly his influence was revolutionary—for he showed beyond all doubt that the tradition had collapsed, and they must break new ground for themselves.
DAY LEWIS. 'Break new ground'—is there any way in which the younger poets seem to you markedly different from the generation that preceded them, apart from the innovations in technique?
STRONG. Speaking broadly, they are much more politically minded: more specifically concerned with social problems. A greater proportion of their poems are addressed to some specific purpose. There is more of what their detractors would call propaganda.

DAY LEWIS. Any poetry which implies a passionate faith in anything *can* be called propaganda . . . (pp. xx–xxi)

We can see how in this discussion politics, as one of the primary ingredients that flavour modern verse, are felt to be possibly unacceptable to some readers, like added yeast that is liable to 'act wild' and give the brew dangerous qualities. Both Strong and Day Lewis are on their guard—the latter disliking the term 'propaganda', the former blaming its use on to others. Day Lewis sees politics as having a beneficial effect on literature, since it produces a variety of styles:

DAY LEWIS. . . . The satire [of modern political verse] had an anarchist irresponsible quality—(hence the attraction of surrealism carrying the modified anarchism of the earlier Auden–MacNeice work to its technical extreme). Where the poet had passed through this stage of dissatisfaction towards a positive political faith, we got a certain amount of 'prophetic' verse, prophetic in the sense that Isaiah's 'Mountain of God' is prophetic—poems which, often very naïvely, but always sincerely, look towards a promised land and which partly aim, by creating an imaginative picture of a better world, to inspire men to work for that world (e.g. Stephen Spender's poem, 'After they Have Tired of the Brilliance of Cities') (p. xxi).

And Day Lewis adds that, although some political verse was intended to be ephemeral and some political poets were 'admittedly propagandist', nevertheless 'any subject which appeals passionately to the poet's imagination is capable of producing a universal and permanent poem'.

We are not, therefore, to think of political literature as necessarily lesser or even necessarily different: it is a stage through which a group or groups of writers happened to pass—a period of literature rather as one would associate, say, the 'metaphysical' poets with a particular era. The special concerns and interests of the writers might introduce elements from outside the usual province of literary art—scientific terms, for instance—but this activity would be simultaneously a symptom and an ingredient.

Such, it appears, are the points being made in this discussion. By the time it was published in 1945 political poetry of either the committed or anarchist kind was becoming or had become, for the time being at least, a thing of the past. Yet although Dylan Thomas's personal, apolitical verse was by then characteristic of the way poetry was developing, in only three years' time Orwell published his essay 'Writers and Leviathan', which argued that 'the invasion of literature by politics was bound to happen', apparently because: 'This is a political age. War, Fascism, concentration camps, rubber truncheons, atomic bombs, etc., are what we daily think about, and therefore to a great extent what we write about, even when we do not name them openly. We cannot help this.' There are those who would argue that this is just a piece of Orwell's obsessive pessimism, that he could never have been the 'happy vicar' which, he claimed, he could have been in the eighteenth century. (There could be few phrases which less aptly describe Jonathan Swift.) But most critics would see the point of saying: 'No one, now, could devote himself to literature as single-mindedly as Joyce or Henry James.'[9] If he were to do so, the implication is, he would neglect so much of 'life' that his work would be narrow; yet if he does concern himself with politics and society then he will be debased as an artist by 'orthodoxies' and 'party lines' and other ephemera. Now Orwell's essay brings us to the second half of this chapter because, it seems to me, behind what he said in 'Writers and Leviathan' and even behind the views of C. Day Lewis quoted above, is the feeling that English literature and politics ought to be separate. Or, at least, that a critic needs to apologize for associating them, by explaining that it is this age with its unprecedented, often foreign, influences that has brought about the reorientation. Yet, paradoxically, both Day Lewis and Orwell are in fact saying that literature *ought* to take account of politics even though they realize that this might for the British create a special problem.

2. The Problem of English Political Literature

In his book *The Writer and Politics* (1948) George Woodcock observed:

> the writer who pretends to eschew political thinking and to devote himself to his art exclusively, is motivated in his actions by the importance which politics holds in the world where he works. The conscious avoidance of becoming implicated shows that in such a writer's mind politics has a place, even if an unpleasant one. The ivory tower is as much a symptom of inescapable social problems as the air raid shelter is of the inescapable evils of War.[10]

This argument goes a step further than any we have encountered so far and comes close to saying that all literature is implicitly political. The 'ivory tower' image, which suggests criticism of writers who ignore the mundane considerations of politics and society, is readily applicable to English Literature, for it seems that our special problem lies in the strength and richness of our literary and linguistic tradition when contrasted with our involvement as a nation in party politics. Perhaps it would be a good idea to consider W. B. Yeats in this context—and not just because he later lived in a tower. His poetic language was English though it had a 'richness of flavour' which derived from across the Irish sea.[11] And his literary traditions, too, were a mixture of English and Irish. Certainly his early poetry seemed to represent a rejection of such aspects of the modern world as politics and mass society. 'To the young Mr T. S. Eliot, in the early Georgian era, Yeats seemed not much more than an interesting survival from the 1890s': an outdated mixture of the Pre-Raphaelite and the Celtic.[12] But the politics which later entered Yeats's life—public and imaginative—were Irish, not English, and the transformation affected every aspect of his creative work: language, style, imagery, form. A lesser poet would perhaps have been submerged by political considerations: a criticism which Auden might have applied to himself since he later suppressed or modified so much of his earlier, overtly political, verse. And Walter de la Mare could have argued, with good reason, that by remaining in his 'ivory tower' he achieved so much more than he could have done in a world outside whose multiplicity of influences would only have dissipated his talents.

It is interesting and rewarding to compare some of the poetry of Yeats and of de la Mare. I think it would be readily agreed that two poems, such as Yeats's 'The Song of Wandering Aengus' and de la Mare's 'The Old Angler', have much in common—especially in their symbols of lost beauty and vitality. In both, the fisherman who caught and lost a beautiful unearthly girl contrasts his increasing age with her eternal and untouchable youth:

> . . . something rustled on the floor,
> And someone called me by my name.
> It had become a glimmering girl
> With apple blossom in her hair
> Who called me by my name and ran
> And faded through the brightening air.

Though I am old with wandering
Through hollow lands and hilly lands,
I will find out where she has gone,
And kiss her lips and take her hands;
And walk among long dappled grass,
And pluck till time and times are done
The silver apples of the moon,
The golden apples of the sun.

('The Song of Wandering Aengus')

. . . she,
Treading the water with birdlike dip,
Shook her sweet shoulders free:

Drew backward, smiling, infatuate fair,
His life's disasters in her eyes,
All longing and folly, grief, despair,
Daydreams and mysteries.

She stooped her brow; laid low her cheek,
And, steering on that silk-tressed craft,
Out from the listening, leaf-hung creek,
Tossed up her chin, and laughed—

A mocking, icy, inhuman note.
One instant flashed that crystal breast,
Leaned, and was gone. Dead-still the boat:
And the deep dark at rest . . .

And he—the cheated? Dusk till morn,
Insensate, even of hope forsook,
He muttering squats, aloof, forlorn,
Dangling a baitless hook.

('The Old Angler')

In the latter poem we find de la Mare's recurrent motif: no meaningful humane answer returns to the seeker or questioner from the natural world. 'Tell them I came, and no one answered,' cries the Traveller in one of de la Mare's best-known verses. Professor Pinto has claimed that 'Echo' (1906) embodied 'the bewilderment and despair of an age which had lost the traditional clues to the labyrinth of the inner life'.[13] The poem ends:

'Who calls?' I bawled thro' my tears;
The wind fell low:
In the silence, 'Who cares? Who cares?'
Wailed to and fro.

Here the echo seems similar to the jumbled echo heard in the caves of Forster's *A Passage to India* which tells the listeners 'everything exists, nothing has value'.[14]

Now de la Mare, who seems the perfect tenant of Woodcock's 'ivory tower', succeeded in reflecting social malaise while retaining a traditionalist 'Edwardian' poetic style. The stilted, slightly archaic, expressions of 'The Old Angler' such as 'with birdlike dip' 'silk-tressed craft', 'leaf-hung creek', seem under no strain or tension. The result is a listlessness which I, at least, find appropriate: there is no sense of a protagonist taking up a challenge. He gives in, albeit miserably, because no answer exists to provide hope or encouragement. Yeats's poem, however, which uses the same symbol (akin incidentally to Eliot's vision of lost beauty at the end of 'The Love Song of J. Alfred Prufrock') has a determination and robustness quite apparent in the movement of the verse:

I will find out where she has gone,
And kiss her lips and take her hands . . .

We are talking here of the development of poetry in a period when lost religious faith was liable to be replaced by some new secular faith—many would claim a political one. Yeats said that he had been 'deprived by Huxley and Tindall of the simple-minded religion' of his childhood and had made 'a new religion' for his poetry from stories, personages and emotions.[15] Clearly his growing interest and involvement in Irish politics from about 1914 provided such ingredients for his verse. Poems like 'September 1913' and 'The Rose Tree' built on Yeats's earlier completely apolitical poetry. The images and symbols of natural beauty are couched in verse whose rhythms carry an intensity of utterance inimitably characteristic of Yeats. The transformation has grown out of early verse in a manner unforeseen by critics and admirers alike. For Yeats, at least, concern with politics inspired in a way that was undoubtedly beneficial to his art, perhaps because Yeats's politics, like his legends, were largely indigenous to the land he wrote about. The 1916 rebellion did not disrupt Yeats's aesthetic vision—it extended it:

We know their dream; enough
To know they dreamed and are dead;
And what if excess of love
Bewildered them till they died?
I write it out in a verse—
MacDonagh and MacBride
And Connolly and Pearse
Now and in time to be,
Wherever green is worn,
Are changed, changed utterly:
A terrible beauty is born.

('Easter 1916')

The incisiveness, the 'bell-beat' of the stress here, are more noticeable than they were in the verse which first gave Yeats a name. But the imagery and symbolism of the passage beginning

Hearts with one purpose alone
Through Summer and Winter seem
Enchanted to a stone
To trouble the living stream.

are of a kind perfectly familiar to readers of the early Yeats. In other words, concern with public affairs gave the poet a catalyst which speeded up the change. But the change was modulated: there was no irreconcilable break with earlier techniques. And an unparalleled ability to suggest by symbol the nature of political and social degeneration was to be revealed in 'The Second Coming' (1921):

. . . somewhere in sands of the desert
A shape with lion body and the head of a man,
A gaze blank and pitiless as the sun,
Is moving its slow thighs, while all about it
Reel shadows of the indignant desert birds.

We may well argue that the difficulty is an unprecedented one: that it is peculiar to this century that politics and society must impinge upon literature because influences such as the mass media and applied science are inescapable. It seems that the poetry even of de la Mare must be read as indirectly but implicitly concerned with social problems. The poetry of W. B. Yeats, it appears, had either to face these influences and pressures, absorb them and use them (which it did magnificently) or remain a Pre-Raphaelite survival, doomed, if not forgotten, to uneasy interpretations. And the poetry of Auden, dedicated wholeheartedly to politics and society? This will need fuller treatment, but there seems to be a consensus of critical opinion that, for all its brilliance, his earlier and most characteristic verse illuminated a narrow space.

At this point if we are to try to decide why Yeats so successfully evolved from the world of Pre-Raphaelite and Edwardian dreams into a poet so much admired by the 'New Country' group we must speculate not only upon great literary and linguistic distinctions but also upon political qualities. For if we speak in the national, not the linguistic, sense of English political literature are we not liable to receive the retort (à la *Lucky Jim*) 'English *what* literature?' or, even more telling, '*what* political literature'? For traditionally, the British have most often been praised by their fellow men for being very non-political in the sense of not easily getting 'hot-under-the-collar' about political affairs— especially party political affairs. Again and again in this century political writers—Russell, Koestler, Orwell, for example—have contrasted Britain with the outside political world.[16] We in Britain, the argument goes, have never taken politics so seriously as to prevent friendly dis- cussion at social gatherings between representatives of competing political parties. Only in Britain, it has been suggested, could you have the title 'Leader of Her Majesty's Opposition'. It is true that many writers and thinkers have been fascinated by ideas and ideologies which come from abroad but the British have been able to absorb them without trouble, rather as Highgate cemetery holds the remains of Karl Marx.

I have been speaking of Britain, but really I should have used the word 'England'. It seems no coincidence that the two British poets to have written unselfconsciously about politics in this century, as if the subject were perfectly natural, were neither of them English: Yeats and MacDiarmid. It would be perhaps extravagant to argue that a Briton needed to be 'Celtic' if he were to write wholeheartedly about politics but the suggestion, for obvious political as well as literary reasons, is attractive. The comparatively untapped and unspoilt lin- guistic and cultural resources, the genuine revolutionary aspirations, must combine to create something different and presumably better than what was, at times at least, scarcely more than fashionable and stimulating in middle-class English society.

Thus *English* writers must have felt an innate refusal to allow ideology to disturb more than the surface of British political life—and this refusal can be extended to the literature. Many writers in Britain, as abroad, have been rebels of a political or quasi-political nature but, almost without exception, they have remained ultimately loyal not so much to the continued political life of the country as to the literary and linguistic tradition to which they belonged. It appears as if there could be no escape from awareness of belonging to a heritage that allowed no alternative. An examination, for example, of Wordsworth's 'rebellion' in this light would stress his revolt in terms of language and metre, and this would in turn reveal the essentially *traditional* nature of his early verse: that it was not a revolt against English verse-forms but a return to earlier forms and methods. And this latent traditionalism would, I suggest, anticipate his later acceptance of non-revolutionary, non-radical, political beliefs. In our own century, therefore, an examination of the 'New Country' poets would reveal a similar development. Whereas in 1938 Louis MacNeice claimed that the group of poets to which he belonged were 'emotionally partisan' and had brought political purpose into their verse,[17] his fellow-poet Stephen Spender had by 1963 so far abandoned an overwhelming interest in relating ideology to verse that politics are scarcely mentioned in his book *The Struggle of the Modern* (intended to discuss 'the problems which writers have created for themselves and are facing in the modern world').[18] And, I suspect, Spender would now discount MacNeice's suggestion of forty years ago that it was the 'New Country' poets and not Yeats and Eliot who were really writing about something—that they alone had a subject and were forging new means to express it.[19] Indeed another of the group, C. Day Lewis, had already written, in *A Hope For Poetry* (1934), of the stylistic debt the 'New Country' poets owed to Eliot and Yeats as well as Hopkins, Owen and D. H. Lawrence, and Day Lewis's whole discussion was to see modern 'political' verse as the new heir to a literary tradition rather than a severance from it.

It follows from what has been said in this chapter that the writer of modern English political literature of the Left was likely to have to face two primary, socially related, problems: one aesthetic, one moral. Robin Skelton puts it well:

> . . . a poet with a *bourgeois* upbringing could not easily speak as a member of the working class. Consequently, he must see himself as the divided creature he is and speak out of the conflict between his environment and his convictions. This sounds well, but leaves the main question unanswered. Is the writer primarily concerned

to produce propaganda, or is his first concern the creation of works of high aesthetic merit? It is no use denying that the most efficient propaganda is likely to be of a low intellectual content. On the other hand to indulge in profound intellectual subtleties is, perhaps, to absent oneself from the Great Struggle, and thus to betray those very values by which one is so concerned to live.[20]

We have already, in considering the nature of political literature, seen Day Lewis's unhappy acceptance (in 1945) of the term 'propaganda'. In 1935, in *Revolution in Writing*, Day Lewis had a tendency 'to place his trust in Marx first and the Muse second', and said that good 'political' verse was 'essentially—though not formally—propaganda' since it was 'bound to have a revolutionary effect on our emotions'.[21] Day Lewis's 'hedging' seems only to confirm what Skelton has claimed and, in any case, the situation of a middle-class English political revolutionary who used his literature to further his aims suggests an atmosphere more suitable for Groucho than Karl. The social and literary traditions of Britain were very unfavourably ranged against him, it seems to me, quite apart from the inherited stability and resilience of the political establishment.

The related moral, and emotional, problem is well discussed by George Woodcock:

> Many of our poets and novelists, particularly in the generations that immediately preceded the war, were involved in sincere and serious attempts to use their powers of thought and writing in order to assist the establishment of social justice. They had their embroilments in politics, ran uneasily in the party packs, and endeavoured to sink their individualities in the collective baying of slogans for such futilities as the Popular Front. Very soon, however, they realised their incompatibility with their party associates and left the razor games of politics for those with thicker skins.
>
> Bred in a liberal tradition of honesty and fair-play . . . they were astonished and hurt to discover the palpable dishonesty and bad faith of 'left wing' politics. Imbued with the intellectual's respect for independence of thought and speech, they resented the scarcely hidden forces which tried to keep them to the 'party lines'. Having at least some concern for truth as a social and individual virtue, they regarded with distaste the cynical cult of falsehood and distortion displayed by the party bosses and propagandists. Moreover, their troubles came not from one side only. Attacked

19

by their fellow writers for deserting the detachment which had been regarded for so long as incumbent on the intellectual, they were at the same time attacked by their political associates because they could not bring themselves to adhere unquestioningly to a body of dogma with which they did not wholly agree.[22]

Woodcock seems to be saying here that the left-wing political writers (especially the 'New Country' group) washed their hands of politics when they found out what a dirty business it was—and that they should not have done so. It is important to recognize in this context the achievement of George Orwell. For he was able to continue his literary work in a progression, not only because he had never been affiliated to a party or orthodoxy, but because he was fascinated by, and masochistically attracted towards, those qualities in politics which dismayed others. It was *because* the business was so dirty that he had to 'smell it out'. His approach might be called European and it resembles that of a Koestler or a Silone. In the context of this discussion he serves as a contrast, as a kind of literary control-experiment, in any examination of modern English political writing. And I feel we can risk the assertion that the most consistently successful English (as opposed to Irish or Scottish) political writing has been produced by men such as Orwell and Wyndham Lewis, who were not, at the time they wrote, committed to an ideology or an orthodoxy.[23]

Thus if we had to restrict ourselves, in defining political literature, to that which is committed to the communication of a party political view and whose *raison d'être is* such a communication, we would find very little in this country. Even the so-to-speak 'hard-core' political writers would raise questions of literary identity and objective. Are Auden and Isherwood writing propaganda in *The Ascent of F6* or are they experimenting with drama? Who is really behind Rex Warner's novels: Thucydides and Karl Marx, or John Bunyan and Franz Kafka? Perhaps it is unwise to ask such questions; certainly there seems to be no definite answer. But at least such speculation draws attention to the fact that our literature (in this century at least) has tended not to take its politics so seriously as the French novel has with Aragon, Brasillach and Camus or the Italian novel with Silone or Russian verse with Mayakovsky. It is for such reasons, I suspect, that Woodcock calls our record 'miserable'. Yet I would have thought that those who are more interested in literature than politics would call this record encouraging. And those who are enamoured of politics should realize that one cannot have it both ways: a liberal democracy with no political censorship must encourage literary rather than political fervours.

But, for all I have said, I shall concentrate in this essay upon the most 'political' literature I can find in the period chosen and select representative examples which most usefully illustrate the imprint upon them of political enthusiasm. It would not be appropriate, even if I had the space, to attempt a critical history of all and any political literature giving each writer a just measure of comment. I will refer to 'cultural politics'[24] only in so far as they guide us to evidence of the kind of committed writing we find in MacDiarmid or Spender—or in the commitedly *un*committed stance taken by Orwell or Huxley. Above all I shall allow broad themes (as indicated by the chapter titles) to dominate the discussion, and within these themes the question of literary form will be the prime consideration. Thus there will occur, from time to time, disturbance of the chronological sequence and certain writers will appear in more than one chapter.

In fact what we are concerned with here is a sport: an unprecedented outgrowth from the main body of work that the student would normally mean by 'English Literature'. This sport exhibited itself initially, perhaps, as a disturbance in the tradition of 'cultural politics' and continued to cause such a tension and a pull away from traditional modes of expression that in the twenties the politicization of literature threatened to change radically the fiction of Forster[25] and, as we have seen, the poetry of Yeats. Yet a sense of uncertainty of form and place *vis à vis* the entire tradition of English literature obviously affected our most committed of political literary writers no less than a Forster or a Yeats —as C. Day Lewis makes admirably clear in his 'interview' with L. A. G. Strong. What should be stressed is the comparative success of what was in essence a new venture, for this country and this language, into the literature of commitment. It developed and flowered, most notably as commitment to 'Leftist' ideology, for about a decade and a half, 1930-45 (though like many rare flowers it was wilting well before it died) and for all its uncertainties and mannerisms must be considered a remarkable achievement despite the criticisms of those who feel commitment detracts from art. Conversely, those who have compared our political literature unfavourably to that of France, Germany and Russia might still agree that though compromise, phlegm and a sense of tradition are sometimes more noticeable than passion in the work of our most committed writers, these virtues (or vices) would certainly be called *political* at Westminster.

Chapter One

The Search for Realism

> What is all human conduct but the daily and hourly sale of our souls? What I am now selling it for is neither money nor position nor comfort, but for reality and power.
>
> Cusins in G. B. Shaw's *Major Barbara*

The last twenty years of the nineteenth century was a time of artistic and intellectual ferment. But the bustle covered a variety of seemingly incompatible strands of action: 'much of the vitality of the period,' claimed Holbrook Jackson, 'much even of its effective vitality, was destructive of ideas and conventions'.[1] If we examine certain trends, generally accepted as characteristic yet unlike each other, we can soon see that their differing qualities could be used by writers in a way that anticipates the future developments of literature and of politics and society.

'Decadence', for example, is a term, at once pejorative and admiring, inevitably employed when discussing the *fin de siècle* period of English literature. Yet factual discussions in prose—especially of political and social questions—are also enormously representative of the time. And, again, there can be found a transcendental view, almost a vision, of society and social life that is unparalleled since the late Middle Ages. All three strands can be detected in Oscar Wilde's *The Soul of Man Under Socialism* (1891), which argued with such passion and conviction that rebels in Tsarist Russia kept copies 'under boards and within mattresses'.[2] '*The State is to make what is useful. The individual is to make what is beautiful.*'[3] Here is the core, I suspect, of Wilde's statement, or plea, and it carries with it many implications about a critical time in the evolution of western society. The word 'make' has behind it all the speculation and worry, which have steadily gathered momentum since the Industrial Revolution, about the power of machines and how they can debase human existence by destroying individuality and creativity. These are thoughts expressed in varied ways by, among others, William Morris, John Ruskin, Gerard Manley Hopkins and a little later—but obsessively—by D. H. Lawrence. '*At present machinery competes against man. Under proper conditions machinery will serve man,*'[4] said Wilde, and in 1891 it was not a hopeless credo voiced by decadent artist, for mechanization surely gave mankind the chance at last for civilized and graceful existence: the word 'make' can mean 'plan', 'decide', even 'force', if necessary. Had not Karl Marx, who lurks uncomfortably behind this and other speculations of the time, argued *deterministically* that such benefits as the withering away of State power would occur in precisely those countries like Britain where mechanized industry was most advanced? And the artist: would he not be left at last with justified freedom to play his part? Or could it be that in any 'ideal' state the artist would be not only less free but *inevitably* less free because of those very mechanistic and deterministic forces that Wilde hoped would liberate the individual? The Utopia and anti-Utopia thus grew beside each other, showing that the very contrariness and uncertainty which we call a cross-road or a crisis will throw up new *genres* to deal with them.

William Morris's *News from Nowhere* (1891) exhibited at least two of those three 'incompatible' strands, while its assumption of the value of good living, of aesthetic delight, might be considered to approach decadence. As with Wilde's piece this 'Utopian romance' includes much political and social discussion of a kind associated with the names of G. B. Shaw and H. G. Wells. But, again like Wilde, Morris projects a vision of ideal (yet humane) beauty of an intensity that demands the epithet religious. And were not these differing qualities already to be found in Morris's associates, the Pre-Raphaelites, who combined visions of a past and pre-industrial splendour with practical considerations of furniture making and interior decoration? Undoubtedly Morris was profoundly influenced by John Ruskin, who in essays throughout the period 1860–84 preached a social gospel against industrialism and its debasing effects on work and art, and indeed on man's whole life. Thus Morris's picture of an ideal future, where man, by abandoning most machines yet retaining an inspired socialism or communism recovered a lost concord with the natural world, includes chapters of discussion and argument more usually found in essays or pamphlets. One chapter entitled 'On the Lack of Incentive to Labour in a Communist Society' contains the following exchange between the narrator and the old man:

'You are very bitter about that unlucky nineteenth century,' said I.

'Naturally,' said he, 'since I know so much about it.'

He was silent a little, and then said: 'There are traditions—nay, real histories—in our family about it: my grandfather was one of its victims. If you know something about it, you will understand what he suffered when I tell you that he was in those days a genuine artist, a man of genius, and a revolutionist.'

'I think I do understand,' said I: 'but now, as it seems, you have reversed all this?'

'Pretty much so,' said he.[5]

It reads rather like those creaking 'phoney interviews' of experts who are being fed prepared questions. But the old man continues with well-argued conviction:

'The wares which we make are made because they are needed: men make for their neighbours' use as if they were making for themselves, not for a vague market of which they know nothing and over which they have no control: as there is no buying and selling, it would be mere insanity to make goods on the chance of their being wanted; for there is no longer anyone who can be *compelled* to buy them. So that whatever is made is good, and thoroughly fit for its purpose. Nothing *can* be made except for genuine use; therefore no inferior goods are made. Moreover, as aforesaid, we have now found out what we want, so we make no more than we want; and we are not driven to make a vast quantity of useless things, we have time and resources enough to consider our pleasure in making them.'

Here is made the kind of point about capitalist consumer society which Leavis and Thompson were to discuss forty years later and which, significantly enough, Orwell considered in non-fiction books like *The Road to Wigan Pier* and also in novels such as *Keep The Aspidistra Flying* and *Coming Up For Air*. Wherever Morris writes with conviction in *News from Nowhere* he tends to be convincing, but when he relies on literary techniques we get wooden conversation or precious archaisms. It is as if the reversal of mechanization has had a linguistic equivalent that brought back expressions of 'Hillo!' and 'quoth I' in the twenty-first century. (Morris was, however, consistent: revolutionary Socialist verse such as 'All For The Cause' and 'A Death Song' is if anything more 'archaic' than the prose of *News from Nowhere*. And in *The*

Dream of John Ball (1886–7), a romance story that in many ways anticipates the form of *News from Nowhere*, the protagonist does, by dreaming, travel into the medieval past and thus justifies the archaic atmosphere in which politics and society are discussed.) His characters tend
to be cyphers and in their perfect health, youthful physique and attitude
to sex, have an uncanny resemblance to the Utopians in Wells's novel
Men Like Gods (1923). But unlike Wells's super-men and -women,
Morris's are believably humane and, in an admirable way, simple. His
greatest success was in creating the atmosphere of a beautiful commu-
nistic society seen at its best in the closing scene of the church feast:

> We went into the church, which was a simple little building with
> one little aisle divided from the nave by three round arches, a
> chancel, and a rather roomy transept for so small a building, the
> windows mostly of the graceful Oxfordshire fourteenth century
> type. There was no modern architectural decoration in it; it
> looked, indeed, as if none had been attempted since the Puritans
> whitewashed the mediaeval saints and histories on the wall. It
> was, however, gaily dressed up for this latter-day festival, with
> festoons of flowers from arch to arch, and great pitchers of flowers
> standing about on the floor; while under the west window hung
> two cross scythes, their blades polished white, and gleaming from
> out of the flowers that wreathed them. But its best ornament was
> the crowd of handsome, happy-looking men and women that were
> set down to table, and who, with their bright faces and rich hair
> over their gay holiday raiment, looked, as the Persian poet puts it,
> like a bed of tulips in the sun.
>
> *(News from Nowhere, p. 235)*

Here there is communicated through precise visualization a genuine,
albeit naïve, faith in man and the value of his existence. But it is significantly one which looks back rather than forward for inspiration.

The uncertainties of those last years of the dying century were also
reflected in the multiplicity of artistic and cultural activities which
tumbled over by force of circumstance into the political and social
fields. Shaw was producing novels of scarcely diluted propaganda and
was shortly to write packages of play-with-preface. Wells would soon
stop his brilliant dreaming and apply (some would say debase) his
talents in 'solving' political and social problems. It was a period notable
for the formation of socialist societies that were often founded and
staffed by the literary and cultivated. The Social Democratic Federation

founded by Henry Mayers Hyndman in 1881 had William Morris as its 'chief supporter', while two years later, the Fabian Society was formed and soon attracted Sidney Webb and G. B. Shaw. This 'socialism' was, as Bonamy Dobrée has said, 'present all through the period' 1830–1914.[6] But it was a mixed and indefinite, semi-political concept deriving from a variety of main influences: Robert Owen, Tom Paine, Karl Marx, J. S. Mill—to say nothing of a host of subsidiary ones dating back to the Garden of Eden. Certainly it was a creed which, as we have seen, inspired writers and if we ask why should it have been so very inspiring we must speculate, with many others who have considered the phenomenon, on the loss of religious faith. Could this loss, so apparent, if sometimes disguised in Arnold, Carlyle, Tennyson and Browning, have lead to the unhappy cynicism of Wilde, the secular faith of Morris, the evolutionary yearnings of Shaw and Wells? Or were the uncertainties, tangible in mixed literary forms and mixed literary activities, only the result of its being the end of an era: Victorian, nineteenth century, Romantic? Could politics replace religion—and, if they did, would it be just another of the 'new' fashions so characteristic of a time which produced 'The New Remorse', 'New Spirit', 'New Human', 'New Realism', 'New Hedonism', 'New Drama', 'New Unionism', 'New Party', 'New Woman', *The New Age* and *The New Review*?

It is usual to interpret Matthew Arnold's famous poem 'Dover Beach' as the perfect utterance of late-Victorian loss of faith, or, as Arnold calls it, Faith. The imagery of 'naked shingles', 'confused alarms of struggle and flight' and 'ignorant armies' which 'clash by night' seems suggestive in Britain of twentieth- rather than nineteenth-century problems. Other verse by Arnold contains similarly disturbing imagery which relates to social malaise: giant inhuman cities where the individual suffers from noise and pollution. 'Lines Written in Kensington Gardens', for example, speaks of 'the huge world, which roars hard by', and of 'the city's jar'. And 'The Future', expressed in terms very reminiscent of 'Dover Beach', clearly regards their disturbing elements as symptomatic of things to come:

> This tract which the river of Time
> Now flows through with us, is the plain.
> Gone is the calm of its earlier shore.
> Border'd by cities and hoarse
> With a thousand cries is its stream.

And we on its breast, our minds
Are confused as the cries which we hear,
Changing and shot as the sights which we see.

And we say that repose has fled
For ever the course of the river of Time.
That cities will crowd to its edge
In a blacker, incessanter line;
That the din will be more on its banks,
Denser the trade on its stream,
Flatter the plain where it flows,
Fiercer the sun overhead.
That never will those on its breast
See an ennobling sight,
Drink of the feeling of quiet again.

In his sentiments, rather than in his style, Arnold seems to be anticipating those three stylistic innovators, Hopkins, Owen and Eliot, so much admired by the political poets Auden, Day Lewis and Spender. It was inevitable perhaps that poets should seek new faiths and that some should find their searches fruitful, for a while at least, in political belief and commitment. But whether or not a writer's search took him to politics, his concerns tended to bring his imaginative consciousness up against the raw edges of realistic experience and into a new world of the ugly, the scientific, the commercial and, of course, the sociopolitical. In fact the writer—as Arnold seems to predict—is to be brought into an atmosphere hitherto 'unpoetical', even 'unliterary'. It is for this reason that such a radical shift was to be required in a writer's consciousness of his task—and, of course, in the reader's. And it was a shift which for some was to create a chasm. The three poets mentioned all developed a new style to communicate uncomfortable, even agonizing, facts, feelings, conditions. All three were for much of their major formative and creative periods isolated with an unprecedented message to get over to an unknown and alienated audience. In the poems of Hopkins, such as 'Binsey Poplars' and more particularly, 'God's Grandeur', we find expressed in new rhythmical tones the effect of mechanized man upon the environment:

Generations have trod, have trod, have trod;
And all is seared with trade; bleared, smeared with toil;
And wears man's smudge and shares man's smell: the soil
Is bare now, nor can foot feel, being shod.

27

And in 'Thou art indeed just Lord' and certain of the 'Terrible Sonnets', Hopkins seems to ask whether God will ignore man and leave the Devil in control.[7] In Wilfred Owen's war poetry Arnold's 'ignorant armies' appear as a betrayed generation sent to an earthly hell created by the powers of technological war. The callousness of governments and the hopelessness of man's political future are expressed, with Owen's characteristic diction, in 'Strange Meeting':

> Now men will go content with what we spoiled.
> Or discontent, boil bloody, and be spilled.
> They will be swift with swiftness of the tigress,
> None will break ranks, though nations trek from progress.

Dissonance and half-rhyme, and sometimes stressed alliteration reminiscent of Hopkins and Browning, were thus used by Owen as a means of communicating unpleasant and unprecedented realities. And in the early poems of Eliot, such as 'The Love-Song of J. Alfred Prufrock' and the 'Preludes', we find a corresponding urban hell in the giant city anticipated by Matthew Arnold. It is 'a hell even more terrible than the trench landscape of Wilfred Owen, because its misery is listless and undramatic'.[8] The imagery is made up of cigarette ends, scraps of paper and deserted streets, while the movement of the verse contains sudden 'plonking' rhymes and rhythms that force the reader into a consciousness of the unpalatable:

> Streets that follow like a tedious argument
> Of insidious intent
> To lead you to an overwhelming question . . .
> O do not ask, 'What is it?'
> Let us go and make our visit.
>
> Six o'clock
> The burnt-out ends of smokey days.
> And now a gusty shower wraps
> The grimy scraps
> Of withered leaves about your feet
> And newspapers from vacant lots;
> The showers beat
> On broken blinds and chimney-pots . . .
>
> One thinks of all the hands
> That are raising dingy shades
> In a thousand furnished rooms.[9]

In such lines Eliot communicates the vision of an atomized society. W. B. Yeats, who, as we have seen, developed a modified style when he turned to the realities of social and political life, has stressed Eliot's stylistic revolution as being one which enabled poetry to deal with the unpleasant realities of the modern world:

> . . . we wrote as men had always written. Then established things were shaken by the Great War. All civilised men had believed in progress, in a warless future, in always-increasing wealth, but now influential young men began to wonder if anything could last or if anything were worth fighting for. In the third year of the War came the most revolutionary man in poetry during my lifetime, though his revolution was stylistic alone—T. S. Eliot published his first book. No romantic word or sound, nothing reminiscent, nothing in the least like the painting of Ricketts could be permitted henceforth. Poetry must resemble prose, and both must accept the vocabulary of their time; nor must there be any special subject-matter. Tristram and Isoult were not a more suitable theme than Paddington Railway Station. The past had deceived us: let us accept the worthless present.[10]

After this statement, which links stylistic changes to rapid social evolution and potential political reappraisal, Yeats quotes some lines from Eliot's 'Preludes' claiming that such 'modernity' has 'passed into young influential poets of today: Auden, Spender, MacNeice, Day Lewis'—poets who were either Communists or possessed by 'an overwhelming social bitterness'. Here, an assessment by a great poet suggests how the early decades of the twentieth century were to encourage, at least for a while, the creation of verse whose style was inseparable from political and social commitment.

In the novel the move towards *stylistic* awareness of social and political realities had begun earlier. Dickens had described the plight of orphans and socially deprived individuals and developed a style which, it might be said, was poised ready for an involvement in politics greater than he exhibited in his portrayals of revolutionary excess in *The Tale of Two Cities* (1859) or in the 'sullen socialism' of *Hard Times* (1854). It is a style of prose close to journalism, sufficiently controlled for the essay or pamphlet, yet with the novelist's selection of material, vocabulary, plot, etc. The socially realistic novels of Samuel Butler, George Gissing or George Moore might or might not bring political discussion or portrayal in their wake but undoubtedly they helped to set the scene in which H. G. Wells, Arnold Bennett, John Galsworthy and later George Orwell were to make their contributions. The 'prevalent didacticism' of the last two decades of the nineteenth century was part and parcel of the 'new' concern with facts, figures and the political and social theories which abounded in essays and inevitably found their way into imaginative prose. This obsessive concern was in turn a symptom of the uncertainty and unease I have mentioned. 'Something was wrong' and the 'profound optimism and complacency' that had been almost universal in England earlier in the century was now irrevocably shaken.[11] A new realism, and with it a factual quality to writing, went hand in hand with a new social awareness. Gissing's *In the Year of Jubilee* (1894), for example, looked hard at the place and role of women in society—suggesting reappraisals, though scarcely encouraging a suffragette movement. The desire to be above all realistic, true to facts, inevitably affected ideas about novel writing. Gissing asked why a woman in a love-scene never had an unsightly pimple on her nose; George Moore, who had modelled himself on that famous naturalist Emile Zola, set his novel *Esther Walters* (1894), concerning the plight of an unmarried mother, in a stable with jockeys.

In his book *Crisis in English Poetry* Professor Pinto chooses two prose passages which describe with utter realism dismal London scenes—one passage to be contrasted with Tennyson's 'The Princess', the other to be compared with T. S. Eliot's 'Prufrock'. The first, from Gissing's *Demos, A Story of English Socialism* (1886) begins: 'To walk about in such a neighbourhood as this is the dreariest exercise to which man can betake himself; the heart is crushed by uniformity of decent squalor'. The second passage from Joseph Conrad's *The Secret Agent* (1907) includes the following:

> the grimy sky, the mud of the streets, the rags of the dirty men, harmonised excellently with the eruption of the damp, rubbishy sheets of paper soiled with printers' ink. The posters maculated with filth garnished like tapestry the sweep of the curbstone.[12]

Now in such passages the novelist is performing 'part of the poet's function of finding words to express his vision of the strange grotesque beauty which is part of hideousness'.[13] The writer, and here we can speak of both novelist and poet, was having to find new order, a new medium, for expression of the ugly or unpleasant. (It is perhaps significant that the early decades of the twentieth century included two writers, Lawrence and Hardy, who were great novelists and great poets.) Thus far the stylistic revolution could really only be objected to by sentimental traditionalists—but the concern for realism brought with it the desire and the opportunity to teach facts and discuss theories. Arnold Bennett, an admirer of Zola, Flaubert and George Moore, would describe London street scenes in the manner of Gissing or Conrad:

> The kerbstone of Holborn was decorated with dustbins at irregular intervals, and all the shops were closed so thoroughly that they looked as if they would never reopen again. A stream of people passed from the east to the west, hurriedly, with a certain gloomy preoccupation . . . The Tube Railway threw up quantities of the same sort of people out of the earth. They were the vanguard of the black-coated workers.
>
> (*The Sinews of War*, 1906)

This resembles the scene that provided Eliot with some of his best poetry in 'The Waste Land': at once a nightmare vision and a searching social comment.[14] Similarly, when Conrad wrote of London evening newspapers being sold briskly 'yet in comparison with the swift, constant march of foot traffic, the effect was of indifference of a disregarded distribution',[15] he too saw a city condemned to soulless mechanical activity. But for some critics a Bennett, a Wells, a Galsworthy and a Shaw would forget the unique powers of literature and write something which degenerated into prosaic factual observation and comment. Thus the passage quoted above from *The Sinews of War* by Arnold Bennett and Eden Phillpotts continues:

> They were the vanguard of the black-coated workers. They all had to be at a particular place at a particular minute; they had the air of trying to catch trains, but they were only trying to avoid fines.

The tendency of 'realistic' novels to concern themselves with data, observations and comments came under severe attack in Virginia Woolf's essay 'Mr Bennett and Mrs Brown' (1924). She argued that in a novel such as *Hilda Lessways* (1911) we could not hear characters' voices, 'we can only hear Mr Bennett's voice telling us facts about rents and freeholds and copyholds and fines'. She claimed that the 'Edwardian' novelists—Bennett, Wells, Galsworthy—had stressed only 'the fabric of things' and by so doing had been allowed to 'palm off' upon the reading public 'a version' of the living reality that constitutes a person's character and life: 'the Edwardians were never interested in character in itself; or the book in itself. They were interested in something outside'. Neither Wells nor Galsworthy tried to portray the reality of a character such as Mrs Brown (a person anyone might meet in a railway compartment): 'I do not think that Mr Wells, in his passion to make her what she ought to be, would waste a thought upon her as she is . . . Burning with indignation, stuffed with information, arraigning civilization, Mr Galsworthy would only see in Mrs Brown a pot broken on the wheel and thrown into the corner.' Perhaps Virginia Woolf's most fundamental criticism of these novelists is as follows:

> it is to express character—not to preach doctrines, sing songs, or celebrate the glories of the British Empire, that the form of the novel, so clumsy, verbose, and undramatic, so rich, elastic and alive, has been evolved.
>
> (*Mr Bennett and Mrs Brown*, 1924)[16]

The suggestion seems to be that such novels are of a lesser literary kind, or even that they are not really novels at all. Here the argument becomes one which would involve poetry. We have seen that C. Day Lewis, in defending political verse, got into difficulties over the term 'propaganda'. It might similarly be wondered whether the realistic texture of the novels of Gissing and Moore, and also of Conrad, encouraged a form of Edwardian novel-writing dealing with the realities of social and political life in which ideas took precedence over imaginative portrayal, or even replaced it.

Now Conrad did write a number of novels which may be called 'political' in the sense that their plots revolve around political events and their characters become involved in political activities. *Nostromo* (1904), *The Secret Agent* (1907) and *Under Western Eyes* (1911) are obvious examples. If one 'message' emerges from them it is that political enthusiasts are dangerous, undesirable people corrosive of human virtues such as loyalty. The following lines from *Under Western Eyes* will illustrate the 'unmistakable dislike of revolutionists' possessed by Conrad:

> . . . in a real revolution—not a simple dynastic change or a mere reform of institutions—in a real revolution the best characters do not come to the front. A violent revolution falls into the hands of narrow-minded fanatics and of tyrannical hypocrites at first. Afterwards comes the turn of all the pretentious intellectual failures of the time. Such are the chiefs and the leaders. You will

notice that I have left out the mere rogues. The scrupulous and the just, the noble, humane, and devoted natures; the unselfish and the intelligent may begin a movement—but it passes away from them. They are not the leaders of a revolution. They are its victims: the victims of disgust, of disenchantment—often of remorse. Hopes grotesquely betrayed, ideals caricatured—that is the definition of revolutionary successes. There have been in every revolution hearts broken by such successes.[17]

A comparison might be made with Gissing's *Demos* which also exhibited fear of socialist militants while supporting the humane credo which they were supposed to serve. Like Conrad, Gissing 'tended to equate' Socialism 'with mob-rule',[18] and also like Conrad he produced novels to be admired more for their characterization and atmosphere than for any particular political or social ideas they succeeded in communicating.

Thus in each of these three works by Conrad the message is not the novel's *raison d'être*. The novel succeeds, like a novel by Thomas Hardy or Henry James, through the enlargement of the reader's imaginative experience. This, I am sure, is what Virginia Woolf would have said and what Dr Leavis no doubt has said. Yet such observations, although valid, do not provide us with any neat categories in which to place different types of political or social novel. As we shall see, Wyndham Lewis in *The Revenge For Love* (1937) was capable of writing a political novel simultaneously realistic, didactic and satirical, *and* 'imaginative' in the mind-enlarging sense that critics use to praise Joyce or Lawrence. There is, however, one general assumption that we can make: a novelist would tend to retain a freedom of movement, of scope, in the creation of his work that was desirable for literature if he did not allow his political affiliations to become his primary driving force, as this surely would limit his technique. But there are many types of political or quasi-political novel: literary dogmatism, like any other kind, has a habit of being refuted 'because it is there', especially in a century when rapidly changing social forces demand an equivalent literary response or even anticipation. Conrad (like Graham Greene) left himself scope for manoeuvre in his political novels because the politics were only a scene or back-drop to the personal tragedies enacted.[19]

Now Conrad had seen political intrigue as squalid: Nostromo, Verloc and Razumov respectively, in the three novels I have mentioned, are forced sooner or later to degenerate—morally and physically—

33

through their involvement. A realistically unpleasant setting increasingly seemed appropriate to writers bent upon telling, in comparison with Conrad, less complex and more straightforward 'home truths' of a social or political nature. In her Preface to the first edition of Robert Tressall's *The Ragged Trousered Philanthropists* (1914) Jessie Pope wrote:

> with grim humour and pitiless realism the working man has revealed the lives and hearts of his mates, their opinions of their betters, their political views, their attitude toward socialism. Through the busy din of the hammer and the scraping knife, the clang of the pail, the swish of the whitewash, the yell of the foreman, comes the talk of the men, their jokes and curses, their hopes and terrors, the whimpering of their old people, the cry of their children.[20]

The novel has received less sympathetic attention in recent years. A. C. Ward claims that like 'other writings of its class . . . the impact is dulled by over-emphasis and repetition'. But he agrees that the troubles of this group of house-painters and decorators are 'convincingly realistic', thus making the book 'a reliable account of working-class conditions in Britain before World War I'. It is a 'classic proletarian novel . . . by an unprofessional writer' which asserts, as its title suggests, that 'employees are philanthropists accepting a pittance for work which produces wealth for employers'. Having given one, Ward asserts: 'a recital of its literary shortcomings has little point'.[21] Here, it seems to me, the critic has been doing something that endangers the development of 'political prose'. Orwell, Koestler and Rex Warner were all to suffer from the faint praise of critics who found their works deficient by the use of arbitrary criteria that derive from novels of a quite different, and irrelevant, kind. It cannot be said too often that literature that anticipates or reflects rapidly changing social or political conditions will appear increasingly varied and thus demand an unprecedented critical response. A novel like Tressall's should not be criticized for what it is not, when positive qualities go unappreciated. *The Road to Wigan Pier* (1937) (biography, essay and at times as much of a novel as *The Clergyman's Daughter* (1935)) has, in its remorselessly realistic account of poverty and hardship, much in common with *The Ragged Trousered Philanthropists*. But critics have never been happy or clear about it; I suspect because it does not conform to preconceived ideas. Kingsley Amis praised *The Road to Wigan Pier* as 'of use to any science-fiction writer in search of a theme' and a fresh cause of dissatisfaction with *1984*',[22] while Tom Hopkinson dismissed it as 'Orwell's worst book' suggesting that it was an uneasy blend of misconceived impressions.[23] In certain passages Tressall's novel uses facts, figures and data, in the manner of Bennett and Wells, together with powerfully realistic, Zola-esque prose, to communicate with effective simplicity the plight of the worker before modern legislation:

> One morning Owen did not get to the yard till ten o'clock and felt so ill that he would not have gone at all if they had not been in sore need of all the money he could earn. The least exertion brought on a violent fit of coughing, and it was only by an almost superhuman effort of will that he managed to get through the work. When he arrived at the yard he found Bert White cleaning out the dirty pots in the paint shop. The noise he made with the scraping knife prevented him from hearing Owen's approach, and the latter stood watching him for some minutes before speaking. The stone floor of the paint shop was damp and slimy and the whole place as chilly as a tomb. The boy was trembling with cold, and he looked pitifully undersized and frail as he bent over his work with an old apron girt about him. Although it was so cold he had turned back the sleeves of his jacket to keep them clean, or to prevent them getting any dirtier for, like the rest of his attire, they were thickly encrusted with dried paint of many colours.
>
> He was wearing a man's coat and a pair of skimpy boy's trousers, and his thin legs appearing under the big jacket gave him a grotesque appearance. There were smears of paint on his face, and his hands and fingernails were grimed with it. But most pitiful of all were his dreadful hob-nailed boots, the uppers of which were an eighth of an inch thick, and very stiff. Across the front of the boot the leather had warped into ridges and valleys which chafed his chilblained feet and made them bleed. The soles were five-eighths of an inch thick, hard and inflexible, and almost as heavy as iron, and studded with hobnails.
>
> (*The Ragged Trousered Philanthropists*, pp. 219–20)

Here, I would suggest, the realism is part of the message: these are the conditions men and boys (and their families) were forced to suffer in an unfair and socially unequal capitalist system. The factual details prevent sentimentality. It is true that pity for man in a harsh and limited environment will produce—as in the case of Wilfred Owen's verse—a restricted, specialized literary form. But, one is tempted to say, so what? No naturalist would criticize a duck for not being a swan. And he would not even be a naturalist if he failed to recognize the special under-water merits of a fish just because he had been shaking his head over its failure to develop the power of flight.

There is an unselfconscious starkness about the way Owen's resolution to commit suicide is presented which I find disturbing. Had literature been written during, rather than after, imprisonment in a concentration camp it would have been, I think, of such a nature. It is the voice of someone who has lost all will other than the desire to tell the truth.[24]

The theatre saw, of course, the development of a new realism that was if anything more remarkable and more noticeable than the equivalents in other branches of literature. Holbrook Jackson first writes of G. B. Shaw as a 'socialist and realist' who, along with H. G. Wells and a host of lesser known names of the 1890s (Richard Whiteing, Cunninghame Graham, Frank Harris, Grant Allen, Robert Blatchford), was using his skill in the propagation of socialist theories.[25] But Shaw became of prime importance because by writing a 'new' kind of drama— an 'Ibsenite' drama—he found a much more successful way of communicating ideas in which he had tried, unsuccessfully, to interest the public in his earlier novels such as *The Irrational Knot* (written 1880) and *An Unsocial Socialist* (1883). Neither received much critical approval even from Shaw himself and the latter work was called by Tindall 'this shocking, second-rate novel'. These were literary efforts dominated by the desire to teach Marxist theories in one case and the value of money in the other. Such passages as the following from the 1883 work indicate the extent to which Shaw was writing tracts masquerading as novels:

> He wished to pay the mason the just value of his work, no more and no less. But this he could not ascertain. The only available standard was the market price, and this he rejected as being fixed by competition among capitalists who could only secure profit by obtaining from their workmen more products than they paid them for, and could only tempt customers by offering a share of the unpaid-for part of the products as a reduction in price. Thus he found that the system of witholding the indispensable materials for production and subsistence from the labourers, except on condition

of their supporting an idle class whilst accepting a lower standard of comfort for themselves than for that idle class, rendered the determination of just ratios of exchange, and consequently the practice of honest dealing, impossible.[26]

It reads like a Marxist text-book, and a boring one at that. What Tressall could make us feel and suffer Shaw could only discuss—in the novel. But in his plays he became quite another writer, not in his subject matter but in his ability to use it with literary effectiveness.

The 'realistic' dramatization of social and class problems, of the hypocrisy, cant and prejudice that Ibsen had mercilessly exposed in such plays as *The Doll's House* (1879) and *An Enemy of the People* (1882), were in Shaw given a wit, irony and charm that owed much to the influence of Oscar Wilde and Samuel Butler. The box-office appeal of Shaw's plays has been confirmed in the success of musical adaptations, so that it may be forgotten how sharp and bitter was the social and political pill which his plays administered—the Prefaces are not, after all, performed.

The real power of money, the naïvety of being content to ignore economic reality and the evil which can be overlooked along with the economics, are all potently expressed in this little exchange from *Widowers' Houses* (1892)

> COKANE. His [Sartorius'] affection for his daughter is a redeeming point—a redeeming point, certainly.
> LICKCHEESE. She's a lucky daughter, sir. Many another daughter has been turned out upon the streets to gratify his affection for her. That's what business is, sir, you see.[27]

Now Sartorius the slum landlord is portrayed as, if anything, less wicked than those like Cokane and Trench who enjoy the luxury of feeling moral without realizing that their money is equally dirty—in fact that it is the same money. And, of course, Trench who had seemed an idealist accepts a marriage that is part of a corrupt capitalist deal. It is reported that during the two performances of the play in 1892 'socialists applauded what others hissed'.[28]

Major Barbara (1905) continued the portrayal of Shaw's 'unpleasant' arguments. What is the message of this play? Clearly Shaw approved of hard thinking in economic matters and Undershaft, the arch-capitalist weapons magnate, seems a Shavian mouthpiece when made to say to his daughter Barbara, lately of the Salvation Army,

. . . you have made for yourself something that you call a morality or a religion or what not. It doesn't fit the facts. Well, scrap it. Scrap it and get one that does fit. That is what is wrong with the world at present. It scraps its obsolete steam engines and dynamos; but it won't scrap its old prejudices and its old moralities and its old religions and its old political constitutions. What's the result? In machinery it does very well; but in morals and religion and politics it is working nearer bankruptcy every year.[29]

Such arguments delivered in the 'no-nonsense' tone of those, like Wells and later Wyndham Lewis, who wrote of cant and hypocrisy and humbug, may yet seem to exhibit old-fashioned, Victorian faith in the perfectability of man through applied science. And, in this play, Cusins, the poet-philosopher, willingly inherits the munitions empire with the declared approval of his betrothed Barbara. Again we may ask: what are we to make of it? Does the play not suggest that the 'right' man (that is the man who has the correct, the real, the rewarding, even the humane, ideas) should try to achieve a benevolent dictatorship, and not be afraid of dirtying his hands with money and industry and, if necessary, armaments? And do not such views imply a distrust of democracy, which is, to use the word that fits Shaw's hard-hitting style, 'unrealistic'? We shall in the next chapter follow the apparent connection between attacking democracy and admiring machinery. And this connection is important because it is revealed in writers' styles: vocabulary, imagery and the whole texture of their work.

Now I have been exploring the way in which Shaw communicated social and political ideas. It seems that he solved his novelistic problems by putting the more propagandist passages in the Prefaces and, as we have seen, by making, in the plays themselves, the didacticism assimilable through wit, humour and a kind of throw-away outrageousness of tone. Yet teaching there is: Shaw wanted his audiences to be educated socially and politically by his plays. John Galsworthy, too, made his own not unsimilar contribution with plays such as *The Silver Box* (1906) and *Strife* (1909) where 'monolithic simplicity' of plot and structure at times equals Shaw's power of witty dialogue as a vehicle for communicating social and political abuses.[30] Yet again, however, it seems valid to ask: are we considering a lesser art-form? Or are Shaw, and Galsworthy after him, whatever they may have intended, extending the dimensions of theatre?

One man of the time was in no doubt: 'The best plays were written by a man trying to preach Socialism. All the art of all the artists looked tiny and tedious beside the art which was a by-product of propaganda.'[31] The whole passage in *Heretics* where G. K. Chesterton makes this assertion is worth study. Having said perceptively that Shaw wrote for 'the vast and universal church of which he is the only member', he continues, with his other eye on Kipling:

> The two typical men of genius whom I have mentioned here . . . are very symbolic, if only because they have shown that the fiercest dogmatists can make the best artists. In the *fin de siècle* atmosphere every one was crying out that literature should be free from all causes and all ethical creeds. Art was to produce only exquisite workmanship, and it was especially the note of those days to demand brilliant plays and brilliant short stories. And when they got them, they got them from a couple of moralists. The best short stories were written by a man trying to preach Imperialism. The best plays were written by a man trying to preach Socialism. All the art of all the artists looked tiny and tedious beside the art which was a by-product of propaganda.[32]

Two of Chesterton's observations of 1905 are of great importance in anticipating the later development of English political literature. Such writing is for him akin to, or a substitute for, religious literature; and, secondly, such writing has a recognizable quality or ingredient irrespective of the author's political views, whether extreme Right or Left and whether play, story or some other literary form. The ingredient seems to involve purpose, commitment, specialized subject-matter, and desire for potent communication. Here we find the assertion that political propaganda can produce good, even great, art and indeed there is the implication that in a time of pessimism or loss of religious faith such writing can produce *the only* true literature. But Chesterton was less than fair to Wilde.

Allan Rodway, in his essay 'The Last Phase',[33] shows some surprise at the similarity between the patriotic verse of Kipling and of Oscar Wilde, though he does not mention that Wilde's 'Ave Imperatrix' (as opposed to the poem of the same name by Kipling) finishes with the most un-Kiplingesque assertion:

> Though childless, and with thorn-crowned head,
> Up the steep road must England go,

> Yet when this fiery web is spun,
> Her watchmen shall descry from far
> The Young Republic like a sun
> Rise from these crimson seas of war.

Yet the two poems are similar in the hymn-like tone appropriate for the exposition of creeds in a faithless era. The religious association of Beauty and Art with political idealism is probably as old as political man—certainly Wordsworth in *The Prelude* accepted the association as one premise of poetic creation, and Yeats was to sing in similar vein of Irish nationalism. Moreover, although Wilde described art as 'perfectly useless' he also claimed, in *The Soul of Man Under Socialism*, that 'The work of art is to dominate the spectator'.[34] Thus Wilde in verse, as well as prose, approached propaganda from art—*The Ballad of Reading Gaol* is perhaps an example of this trend—while Kipling, travelling in the reverse direction, turned propagandist verse into 'something genuinely original'.[35]

There seems to be a grudging admission that Kipling was, at times anyway, a great stylist both as poet and prose-writer, by those critics who dislike his political views. And even critics who are perhaps more sympathetic to his views appear to be on the defensive.[36] Kipling's work raises a question felt more acutely in a novelist such as Céline: to what extent does literature communicating morally indefensible views remain good literature? Is it incurably tarnished? (Dr Steiner has made such questions peculiarly his own, especially in the field of political writing.)[37] Certainly Orwell's approach to Kipling seems healthy and positive:

> It is no use claiming . . . that when Kipling describes a British soldier beating a 'nigger' with a cleaning rod in order to get money out of him, he is acting merely as a reporter and does not necessarily approve what he describes. There is not the slightest sign anywhere in Kipling's work that he disapproves of that kind of conduct—on the contrary, there is a definite sign of sadism in him, over and above the brutality which a writer of that type has to have. Kipling is a jingo imperialist, he is morally insensitive and aesthetically disgusting. It is better to start by admitting that, and then to try to find out why it is that he survives while the refined people who have sniggered at him seem to wear so badly.[38]

Yet sensible as it is, Orwell's approach seems to suggest that somehow the good (writing ability) can be separated from the bad (political and racial prejudices). I doubt whether Orwell really felt this to be possible: he believed that political affiliations—even when they were not consciously communicated in writing—permeate the style, the texture, the very atmosphere of literature, because strongly-held beliefs are ultimately inseparable from a writer's emotions, from his very psyche. Bad politics and good writing could mix perfectly well—but *both* qualities would permeate the literature. Thus when a reader approaches any of Kipling's work he is likely to bring with his interest an awareness that Kipling has a distinct reputation, and that his writing has been seen as symptomatic of an imperialist's world-view. When the reader comes across a passage such as the following from a well-known story he will feel duty-bound to take note and say with recognition, 'Ah!'. Kipling is describing the Indian railway:

> There are no cushions in the Intermediate class, and the population are either Intermediate, which is Eurasian, or Native, which for a long night journey is nasty, or loafer, which is amusing though intoxicated. Intermediates do not buy from refreshment-rooms. They carry their food in bundles and pots, and buy sweets from the native sweetmeat-sellers, and drink the roadside water. That is why in the hot weather Intermediates are taken out of the carriages dead, and in all weathers are most properly looked down upon.[39]

Presumably such a passage communicates what is unacceptably imperialist, and the humorous, 'Just-so Story' tone of 'most properly looked down upon' can only aggravate further a reader's dislike of earlier references to 'nasty' natives. And yet there are people of professed left-wing and humanist views who will argue that the poem 'Loot' (where, as Orwell has said, the 'nigger' is beaten with cleaning rods 'to show you everything 'e owns')[40] must be seen as a faithful account of how the British soldier will behave in such a situation—just as in 'That Day' the cowardice under fire of Tommy Atkins is more concerned with frank realism than with any condemnation of military behaviour:

> . . . I 'eard a beggar squealin' out for quarter as 'e ran,
> An' I thought I knew the voice an'—it was me!

An argument can indeed be made that in such poems as 'That Day' and 'Stellenbosch' Kipling is only anticipating the Siegfried Sassoon of 'The General' and 'They': that Kipling, like Sassoon, was telling those outside the experience what it was really like—the political or social views being only of secondary importance, whatever the writer may have intended. It is interesting to note that both Siegfried Sassoon and E. M. Forster liked to read the poetry of T. S. Eliot in the dark days of the Great War. I suspect that far from finding Eliot mainly a 'relief' as Orwell has suggested, writers found a kindred spirit communicating the realities of loneliness in the alien environment of a big modern city.[41]

If we search for definitive statements as to the worth of late nine-teenth and early twentieth century political literature, or even as to its essential qualities, we are forced to accept or reject opinions rather than facts. Except perhaps one: the general movement of writing in the period 1880–1920 was towards a realism (whether looking out at society or into the workings of the mind) which steadily brought most literature into the arena of social and political problems from which perhaps the bulk of it was not to escape until authoritarianism and World War threatened literature itself. And, in addition to this demonstrable trend, we can with justification suspect that political beliefs would increasingly fill the void created by the loss of religious faith.

Chapter Two

Flirtations with Authoritarianism

We are the first men of a Future that has not materialized.
>   P. Wyndham Lewis, *Blasting and Bombardiering*

. . . far above and far as sight endures
Like whips of anger
With lightning's danger
There runs the quick perspective of the future.
>   Stephen Spender, 'The Pylons'

A writer on English political literature must feel when he contemplates the 1930s that at last he has arrived and that foreign influences—political as well as stylistic—really begin to show. Whatever doubts and equivocations there may have been about the political nature of the work of, say, Galsworthy or Kipling or D. H. Lawrence, surely Auden, Spender, Day Lewis and MacNeice (dubbed, as a group, 'MacSpaunday' by Roy Campbell) left no doubt that the readers of their verse were not only learning political truths but being made to feel political emotions. All this may be true, but it is interesting to observe that the 'New Country' poets felt it necessary to add to the effect of their verse by stating, in prose, their intentions and, as they saw them, achievements. George Orwell, in his essay 'Inside The Whale', quoted from Louis MacNeice's *Modern Poetry* (1938), intending to illustrate his criticism of the 'New Country' or 'New Signatures' group:

> The poets of 'New Signatures', unlike Yeats and Eliot, are emotionally partisan. Yeats proposed to turn his back on desire and hatred; Eliot sat back and watched other people's emotions with ennui and an ironical self-pity . . . The whole poetry, on the other hand, of Auden, Spender, and Day Lewis implies that they have desires and hatreds of their own and, further, that they think some things ought to be desired and others hated.

43

And again:

> The poets of 'New Signatures' have swung back . . . to the Greek preference for information or statement. The first requirement is to have something to say, and after that you must say it as well as you can.

'In other words,' Orwell continues, ' "purpose" has come back, the younger writers have "gone into politics",' but, Orwell adds, 'Eliot and Co. are not really so non-partisan as Mr MacNeice seems to suggest.'[1]

Now such a critical and implicitly condemnatory (even at times mocking) approach to these writers can tell us a great deal. Our attention is drawn to their essentially *grouped* activities as literary men—not that they actually were all the same but that they thought of themselves as a group and were thought of at the time as a group. One of Orwell's complaints is that 'their criticisms of one another's work have always been (to put it mildly) good natured' (p. 560). Moreover, and this would be a profounder criticism, if a group of writers are politically inspired is not this potentially collectivist, even authoritarian? Certainly Orwell's critique seems to suggest this idea: 'Suddenly we have got . . . into a sort of Boy Scout atmosphere of bare knees and community singing.' Indeed their politico-literary activities are seen as a substitute for religion: 'The typical literary man ceases to be a cultured expatriate with a leaning towards the church, and becomes an eager-minded schoolboy with a leaning towards Communism' (p. 559). From such group leanings, albeit Left leanings, Orwell had already, by 1937, dissociated himself and was to gain literary and personal recognition through that dissociation.

But what of the literary Right? Was there a similar polarity observable to the keen eyes of Orwell (whose political views were hardly Red, never Blue but increasingly jaundiced)? Perhaps he was too readily able to discover political orthodoxies. Although he called Yeats, Joyce, Eliot, Pound, D. H. Lawrence, Wyndham Lewis and even Aldous Huxley 'reactionary', he felt they scarcely formed a 'group' and admitted that 'several of them would strongly object to being coupled with the others' (p. 555). However, if we waive this objection on the grounds that subjective preferences are scarcely relevant, are we left with a right-wing politico-literary group as *The Reactionaries* would suggest? And if we decide that there was explicitly or implicitly a group, is it discernible in ideology only or is it apparent also in the nature, the texture, of the literature produced by these 'reactionaries'?

If we look at the way the Left writers of the 1930s regarded the so-called Right, I think it will become clear that the 'reactionaries' *were* regarded as a group, but in a very special sense, and that the two groups resembled each other not only stylistically (which is to be expected since influences upon subject-matter inevitably often created identical problems) but also ideologically (which may be more surprising but seems, to me at least, equally inevitable).

There is, for example, in the literature of the late nineteenth century and earlier decades of this century a fascination with machines and with the products of technology that affected the imagery and metre of certain poetry and which, I suggest, reflected, on the part of the writers concerned, an authoritarian world-view. It also emerges in the work of certain prose writers. This authoritarianism stems, I think, from a belief that technology properly used could solve social problems and that, therefore, the right government must be found to direct such enterprise. However, behind this rational approach to the use of technology lay an irrational attraction felt for machines and their immense inhuman power. The names associated with the trend are W. E. Henley, Kipling, Shaw, Wells, Wyndham Lewis, W. H. Auden, Stephen Spender and Roy Campbell.

Henley, as an editor, encouraged Kipling, Shaw and Wells, and as a poet influenced, by his harsh, realistic style, the poetry of T. S. Eliot. With Kipling, Henley shared 'the dream of unending progress through empire and machine'[2] and his last poem 'A Song of Speed' tells of a ride in a 1901 Mercedes whose pipes and cylinders he handled in 'religious awe':

> . . . this Thing,
> This marvellous Mercédes,
> This triumphing contrivance,
> Comes to make other
> Man's life than she found it:
> The Earth for her tyres
> As the sea for his keels;
> Alike in the old lands,
> Enseamed with the wheel-ways
> Of thousands of dusty
> And dim generations, . . .
> Thus the Mercédes
> Comes, O, she comes,

45

> This astonishing device,
> This amazing Mercédes,
> With Speed—
> *Speed in the Fear of the Lord*

A comparable feeling for engines is shown in Kipling's poem 'Mac-Andrew's Hymn' where the mechanical rhythms of the verse communicate 'the intimate spiritual connection between Calvinism and modern industrialism'.[3]

The 'purring dynamos' worshipped by MacAndrew are humorously portrayed in H. G. Wells's well-known short story 'The Lord of the Dynamos' where a native of indeterminate racial origin kills for his mechanistic master. A cynic might suggest that Wells was at times scarcely more advanced than the native in his admiration of what mechanization might achieve in a properly organized international social and political system—though he would be wrong to do so. It is in the later controversial prose of Shaw and more particularly Wyndham Lewis that a recognizably bombastic and authoritarian note is found. In the case of Shaw there is no particular connection with machines, though I think—despite his Preface to *Back to Methuselah* (1921)—he was attracted to the deterministic nature of evolution. He, like Wells and Samuel Butler before him, believed that man could, and no doubt would, develop the techniques of social improvement just as he had developed the bicycle and the motor-car. In Wyndham Lewis, the Futurist—or in his case Vorticist—connection of machine-power with aesthetic and political ideals reached for a time its English apotheosis, as the title of his 1914 magazine *Blast* would suggest. The texture of the prose written by Shaw in his political essays of the 1920s and 1930s is often very similar to Wyndham Lewis's (and indeed to some of Wells's). *The Intelligent Woman's Guide to Socialism, Capitalism, Sovietism and Fascism* (1928) by Shaw contains absurdly laudatory and unrealistic pronouncements about the Soviet Union: 'mistakes are not hushed up in Russia . . . Russia never ceased to fill her workers with hope and self-respect'.[4] In *Everybody's Political What's What?* (1944) Shaw launches into an attack on democracy which in style as well as content is extremely reminiscent of Wyndham Lewis in such books as *The Art of Being Ruled* (1926):

> Complete political standardization, with the suppression of the last vestiges of the party system, will rescue masses of energy otherwise wasted in politics for more productive ends. All the

humbug of a democratic suffrage, all the imbecility that is so wastefully manufactured, will henceforth be spared this happy people.

(*The Art of Being Ruled*)[5]

A nearly desperate difficulty in the way of its realization [democracy's] is the delusion that the method of securing it is to give votes to everybody, which is the one certain method of defeating it. Adult suffrage kills it dead. High-minded and well-informed people desire it: but they are in a negligible minority at the polling stations.

(*Everybody's Political What's What?*)[6]

The tone is one of absolute certainty: no fault in what is said could possibly exist; 'I know all the answers,' it seems to say. It is a kind of prose which mixes long abstract terms with shouts of 'humbug', 'cant', 'rubbish'. It is in fact the language of writer turned orator—an orator whose glibness and belief in 'obvious' straightforward solutions would be implicitly authoritarian even if the sentiments were not directly so. Such quotations, from writers who ostensibly should have represented the opposite ends of the political spectrum seem to confirm W. Y. Tindall's comment: 'From right as well as left, artists, seeking order, kicked at the decaying body of liberalism' (*Forces in Modern British Literature*, p. 83). In fact, with characteristic bluntness, Wyndham Lewis was happy to rationalize what was new in post-Great War European politics: '*Fascismo* is merely a spectacular marinettian flourish put on to the tail, or, if you like, the head, of marxism: that is, of course, fascism as interpreted by its founder, Mussolini' (*The Art of Being Ruled*, p. 369). The approach of Wyndham Lewis, and the other writers mentioned, to politics, society and even the arts was one which was liable to see these phenomena in terms of trends, percentages and measurable forces—indeed in scientific or mechanical terms: 'What will shortly be reached will be a great socialist state such as Marx intended, rigidly centralized, working from top to bottom with the regularity and smoothness of a machine' (*The Art of Being Ruled*, p. 370).

But in Wyndham Lewis's case, behind the rationalization lay a fascination. For years he had loved machines and was attracted by their power, as his accounts of preferring guns to horses during the Great War would confirm.[7] And such pictures as 'A Battery Shelled' give evidence of an attraction towards machines which he could express in

47

more than one art form. It is significant that his primary move into a
kind of journalism (the manifesto *Blast*) should have condemned
outright, and often in capital letters, so many aspects of the English way
of life but approved of England the 'industrial island machine'.[8]

Roy Campbell, a South African, has been described by W. Y.
Tindall as 'another, lesser Lewis', whose disciple he was (*Forces in
Modern British Literature*, p. 89). I suppose Campbell has produced the
most purely Fascist verse written in the English Language. ('Fascist'
is not a word to be used with impunity, but here it is clinical.) This is
part of 'A Song for the People' (1930):

> A shapeless mass to any rhythm worked,
> See how its legs to raucous music stir
> As if some string of sausages were jerked
> And tugged, and worried by a snarling cur!
> Funnelled with roaring mouth that gorp like cod
> And spit the bitten ends of thick cigars,
> This is the beast that dares to praise its god
> Under the calm derision of the stars!
> When from the lonely beacons that we tend
> We gaze far down across the nameless flats,
> Where the dark road of progress without end
> Is cobbled with a line of bowler hats.
>
> Searching the lampless horror of that fen,
> We think of those whose pens or swords have made
> Steep ladders of the broken bones of men
> To climb above its everlasting shade:
> Of men whose scorn has turned them into gods,
> Christs, tyrants, martyrs, who in blood or fire
> Drove their clean furrows through these broken clods
> Yet raised no harvest from such barren mire.

The violence and harshness of the vocabulary, the mechanical regularity
of the metre, suggest at times a modern, cruder Pope, at times a Mac-
Diarmid of the Right (whom, incidentally, Campbell bitterly attacked).
Here, as in other less extreme poems, people are seen from afar as
'masses' which an authoritative power must channel like machine-
fluid. Auden or even Spender tended in the era between the Wars to
view social problems from a distant vantage point whose look-out is
assisted by the techniques of applied science. But Campbell viewed the

masses themselves as a problem in a Nietzschean way reminiscent of Wyndham Lewis or D. H. Lawrence at their most intolerant.

Now in the passages quoted above from MacNeice's *Modern Poetry* we can see something of the special sense in which writers like Yeats and Eliot were regarded as a reactionary group by the Left poets of the 'Pink Decade'. Stephen Spender, looking back in 1953, also made a firm distinction between the writers of the twenties and those of the thirties. The latter were committed politically, emotionally and in a real sense aesthetically to the destruction of Fascism, which they seemed to regard as a monstrous death-throe of 'laissez-faire' capitalism. Indeed so total did they feel their commitment that it left them in some doubts as to whether they should be men of letters or men of action.

> We were [records Spender] divided between . . . artistic and . . . public conscience, and unable to fuse the two. I now think that what I should have done was either throw myself entirely into political action; or, refusing to waste my energies on half-politics, make my solitary creative work an agonized, violent, bitter state-ment of the anti-fascist passion.
>
> (*World Within World*, p. 174)[9]

A writer who was not thus committed, so it seemed at the time, to the Left writers of the 1930s, was in effect pro-Fascist, even if his literary powers were concerned mainly with style, technique, and form and not (as perhaps it already seemed in the case of Ezra Pound or Wyndham Lewis) explicitly pro-Fascist. To quote again from Spender:

> The sense of political doom, pending in unemployment, Fascism, and the overwhelming threat of war, was by now so universal that even to ignore these things was in itself a political attitude. Just as the pacifist is political in refusing to participate in war, so the writer who refuses to recognise the political nature of our age must to some extent be refusing to deal with an experience in which he himself is involved. . . . A pastoral poem in 1936 was not just a pastoral poem: it was also a non-political poem. (p. 215)

The purpose of this study is not to examine ideologies, but by now it should be apparent that for a writer of committed left-wing literature of the 1930s the distinction between a poem's form (or that of a play or novel) and its political or social purpose was becoming blurred, or even indiscernable. One way of illustrating this mutual involvement of ideology and style is to examine the Auden, Spender, Day Lewis group of poets in order to see how their poetry exhibited three concerns collectivism, 'religion' and emotion.

The first of these concerns or attributes is generally admitted as characteristic of the thirties' poetry. Robin Skelton has spoken of its 'obsession with ideas of community, and . . . obsession with the notion of war'.[10] If you put these obsessions together you will get, I suggest, a collectivist or even potentially authoritarian atmosphere. Day Lewis's 'The Magnetic Mountain' (1933), dedicated to W. H. Auden, quotes from Rex Warner's 'Hymn' (1933) as an epigraph:

> Come, then, companions, this is the spring of blood,
> Heart's heyday, movement of masses, beginning of good.

Orwell, who had once spoken contemptuously of Auden as a 'gutless Kipling', continued, even during his apology, to be amused by the 'atmosphere of uplift', the 'pure scout-master' tone of the early poetry of this group (*CEJL*, p. 561). Inevitably Orwell shied away from their collective persuasion, from any attempt to substitute what in his opinion would have been one form of domination for another. It might be true that Marx and Freud could be seen as liberating influences, telling people how they had for centuries been robbed and restricted by the vested interests of those in power, but was not the key-note of this new poetry the desire to establish a new 'enlightened' collectivist *system*? Yet, whatever criticisms an outsider might make, there is no doubting the sincerity of the group and their belief that now, if ever, was the chance to do something. As Spender in *World Within World* remarks:

> I was 'political' not just because I was involved, but in feeling I must choose to defend a good cause against a bad one. Auden remarked to me at the end of the war that he was political in the 1930s just because he thought something could and should be done.[11]

Most commentators make Auden the leader of the band. But Tindall has stressed the precedence of Hugh MacDiarmid—not so much in his style as in his ideology.[12] His hatred of the bourgeoisie meant that the 'New Country' poets were in a sense, by following MacDiarmid's lead, supporting a cause dedicated to their destruction. MacDiarmid has always been, however, in danger of placing himself in an equally ludicrous situation. For he has presented himself as a poet of the (Scottish) people, writing verse which every working man or woman must understand if it is to be justified.

Are my poems spoken in the factories and fields,
In the streets o' the toon?
Gin they're no', then I'm failin' to dae
What I ocht to ha' dune.

Gin I canna win through to the man in the street,
The wife by the hearth,
A' the cleverness on earth'll no' mak' up
For the damnable dearth.

('Second Hymn to Lenin', 1935)[13]

And yet the editors of his selected poems, both of them Scottish scholars, found that MacDiarmid's verse posed 'special problems for the reader'.[14] Indeed in this poem the poet seems to admit to the kind of literary problems which 'political poetry' was raising for C. Day Lewis:

Poetry like politics maun cut
The cackle and pursue real ends,
Unerringly as Lenin, and to that
Its nature better tends.

Wi' Lenin's vision equal poet's gift
And what unparalleled force was there!
Nocht in a' literature wi' that
Begins to compare.

If a poetry of expediency, a perfect socialist realism, is to be achieved that will bring the poet 'face to face/Wi' the human race', it would surely be more expedient to employ language that millions rather than hundreds will readily appreciate. And expediency was very much a part of what MacDiarmid had to say in the era that links his name with Auden's:

As necessary, and insignificant, as death
Wi' a' its agonies in the cosmos still
The Cheka's horrors are in their degree;
And'll end suner! What maitters 't wha we kill
To lessen that foulest murder that deprives
Maist men o' real lives?

('First Hymn to Lenin')[15]

We may well recall Auden's later qualms about 'necessary murder'.[16] Here I think is the key distinction between MacDiarmid and 'these pseudos' as he later called the 'New Country' poets, for the Scot remained ideologically constant.[17] Yet, paradoxically, his 'Third Hymn to Lenin' (1957), where he spurns any possible connection with Auden, most resembles that poet's style in its imagery and in its wide-angled view of social evolution. He is of course addressing Lenin:

> On days of revolutionary turning points you literally flourished,
> Became clairvoyant, foresaw the movement of classes,
> And the probable zig-zags of the revolution
> As if on your palm;
> Not only an analytical mind but also
> A great constructive, synthesizing mind
> Able to build up in thought the new reality
> As it must actually come
> By force of definite laws eventually,
> Taking into consideration, of course,
> Conscious interference, the bitter struggle
> For the tasks still before the Party, and the class it leads
> As well as possible diversions and inevitable actions
> Of all other classes.

Although MacDiarmid's verse is of uneven quality, due perhaps to uncertainty of style—Scottish Lallans, English abstract—at his best the note of conviction rings true in a Yeatsian manner.[18] At others the tone of invective and diatribe detracts from the verse because the reader senses a lack of precision—or worse, a lack of control. For wholehearted, single-minded political conviction written in intense communist realist (even Expressionist) terms, only a work such as Sean O'Casey's play *The Star Turns Red* (1940) equals the verse of MacDiarmid; but the Irishman's note is shrill, his vision naïve, and in the year following the Nazi–Soviet pact the play must surely have seemed *passé* if not irrelevant. And at the opposite end of the political spectrum Roy Campbell was, perhaps, even better than MacDiarmid at handling those strong political convictions which might be shouted at a public meeting.

And so there seems no reason to argue with those who make Auden the primary stylistic innovator of political verse to have emerged in the early thirties. Yet the innovations have met with a mixed response. The atmosphere of 'uplift' mentioned by Orwell occurs in dozens of poems published in the early thirties, and parodied by William Empson in 'Just a Smack at Auden', which begins:

Waiting for the end, boys, waiting for the end
What is there to be or do?
What's become of me or you?
Are we kind or are we true?
Sitting two and two, boys, waiting, for the end.

Two of Auden's *Poems* (1930), Nos. XII and XXX, anthologized by Skelton (*Poetry of the Thirties*), exhibit the essential characteristics. The language may be colloquial, consciously awkward, or even approach office-jargon:

We made all possible preparations
Drew up a list of firms,
Constantly revised our calculations
And allotted the farms,

Issued all the orders expedient
In this kind of case:
Most, as was expected, were obedient,
Though there were murmurs, of course.

('Let History be my Judge')

Or it may be militantly intellectual, touching freely on psychological, economic and political topics which systematize the view of man that sees him as a unit in the phenomena of social malaise:

Sir, no man's enemy, forgiving all
But will its negative inversion, be prodigal:
Send to us power and light, a sovereign touch
Curing the intolerable neural itch,
The exhaustion of weaning, the liar's quinsy,
And the distortions of ingrown virginity.
Prohibit sharply the rehearsed response
And gradually correct the coward's stance;

('Petition')

The tone is one of youthful exhortation: exuberant, clever, convinced. Together such early poems formed a manifesto. And the literary influences revealed in these lines are those we would expect to find since they derive from those poets admired in Day Lewis's *A Hope For Poetry* (1934): Hopkins, Owen, Eliot, Yeats, Hardy. (A group notable, not for its socialistic leanings, of course, but for its innovatory powers in modern verse.) The half-rhymes and alliterations of XII encourage the

53

strident, challenging, punning tone appropriate to the poem: 'firms/ farms' and 'case/course' go on to 'abuse/boys' and 'anyone/win'. (Again, the influence of Eliot suggests a conscious break with the literary past. Because the liberating message is new?) His friend Christopher Isherwood has said that to appreciate Auden's early verse the reader has to realize that he was 'essentially a scientist'.[19] Thus the terms, even the jargon, of science and especially the social sciences, abound in much of Auden's early, and most politically committed, work. Terms such as 'neural itch', 'quinsy', 'distortions', 'ingrown' and 'rehearsed response' build on Eliot's 'patient etherised upon a table'. The literary innovation is intended to encourage political and social innovation—or so it seems. The lists of industrial objects—chimneys, bridges, wharves, canals, tramlines, trucks, rails, power stations, pylons, high-tension wires etc., of the poem beginning 'Get there if you can and see the land you once were proud to own', are further examples of how a social and political viewpoint being urged in verse can ultimately affect the whole shape, indeed the entire technique, of writing. Such lists also suggest a total, even lofty, view of society seen as from an aircraft. The 'country houses at the end of drives', the 'new styles of architecture' ('Petition') are significantly generalized—a particularity could be too easily disputed, too demonstrably debatable. But a general truth is, in the century of mass society, so much more important. This at least seems to be both political message and justification for a poetic technique that derives from Hardy's *The Dynasts*. Dr Rodway has drawn attention to the 'panoramic view' of the following lines with their recurrent images of airman and hawk:

> Consider this and in our time
> As the hawk sees it or the helmeted airman:
> The clouds rift suddenly—look there
> At cigarette end smouldering on the border.

('Consider')[20]

Auden has said that he valued most in Hardy 'his hawk's vision, his way of looking at life from a very great height',[21] and this fusion of technique and symbol was popular with other poets of the group and is apparent in, for example, Day Lewis's *The Magnetic Mountain* and Spender's 'Landscape Near an Aerodrome'. The airman-hawk image seems to have symbolized a militant, omniscient, Christ-like saviour, whose aesthetic and moral beauty has been anticipated for the group by Hopkins's 'Windhover'.

But, of course, such poetry for all its effectiveness (or all its absurdity)[22] raised problems of interpretation. Quite apart from the fact that very few people read it, and perhaps even fewer understood it, those who got the message jibbed at it—or at least at its implications. For other groups in Europe harangued from the vantage-point of assumed superiority. To quote one contemporary observer, Julian Symons:

> I was amused to read the other day in Richard Hoggart's brilliant book about Auden that 'In *The Orators* the important figure of the Airman symbolizes the forces of release and liberation': amused because I remembered how anxiously this point was debated immediately after the book's publication. Was not the Airman, we asked ourselves, a Fascist?
>
> > The few shall be taught who want to understand,
> > Most of the rest shall love upon the land;
> > Living in one place with a satisfied face
> > All of the women and most of the men
> > Shall work with their hands and not think again.
>
> Were not these Fascist sentiments? Didn't Auden clearly approve of them?[23]

As might be expected George Orwell also had qualms about the way Auden looked at society as if through the wrong end of a telescope. The generalized view of man's political and social behaviour found in the later and more mature poem 'Spain' (again technique and message are inseparable) lead Orwell to comment on the following stanzas:

> To-morrow for the young, the poets exploding like bombs,
> The walks by the lake, the weeks of perfect communion,
> To-morrow the bicycle races
> Through the suburbs on summer evenings. But to-day the
>   struggle.
>
> To-day the deliberate increase in the chances of death,
> The conscious acceptance of guilt in the necessary murder:
> To-day the expending of powers
> On the flat ephemeral pamphlet and the boring meeting.

The second stanza is intended as a sort of thumb-nail sketch of a day in the life of a 'good party man'. In the morning a couple of political murders, a ten-minutes' interlude to stifle 'bourgeois' remorse, and then a hurried luncheon and a busy afternoon and evening chalking walls and distributing leaflets. All very edifying. But notice the phrase 'necessary murder'. It could only have been written by a person to whom murder is at most a *word*. Personally I would not speak so lightly of murder. It so happens that I have seen the bodies of numbers of murdered men. Therefore I have some conception of what murder means—the terror, the hatred, the howling relatives, the post-mortems, the blood, the smells.[24]

Here again we may observe that a writer's political viewpoint (albeit one of disengagement from generalized truths deriving from 'isms', in this case Marxism) will have a profound effect on style. Orwell crusaded for clarity of prose, for referential nouns, because he considered them politically desirable and he made this crusade the very substance of *Homage to Catalonia*, *Animal Farm* and *1984* by writing clear prose 'like a window pane'[25] and inventing, for satirical purposes, the ideal language of distortion, 'Newspeak', whose non-referential abstractions mirrored only the obsessive teachings of authoritarianism.

I have mentioned the 'religious' (some would claim 'religiose') character of 1930s' left-wing verse. The close association of political and quasi-religious ideals was, of course, to be expected—especially perhaps among a literary group which observed and admired from afar. To say that 'It became as normal to hear that so-and-so had "joined" [the Communist party] as it had been . . . when Roman Catholicism was fashionable, to hear that so-and-so had "been received" '[26] is really only to echo Freud: 'If another group tie takes the place of the religious one—and the socialistic tie seems to be succeeding in doing so—then there will be the same intolerance towards outsiders.'[27] Intolerance? Yes, though 'contempt' might be a more accurate word. The most characteristic quality, however, is best described by the phrase: 'communal sacrament'. Skelton uses this when discussing the militant idealism of Rex Warner and Michael Roberts in whose minds revolution and war were becoming almost synonymous. They were acts which could purify by cleansing the world of 'pettiness and selfishness' and by involving the individual in communal suffering.[28] Inevitably Warner's 'Hymn' may be compared with Rupert Brooke's 1914 sonnets, where young soldiers probably doomed to drown in mud are seen almost as novitiates ready for baptism in holy water. Indeed such was the fervour of John Cornford, killed at the age of twenty-one, that the poetry he wrote during the Spanish Civil War is for many painful to read because it seems a permanent testament to the betrayal of political idealism (which Orwell was to record with such passion and clarity in *Homage to Catalonia* (1938)). He was just too good a man whose personal sacrifice was scarcely to be noticed by authoritarian governments committed to a power struggle. Cornford's 'patriotism'—albeit 'deracinated'[29]—is just as unrealistic as Brooke's and no less sincere:

> . . . in Spain
> Our fight's not won till the workers of all the world
> Stand by our guard on Huesca's plain
> Swear that our dead fought not in vain,
> Raise the red flag triumphantly
> For Communism and for liberty.[30]

Even in a poem such as this (which some might claim resembles the cries of Prince Hal no less than those of Rupert Brooke) there are elements peculiarly 'thirty-ish'. As in Auden's 'Spain' the idealism both communicates, and is given form by, the political philosophy. The dialectical thought, the certainties based on propagated notions of past, present and future, are uttered as incantation or catechism—or both at once.

> The past, a glacier, gripped the mountain wall,
> And time was inches, dark was all,
> But here it scales the end of the range,
> The dialectic's point of change,
> Crashes in light and minutes to its fall.
>
> Time present is a cataract whose force
> Breaks down the banks even at its source
> And history forming in our hand's
> Not plasticine but roaring sands,
> Yet we must swing it to its final course.
>
> The intersecting lines that cross both ways,
> Time future, has no image in space,
> Crooked as the road that we must tread,
> Straight as our bullets fly ahead.
> We are the future. The last fight let us face.[31]

Once again in trying to delineate the essential qualities of the verse we find ourselves placed uncomfortably between politics and religion.

I have mentioned the intolerance and contempt of those outside the group—or, if you prefer, those outside history—which Freud had predicted for political parties of the Left as the inheritors of religious bigotry. In *The Magnetic Mountain* C. Day Lewis, usually considered the most indebted stylistically of Auden's disciples, contrasts

> Lipcurl, Swiveleye, Bluster, Crock and Queer,
> Mister I'll-think-it-over, Miss Not-to-day,
> Young Who-the-hell-cares and old Let-us-pray,
> Sir Après-moi-le-déluge

with his heroic friends, Wystan and Rex, 'all of you that have not fled'. 'Heroic' is not an exaggerated adjective for the poet to use. Earlier he had said he would 'hit the trail for that promising land' where he might 'catch up with Wystan and Rex my friend'. And Auden is again idealized into 'lone flyer, birdman, my bully boy!' whose born right is 'wing-room' and 'kestrel joy'. Poem 16 concludes:

> Gain altitude, Auden, then let the base beware!
> Migrate, chaste my kestrel, you need a change of air![32]

As well as a Christ-figure suggested by the symbol of chaste kestrel looking down from pure element (the poem abounds with phrases that echo Hopkins)[33] are we not being confronted with a simplified, almost Manichean moral system where the politically right and wrong get their just deserts—by force if necessary? Lipcurl *et alia* 'haven't a chance' because 'We are going about together, we've mingled blood':

> Scavenger barons and your jackal vassals,
> Your pimping press-gang, your unclean vessels,
> We'll make you swallow your words at a gulp
> And turn your back to your element, pulp.
> Don't bluster, Bimbo, it won't do you any good;
> We can be much ruder and we're learning to shoot.
> Closet Napoleon, you'd better abdicate,
> You'd better quit the country before it's too late.

> (Poem 20)

The tone is forceful, even vital, but adolescently so, and adolescence is very much a relevant quality because the hatred—and the love of the leader—are of a kind exhibited by a hitherto powerless group, feeling its identity and authority for the first time. If the leader is a god symbolized by a beautiful creature (kestrel), so the villains become 'devils' with bestial characteristics (scavengers, jackals, etc.). Such a technique had already been used by no less a writer than T. S. Eliot in verse and prose.[34] Thus when Rex Warner told the typically complacent bourgeois:

> Come with us, if you can, and, if not, go to hell
> with your comfy chairs, your talk about the police,
> your doll wife, your cowardly life, your newspaper,
> > your interests in the East,
> You, there, who are so patriotic, you liar, you beast![35]

the final word of the passage may not be simply transposed public school slang but symptomatic of poetry's growing involvement, during the 1930s, in the language of propaganda.[36]

Critics of the 'New Country' poets have always drawn attention to their *separateness* as a group.[37] They were bourgeois writers, ashamed of their politically unfashionable origins, who attacked the bourgeoisie with vehemence caused by self-confessed guilt. They wrote esoteric and allusive verse that was highly indebted to the most reactionary of literary coteries, yet they were supposed to be addressing the masses. In so far as they did use popular language and speech rhythms, they produced a new left-wing jingoistic verse reminiscent sometimes of Rupert Brooke and at others of Rudyard Kipling. Above all they were separated from the Communist fountain-head, the Soviet Union—they were, to use Richard Crossman's term, 'Worshippers from Afar'.[38] Literature produced in such circumstances is likely to have many disadvantages (not the least of which is uncritical love), but these can be offset by intensity of vision. Poem 32 of *The Magnetic Mountain*, for example, beginning:

> You that love England, who have an ear for her music,
> The slow movement of clouds in benediction,
> Clear arias of light thrilling over her uplands,
> Over the chords of summer sustained peacefully;

successfully transfers the feeling for rural beauty (developed in the first stanza through the extended metaphor of music) into sorrow for the run-down countryside casually destroyed by the unplanned spread of industry whose profits go to the selfish few. And the sorrow and sensitivity for ordinary people 'happy in a small way' is again effectively transmuted into the anger and determination of the final lines.

> You above all who have come to the far end, victims
> Of a run-down machine . . .
> You shall be leaders when zero hour is signalled,
> Wielders of power and welders of a new world.

Similarly the single vision is maintained in a narrative poem, 'The Nabara' (1938), which tells of the courageous exploits of a small fleet of Republican trawlers who engage in battle a rebel cruiser armed with German guns. Because it is an account of an actual incident the poet is able to give a definite and meaningful setting to fervently held political ideals. The reader is shown that 'Freedom is more than a word' since the

> Simple men who asked of their life no mystical splendour,
> . . . loved its familiar ways so well that they preferred
> In the rudeness of their heart to die rather than surrender . . .

There is no doubt that the Spanish War gave the left-wing poets of the thirties a focus that was tangible. 'The Nabara' has a relaxed and masculine assurance controlling and directing the emotion that in earlier poetry by C. Day Lewis threatened always to get out of hand.

Emotion is of course a driving-force in much of the poetry under discussion. The poet who said of the poets killed in Spain, 'This martyrdom was perhaps the greatest contribution made by creative writers in this decade to the spiritual life of Europe,'[39] was expressing a credo which impinges on the whole idea of what poetry should be and what it should achieve. This poet was Stephen Spender, who has been called the Shelley of the group. Indeed Spender compares the vain search for social justice of his contemporaries with the struggles and failures of Wordsworth, Coleridge and Shelley. And John Lehmann in *New Writing in Europe* (1940) also finds it necessary to use the Romantic Revival as a yardstick for judging the nature of Spanish War verse. He quotes Wordsworth's dictum: 'The true sorrow of humanity consists in this; not that the mind of man fails, but that the course and demands of action and life so rarely correspond with the dignity and intensity of human desires . . .'.[40] The Spanish War was one of those 'rare occasions' when the intensely felt emotion corresponded with the physical reality. But for Spender, I suspect, the entire decade was such an occasion since he did not depend so much on a sense of shared political commitment as many of the other Left poets did.[41] His was always a personal view rather than a collective one and his sense of humour (seen in prose rather than verse) detected the bizarre and the ludicrous in political behaviour. His account of his brief association with the Communist Party reads like a plot for N. F. Simpson and thus his undoubted dismay at the Nazi–Soviet pact of 1939 would be more of sympathy for others than a sudden feeling of revulsion on his own behalf.[42]

He did, however, like to observe and record in his poetry what was being done in the interests of the socially deprived—and what ought to be done. In his famous poem 'The Landscape near an Aerodrome' (1933) the travellers in that familiar symbol of elemental omniscience (the aeroplane) 'see what is being done'. And what is it they see? The rural 'miles of softness' give way to 'a fraying edge' of industrial and urban development which, when observed at its core, becomes 'the landscape of hysteria'. These are potent images since the social malaise observable to the psychologist is communicated in a hushed and beautiful atmosphere reminiscent of a surrealist painting. It is not until the aircraft lands that the passengers can hear the tolling bell and find that 'Religion' blocks the sun.[43] Spender has been criticized for this final (apparently Marxist) swipe at the Church and I suppose it could be argued that, coming at the end, the reference is too noticeable and is made to seem the main point of the poem. But what is in my opinion far more significant is the admiration of the machine: the airliner 'more beautiful and soft than any moth'. In one sense, of course, the airliner not only provides the means for seeing what is wrong with society but symbolizes what is right. Here at least is a scientific achievement whose aesthetic appeal seems to confirm that *if* man organized himself properly in an unselfish, socially-conscious way he could make a society as perfect and as beautiful as the aircraft. This way of thinking might justly be termed Utopian and, of course, echoes H. G. Wells who continued to praise the aircraft (even in 1942!) as symbolic of man's collective achievement.[44] In this politically naïve sense the aircraft's pristine beauty is to be contrasted with the haphazard development and decay of *laissez-faire* capitalism whose inherent selfishness results in deprivation and cruelty:

> . . . chimneys like lank black fingers
> Or figures frightening and mad: and squat buildings
> With their strange air behind trees, like women's faces
> Shattered by grief.

In a more profound sense, however, this poem is not just about different political and social systems but in its form and vocabulary

61

is symptomatic of the unprecedented cultural developments of this century. In this sense Spender has taken certain qualities of modern art (found also in Auden's work and, even more, in Wyndham Lewis's) and pushed them to their logical or illogical conclusions.[45] 'The Landscape near an Aerodrome' (1933) should be read in conjunction with 'The Express' (1932) and 'The Pylons' (1933). These three, and especially 'The Express', may be thought of as some of the few English Futurist poems. The term 'Futurist' seems appropriate since not only does the appeal of the machine have political and social significance but the form of the poems is an essential part of their message. Here again art and propaganda are inseparable and the ancestry of the form seems to derive from Marinetti and Mayakovsky with, no doubt, help from Wyndham Lewis and Ezra Pound in the midwifery department. Those who find it strange that an important artistic movement should exercise its influence upon opposite ends of the political spectrum should remember that machine-worship was a feature of the extreme socialist movements which were later called Communist and Fascist. The idea of a perfectly organized state, as uncomplicated, predictable and impartial as a machine, was common to both.[46] In any case 'Futurist' would be an acceptable description of such poems by Spender on his own terms: 'Like most movements . . . futurism . . . represents a tendency wider than the movement itself . . . By futurism is meant concentration on those aspects of the present which seem least related to the past, most prophetic of the future.'[47] There are moments in Spender's early verse when 'Futurist' is the *only* possible term to use. The dead Communist worker in 'The Funeral' is 'one cog in a golden and singing hive'. Despite the mixture of metaphors here one is reminded of Zamiatin's *We* (first published in English in 1924 and influential upon *Brave New World* and *1984*) where, contrary to Spender's images, the images of a machine-community are intended to be anti-Utopian:

> I watched how the workers . . . would bend down, then unbend and turn around swiftly and rhythmically like levers of an enormous engine . . . I watched the monstrous glass cranes . . .; like the workers themselves they would obediently turn, bend down . . . All seemed one: humanized machine and mechanized humans. It was the most magnificent most stirring beauty, harmony, music! . . . I descended and mingled with them, fused with their mass, caught in the rhythm of steel and glass.[48]

'The Express', too, has all the 'Futurist' qualities that place the poem mid-way between art and politics. It was the Futurists who claimed that trains, or even armies, were man's greatest achievements (for aesthetic as well as organizational reasons). In 'The Express' the train begins as 'manifesto' and 'statement', and travels out of the ugly and chaotic city into the countryside where 'she' accelerates deterministically into an ideal beauty of cosmic significance:

> . . . always light, aerial, underneath,
> Retreats the elate metre of her wheels.
> Steaming through metal landscape on her lines,
> She plunges new eras of white happiness,
> Where speed throws up strange shapes, broad curves
> And parallels clean like the steel of guns.
> At last, further than Edinburgh or Rome,
> Beyond the crest of the world, she reaches night
> Where only a low streamline brightness
> Of phosphorus on the tossing hills is white.

At times it seems as though Shelley and Marx (as well as Freud)[49] were vying with each other to influence the writer, both poetically and politically. And in the final three lines of the poem a further dimension is added to its thought:

> Ah, like a comet through flame she moves entranced
> Wrapt in her music no bird song, no, nor bough
> Breaking with honey buds, shall ever equal.

Here, as in the opening words of 'The Landscape Near an Aerodrome' and throughout 'The Pylons', technological and organic forms are compared—to the latter's clear disadvantage. It is as though applied science provided the next step forward in evolution thus deifying man in the manner of Wells's *Men Like Gods*.

'Writers and Manifestos', a chapter in Spender's *The Destructive Element* (1935) suggests that he was very interested in Soviet concepts of 'political literature'. For example, he thought such statements as the following from Selivenovsky's *Poetry of Socialism* were 'excellent':

> To become an artist of socialism means, if you come from the intelligentsia, that not only must you be convinced that the ideas of socialism are correct, but that you must alter your previously-formed poetic style. It means that you must overcome and discard many of your former ideas about life: you must change your way of looking at the world.[50]

In Spender's chapter such 'admirable and honest' declarations are set against the tragic conclusions to other literary careers which commenced with state blessing but ended in suicide or exile—those for example of the 'Futurists' Mayakovsky and Zamiatin. I am sure that Spender always believed that an artist could, theoretically or ideally, produce art devoted to the propagation of political or social ideas, yet still retain an essential independence. But he seems to have come to believe that, in practice, such art is liable to become heresy or dogma—according to the attitudes of state power. 'Socialist' came to mean for Spender, I suspect, something closer to William Morris than to Marx or Lenin.

If I sound uncertain about Spender's political affiliations at the time he wrote political poetry in the 1930s it is because Spender himself seems to have been uncertain. 'Communist', 'Socialist', 'Marxist', 'Liberal' are all terms which he used and which might be associated with his beliefs. 'Marxist' is the most appropriate since it is the most closely related to his literary strivings: the emotional impetus that drove him to write. D. E. S. Maxwell in *Poets of the Thirties* suggests that measuring a society through the 'synthesis of marxism and psychoanalysis' encouraged Spender both in his personal problems and his creative ones.[51] Whether he was able in his verse 'to relate the public passion to my private life' (as he said he wished to in *The Destructive Element* and *World Within World*) is debatable. A poem like 'The Express' has the advantages of homogeneity—the intensely pictured symbol never blurs —but it has the disadvantages of imprecise idealism. However, when Spender dealt with a real event, as in 'Vienna' (1934), that had the size and scope offering substantial poetic utterance, there was a tendency for different literary influences to direct his course, just as in his emotional and political life differing or even incompatible forces held sway from time to time. Although the subject of 'Vienna' is Dolfuss's suppression of Viennese socialists, set against the emotional world of a 'love relationship', the poem seems at times an exercise in post-Eliot versification reminiscent of *Prufrock* or *Portrait of a Lady*:

> In the middle of reading, or walking on the town pavement,
> Or through the smoke of afternoon talk,
> I would strain my sense . . .

and

> Ignorant of history, all the day
> Traffic shivered my bones like a malaria.

Indeed the earlier poetry of Auden, Day Lewis and Spender (and Louis MacNeice whose verse seems more relevant to the next chapter) has a certain inevitable unevenness that derives from their essentially experimental, pioneering approach to writing. The admixture of ideas, influences, passions, uncertainties gave to their verse an atmosphere at once immediate and immature—as contemporary as a landing airliner, the most recent technical gadget, today's political assassination. Yet these observations are not to imply the creation of ephemera: their poems were unprecedented (in English at least) and their substance is still undigested. For by the late 1930s, and certainly by 1939, all poets were seeking sanctuary inside themselves, away from the powers of mass society, and few English poets have since then sought so courageously to make moral sense of twentieth-century political life.

Chapter Three
The Despair of Systems

> . . . Left and Right will shriek till youth is old,
> And each a worm-cast on the unwashed sand.
>
> Helen Spalding,
> 'On Hearing a Symphony Followed by a Political Tirade'

The previous chapter began by associating literature and politics through the observations of Louis MacNeice. This chapter should begin with dissociation from politics—and the process will again involve MacNeice. In his invaluable book on the thirties Julian Symons quotes a report from the *Evening Standard* concerning Auden and his collaborator in some remarkable plays, Christopher Isherwood, both of whom had recently left Europe for America:

> The young pair are not wholly impressed with the New World They shut themselves up in a flat in one of the city's less fashionable slum districts. Here, in conclave, they proceeded to evolve a new philosophy of life. Its main principle, I gather, is a negation of Auden's previous thesis that art is inseparable from politics.[1]

What, exactly, was occurring? The answer is that nothing exact was occurring—or rather than in Britain a significant diversification of literary form was appearing, symptomatic of revulsion from commitment, especially political commitment. (Significantly, foreign influences were now becoming more stylistic than political.) 'September 1, 1939', that fine poem which Auden was later to suppress, speaks in a way that suggests involvement in some unspecified, but quasi-Christian, morality as the only solution to the plight of civilized man:

> Into this neutral air
> Where blind skyscrapers use
> Their full height to proclaim
> The strength of Collective Man,

> Each language pours its vain
> Competitive excuse:
> But who can live for long
> In a euphoric dream;
> Out of the mirror they stare,
> Imperialism's face
> And the international wrong.

If engagement in politics is likely to lead to 'mismanagement and grief' what alternative do men and women have, composed as they are 'of Eros and of dust'? It seems to be 'a change of heart' that alone could help to create a more perfect society, indeed a more perfect world:

> . . . the error bred in the bone
> Of each woman and each man
> Craves what it cannot have,
> Not universal love
> But to be loved alone.

Both the ethics and the versification here anticipate another of Auden's poems, 'In Memory of W. B. Yeats':

> In the nightmare of the dark
> All the dogs of Europe bark,
> And the living nations wait,
> Each sequestered in its hate;
>
> Intellectual disgrace
> Stares from every human face,
> And the seas of pity lie
> Locked and frozen in each eye.

The noticeable rhyme and rhythm are still suggestive of the thrusting intellectual brilliance of a young man with ideas. But the choice of words, the subject-matter and the 'message' are more suggestive of contemplation from afar. What is, and what should be, are still firmly conceived but there is no longer any confidence that achievement can be the result of decisive human action, and in particular of political action.

I would suggest that Auden, who for more than a decade had been if not the hub at least at the centre of British political literature, should be taken as characteristic of the new approach—one which Stephen Spender had come to share:

67

After my return from Spain I reacted from the attempt to achieve Communist self-righteousness towards an extreme pre-occupation with the problems of self. I wrote poems in which I took as my theme the sense of being isolated within my personal existence: but I tried to state the condition of the isolated self as the universal condition of all existence.[2]

Political concerns were being transmuted into social or moral concerns; literary forms changed more slowly but inevitably they too altered. Indicative of the shift from commitment towards an inward-looking, self-questioning debate on where man stood in society, in the world or even in the universe, is the variety of literary styles to appear in the late thirties. Popular psychology and surrealism, already found as we have seen in the poetry of the 'New Country' group, appeared with increasing relevance in writing which examined the role (or plight) of the individual, rather than the group, bound to exist in mass society. Thus the new 'political' literature tended to be, paradoxically, anti-political. The dramatic collaborations of Auden and Isherwood, especially *The Ascent of F6* (1937) and *On the Frontier* (1938), the 'Kafkan' novels of Rex Warner, *The Wild Goose Chase* (1937), *The Professor* (1938), *The Aerodrome* (1941), Edward Upward's *Journey to the Border* (1938) and Stephen Spender's play *Trial of a Judge* (1938) are all works which portray or dramatize what is in fact the author's (or authors') inner debate. By moving away from almost direct *participation* in politics, political literature became more literary but less immediate. By the late 1930s and early 1940s generic terms such as allegory, satire, parody, fable, pastiche had become increasingly applicable. Thus the Ostnian Air Cadets in *On the Frontier*, with their facile faith in authoritarian government, seem unconsciously to resemble a younger Auden as pictured by Cecil Day Lewis! It is the politically uncommitted Eric and Anna whom the reader has to admire, despite their powerlessness:

> We found our peace
> Only in dreams.[3]

Similarly, in the football match brilliantly portrayed as a surrealist allegory of Fascism versus Democracy, the Cons whom we (like the observer George) rightly hate for winning through brutality and trickery, possess, despite their female bodies, the kind of collective animal power which their creator Rex Warner had once so much admired:

THE DESPAIR OF SYSTEMS

. . . it soon became evident that in the tight scrums the light Pro forwards were no match for their heavier opponents. As the ball was put into the scrum, the Cons, with what seemed the lurching lunge of a tortoise, pushed the Pros back a yard, and, keeping the ball between the second and third ranks of their pack, began to move slowly down the field, carrying the struggling Pros in front of them. 'Shove, boys! For God's sake shove!' shouted the Pro captain with tears running down his face, as he saw the slow moving mass bearing down upon his goal line, and the vain efforts of his hopelessly outweighted men, and George too, though he could not but admire the accurate formation of the Cons, was on the whole disgusted by so unambitious and so overwhelming an attack.[4]

And so it is to be expected that the overall trend of Auden's involve-ment in experimental, often Freudo-Marxist, drama suggests, in its style no less than its sentiments, a change of attitude—even 'a change of heart'—*vis à vis* extremist and committed political beliefs. In his play, *The Dance of Death* (1933), for example, Auden had used pastiche, parody and cockney choruses to portray and satirize the death-wish of bourgeois society. After a 'wild goose chase' to find the English revo-lution the Dancer's death significantly heralds the entrance of Karl Marx. Similarly *The Dog Beneath the Skin* (1935) is 'a grand mixture of serious poetry and sheer doggerel of music-hall, cabaret and charade styles'.[5] Here again, as in so much produced by the 'New Country' poets, the psychological and political (especially Marxist) elements are fused. Apparently Homer Lane's ideas were behind an earlier play influential upon *The Dog*, and clearly Auden and Isherwood were better at sharing these ideas, so well discussed in *Lions and Shadows* (1938), than in creating a convincing homogeneous play for their com-munication.[6] In *The Dog*, as in *The Dance*, a series of picaresque inci-dents is woven into a fable about the quest of a village boy for the long-lost heir to the Manor. When Sir Francis Crewe, the heir, reveals that he has been disguised as a dog, he tells the ruling class of the village how they look from 'a dog's-eye view': 'As a dog, I learnt with what a mixture of fear, bullying, and condescending kindness you treat those whom you consider your inferiors, but on whom you are depen-dent for your pleasures.'[7] On leaving to fight the class war with a group of Pressan Ambo village boys and having been told by General Hotham that he is a traitor, Francis replies: 'Traitors to *your* Pressan General:

not ours!' It is, significantly, the representatives of the ruling class who now become animals 'barking, mewing, quacking, grunting, or squeaking, according to their characters' (p. 178). Thus the theatrical experiments of Auden and Isherwood recall T. S. Eliot's verse parodies of the popular song and also anticipate Ionesco in their use of 'Expressionist' symbolism. Yet, although the poet and novelist appear to have relished their collaboration, this play seems uncertain and unpolished, it uses too many esoteric jokes and allusions and certainly would have appealed only to a minority audience.

Their next play *The Ascent of F6* (1936) seems to have behind it the lives of men like T. E. Lawrence as a means of exploring what really motivates someone destined to be a leader. Here, as in all the plays by these authors, 'Ostnia' and 'Westland' are recognizable types of European nation-state each of which blames the other for heightening tension. Such polarization into absurd political extremes reaches its satirical height in *On the Frontier* (1938). And so the influences of Freud and of Kafka encouraged a psychological exposure of motives, on an individual and social scale, peculiarly suited to literature which portrayed and now increasingly condemned totalitarian society. Thus Auden's involvement in political drama took him steadily through from an entrenched 'Communist' position to one which by the late 1930s was far less committed and which now used psychological and sociological insight as a means of condemning the kind of fixed, 'dyed-in-the-wool', political attitude of which he himself might have been accused ten years before.

Both Stephen Spender and Rex Warner portrayed in their writing of the late thirties and early forties the helplessness of a liberal confronted by Fascism. Spender's play *Trial of a Judge* (1938), like 'Vienna', benefits from its basis in real events (in this case the Potempa murders). This 'tragic statement in five acts' most successfully uses verse to communicate the atmosphere of Nazism as it impinges upon the shocked consciousness of the Judge who realizes how futile his 'resistance' has been. Moreover, his attempt to compromise does not save him, for he had dared even to think the Communists and not the Nazi terrorists should be acquitted. Ultimately the Judge himself is 'judged' by forces so alien he can scarcely comprehend them—though he can describe and explain them:

> I speak from the centre of a stage
> Not of a tragedy but a farce

Where I am the spiritual unsmiling clown
Defeated by the brutal swearing giant
Whose law is power, his order
Nature's intolerant chaos;
Here my defeat shows bare its desert
In which emptiness wins and force levels
Wastes meaningless except to mockery.
Laugh if you will at the mind's and body's weakness
Yet if you multiply my single death
By all the deaths for which it is one precedent,
You see in my fall the fall of cities,
In this my innocent injured protest,
The massacre of children; in the triumph
Of those who hold me here
Your history clamped in iron; your word ground
Beneath the oppression of an age of ice.[8]

The choruses of 'black prisoners' and 'black troop leaders', who speak with powerful rhetoric expressive of extremism and intolerance, resemble certain speeches (and the use of colours) in O'Casey's 'Expressionist' play *The Star Turns Red* (1940). But whereas Spender's drama reveals the nightmare vision of political lunacy—a glimpse of a degenerate civilization—in the coarse violence of Fascist language, O'Casey's 'purple passages' tumble into bombast and, in the case of Red Jim, sentimentality. It is significant that O'Casey's hero, unlike Spender's, could allow of no 'liberal' moderation and remains as politically rigid as the Fascist enemies he confidently expects to destroy:

We fight on; we suffer; we die; but we fight on.
Our altar is the spinning earth, chanting reveille to the newborn,
    sounding the Last Post over those sinking back into her bosom
    when the day's well-done work is over.
Our saints are those who fall bearing a roll on the drum of revo-
    lution.
We fight on; we suffer; we die; but we fight on.
Till brave-breasted women and men, terrac'd with strength,
Shall live and die together, co-equal in all things;
And romping, living children, anointed with joy, shall be banners
    and banneroles of this moving world!
In all that great minds give, we share;
And unto man be all might, majesty, dominion, and power![9]

Such writing seems to me to show a sad decline as (political) litera-
ture, even as propaganda, from the anti-extremist *The Shadow of a
Gunman* (1923), *Juno and the Paycock* (1924), and *The Plough and the
Stars* (1926), and the anti-war *The Silver Tassie* (1929)—also an
'Expressionist' play—where humour and tragic irony had been
combined, with immense success.

Now 'a change of heart', unless universal, is not enough to defeat
authoritarianism; so where does this leave the good, the right-thinking
and right-feeling individual? In gaol or on the scaffold—or worse. Rex
Warner's later novels *The Professor* (1938) and *The Aerodrome* (1941)
are evidence of the increasing bewilderment and despair of the erstwhile politically orientated writer who, on losing commitment, found
little faith in man or in his ability to cope with the problems of social
organization. By the early 1940s the appalling social and political scene
showed itself in the merging of two hitherto distinct novelistic forms.
The allegory or commentary which portrayed at one remove the actual
political realities (*The Professor* or Koestler's *Darkness At Noon* (1940))
became increasingly indistinguishable from that potent *genre*, the anti-
Utopia (Zamiatin's *We* (1924), Huxley's *Brave New World* (1932)
Orwell's *1984* (1949)). In other words the most imaginative writer
would be hard put to it to create a terrestrial hell more convincing than
Auschwitz. But the impact of social and political evolution upon
literary form was of course inevitable. The anti-Utopia itself was
scarcely credible before man's mastery of science and technology had
given him the power to enslave with unprecedented near-perfection.

It is usual for Orwell to be placed in a line of British novelists who
may or may not be satirical but who certainly qualify as 'novelists of
ideas'. Samuel Butler, Gissing, Wells, Huxley, and less certainly,
Dickens would spring to mind. The genesis and evolution of anti-
Utopian writing clearly owed much to most of these and it is for this and
other stylistic considerations that Orwell tends to be associated with such
novelists in critical accounts of his work. But before looking at the best-
known contribution that Orwell has made to political literature (indeed
to any literature) it seems that in the context of this account it is worth
considering Orwell as the communicator of anarchism. For he, almost
alone among important writers of political literature, made dissociation
from party politics his *credo*. The road to *1984* started as a tiny track that
took the author from prep-school to public school, to Burma, to Paris,
to Wigan, to the B.B.C., to *Tribune*, to Jura, to death. All this is well-
known. But because of his early stand *against* politics, because for him

politics gave off a nasty smell, Orwell was ahead of his time and writers, for example Louis MacNeice, whom as we have seen he sharply attacked, came later to resemble him in their attitudes to political behaviour. (Stephen Spender, who later became his close friend, seems to have moved nearer to Orwell's position on politics just as Wyndham Lewis moving in the reverse direction came increasingly to accept Orwell's approach to politics and admire its expression in *Animal Farm* and *1984*.)[10]

There was a body of writing produced in the middle to late 1930s to which the term 'anarchist' is applicable. The anarchism is directed not only against society but, not unnaturally, against society's moral views—even against anyone's desire for comfort and security. This kind of writing (prose and verse) communicates a desperate hatred through terms and images of sado-masochistic violence and contemptuous description of the synthetic and the standardized products of capitalist mass society, whose demise is predicted with more relish than confidence. Overall there looms a prevailing death-wish and the only relief is provided by a 'sick humour' often expressed through 'plonking' rhymes and rhythms reminiscent of Ogden Nash or even Harry Graham.

Dr Rodway has called Auden, Spender, Day Lewis and MacNeice 'Social Poets'.[11] MacNeice seems to have become in the 1930s, and the ensuing decades, increasingly *anti*-social. The anarchist note, the telling contempt of *laissez-faire* capitalism—however much it may have been modified by humour—recurs in 'Christmas Shopping', 'Bagpipe Music' (1938) and, most characteristically, in the much later poem 'Jigsaw II' (1957) which finishes:

> Property! Property! When will it end
> When will the Poltergeist ascend
> Out of the sewer with chopper and squib
> To burn the mink and the baby's bib
> And cut the tattling wire to town
> And smash all the plastics, clowning and clouting
> And stop all the boxes shouting and pouting
> And wreck the house from the aerial down
> And give these ingrown souls an outing?

MacNeice, it seems to me, never rediscovered his earlier ability to *reflect* political events as exhibited in the twenty-four cantos of *The Autumn Journal* (1938) where the atmosphere of 'Munich' and the

73

Spanish War is irresistibly conjured up through evocative references to everyday matters shadowed by crisis.

In the play *The Ascent of F6* by W. H. Auden and Christopher Isherwood there are dialogues between a typical bourgeois married couple (Mr and Mrs A) whose dependence on salary and suburb has, as they are at least aware, made their lives a meaningless, sterile routine that the verse's expected rhymes and rhythms reinforce:

> The eight o'clock train, the customary place,
> Holding the paper in front of your face,
> The public stairs, the glass swing-door,
> The peg for your hat, the linoleum floor
> The office stool and the office jokes
> And the fear in your ribs that slyly pokes:
> Are they satisfied with you?
> Nothing interesting to do,
> Nothing interesting to say,
> Nothing remarkable in any way;
> Then the journey home again
> In the hot surburban train
> To the tawdry new estate,
> Crumpled, grubby, dazed and late:
> Home to supper and to bed.
> Shall we be like this when we are dead?[12]

A distrust of what mass society could do to enslave man by using science and technology was later to be expressed by Auden in *The Unknown Citizen*. Much earlier, before he emigrated, Auden (who seems to have had an irrepressible gift for versification whose logical extension is the Clerihew) had pilloried the thoughtless scientist in his poem about 'Honeyman's N.P.C.'.[13] James Honeyman sells his lethal gas to a foreign power and, though all he 'innocently' wanted was wealth and fame for himself and his family, sees them choked by his own creation. The violence, always latent in society, is almost sadistically forced upon the reader in the 'sick' ballads now called 'Miss Gee' and 'Victor'. Although Auden did not develop fully a strain of verse which communicated the plight of man systematically dehumanized by the government of mass society, all the elements are to be found in the former poem (set to the tune of 'St James's Infirmary'). The church and the capitalist orthodoxy have literally used up Miss Gee until, in a conclusion where Freud and Marx are vindicated, the only bit of the poor lady that is left is donated to Moral Rearmament:

> They laid her on the table,
> The students began to laugh;
> And Mr Rose the surgeon
> He cut Miss Gee in half.

> Mr Rose turned to his students,
> Said: 'Gentlemen, if you please,
> We seldom see a sarcoma
> As far advanced as this'.

> They took her off the table,
> They wheeled away Miss Gee
> Down to another department
> Where they study Anatomy.

> They hung her from the ceiling,
> Yes, they hung up Miss Gee;
> And a couple of Oxford Groupers
> Carefully dissected her knee.

Sadistic violence and slapstick humour had, apparently gratuitously, been a feature of Evelyn Waugh's 'funny' novels such as *Decline and Fall* (1928) and *Black Mischief* (1932)—although intentional anger with modern society was later to combine well with violence in *The Loved One* (1948). The incipient anarchism of writing which combines violence with humour seems to have anticipated post-war trends both in literature and in social behaviour. But in the late thirties and early forties the 'Angry Young Men' and 'Liverpool Poets' were, if not just flashes in their father's eyes, probably playing soldiers or making paper aeroplanes. The violence invoked to smash the shiny products of capitalism and mass society had a much closer literary outlet in the growth of the anti-Utopian fiction of Huxley and Orwell. John Betjeman's famous poem 'Slough' (1937) expresses in verse, which again sports the familiar accentuated rhyme and iambic rhythm, a veritable anti-Utopian world-view. All the elements are there: the synthetic food feeding synthetic minds, the destruction or dehumanization of the little man by economic or governmental power, and the uncontrollable urge of the writer to smash—in this case significantly with bombs—this man-made hell. At such a point a writer's next step was clear: why could he not portray an authoritarian society which had been *planned* as ideally unpleasant by the only self-perpetuating government it had ever had, or was likely to have? Here indeed would be a genuine and original contribution to political literature.

Of course Eugene Zamiatin and Aldous Huxley had already pictured such societies—as indeed had H. G. Wells, who taught them both—but their visions were of the distant future.[14] Orwell's *1984* was uncomfortably close and might just as easily have been given the title *1948*, while *Animal Farm* (1945) was prevented only by its fabulous animals from documenting exactly the 'betrayal' of the Russian revolution—or indeed of any revolution that leads to tyranny. Orwell's anti-Utopian vision grew from an anarchistic dislike of mass, or collectivist, society but it was a dislike doomed to change to despair. The Orwellian hero (really an anti-hero) of the early novels becomes a rebel-observer who sees what he dislikes with 'the intimacy of hatred'.[15] It is of course significant that the rebel-observer—Gordon Comstock in *Keep The Aspidistra Flying* (1936) or George Bowling in *Coming Up for Air* (1939)—comes later to conform to the dictates of the society which has simultaneously repelled and attracted him. Just as Winston Smith in *1984*, the last man to write 'Oldspeak' passionately, gets his only unclouded satisfaction in life by writing lying propaganda in the dehumanized 'Newspeak', so Gordon Comstock, initially a poet, becomes a coiner of the very advertising clichés he had so much despised. 'It was what, in his secret heart, he had desired' (p. 253). Winston Smith's final love of Big Brother is clearly a development of Comstock's acceptance of the 'Money-God's' embrace. Yet, in an earlier point in the novel, Comstock had been recognizably a 'drop-out' whose intense hatred of society suggested at times a death-wish and at others subversion. His thoughts on the kind of society of which commercial advertising was symptomatic are remarkably similar in vocabulary and in tone to the explosive utterances of Louis MacNeice and John Betjeman quoted above:

> The sense of disintegration, of decay, that is endemic in our time, was strong upon him. Somehow it was mixed up with the ad-posters opposite. He looked now with more seeing eyes at those grinning yard-wide faces. After all, there was more there than mere silliness, greed, and vulgarity. Corner Table grins at you, seemingly optimistic, with a flash of false teeth. But what is behind the grin? Desolation, emptiness, prophecies of doom. For can you not see, if

you know how to look, that behind that slick self-satisfaction, that tittering fat-bellied triviality, there is nothing but a frightful emptiness, a secret despair? The great death-wish of the modern world. Suicide pacts. Heads stuck in gas-ovens in lonely maisonettes. French letters and Amen Pills. And the reverberations of future wars. Enemy aeroplanes flying over London; the deep threatening hum of the propellers, the shattering thunder of the bombs. It is all written in Corner Table's face.

(Keep the Aspidistra Flying, p. 21)

Now it could be argued that George Orwell was an 'egotistical' writer almost in the Keatsian sense since all the novels have much in common and all of them have a central character (the rebel-observer) who essentially is a recreation of Orwell himself. And Orwell said more than once that he hoped the coming war would bring with it a revolution that would finally destroy capitalism even if 'the London gutters will have to run with blood';[16] indeed he wrote to Herbert Read suggesting that, once the war started, subversive printing-presses should attack the Chamberlain government.[17] Later, Orwell's war-time diary was to reveal thoughts almost identical to those of Gordon Comstock:

Always, as I walk through the Underground stations, [I am] sickened by the advertisements, the silly staring faces and strident colours . . . How much rubbish this war will sweep away . . . so much of the good of modern life is actually evil that it is questionable whether on balance war does harm.[18]

In *Coming Up for Air* George Bowling enters a 'milk-bar' where everything is 'slick and shiny and streamlined; mirrors, enamel, and chromium plate' with 'a sort of propaganda floating round, mixed up with the noise of the radio, to the effect that . . . nothing matters except slickness and shininess and streamlining'. And, it is added, 'Everything's streamlined nowadays, even the bullet Hitler's keeping for you'. The climax of this scene is when Bowling tries to bite a rubberized sausage that explodes into 'bombs of filth bursting inside your mouth'.[19] The imagery of bombs and dismembered limbs recur in this novel and later in *1984*, prompting Anthony West to claim that such scenes 'repeat themselves with manic violence and a generalized sadism that is clearly beyond control'.[20] But, as we have seen, Orwell was in good literary company in his preoccupation as a writer with violence directed against societies already so badly off course that destruction could be seen as purgative.

Nevertheless Orwell volunteered for military service and bitterly resented his failure on medical grounds to join the army. By the 1940s Orwell was seeing with increasing clarity that what he really feared was neither capitalism nor communism but the essential features of both carried to their logical extensions: a collectivism that could be described as mega-totalitarian. It would be a superstate using every scientific and technological means to control the population. With a growing group of 'pessimists' that included Arthur Koestler, Bertrand Russell and Ignazio Silone, Orwell feared man's 'infinite malleability': that it might be 'just as possible to produce a breed of men who do not wish for liberty as to produce a breed of hornless cows'.[21] Gordon Comstock saw in the advertisements 'Modern man as his masters want him to be: a docile little porker, sitting in the money-sty, drinking Bovex'. The imagery here, by looking forward to *Animal Farm* and *1984*, tells us something about the strengths and limitations of the anti-Utopian literary form. For just as George Bowling when he bites into the rubber-skinned sausage and tastes the modern world recognizes its *erzatz* quality, so the writer of an anti-Utopia must necessarily do without subtle characterization. Only the rebel has uniqueness and, since he is doomed to be standardized by force, the novelist's real concern is the extinction of the psyche rather than its extension.[22]

The anti-Utopia derives, of course, from the *Utopia* of Thomas More and, before him, of Plato and his *Republic*. Although the inversion of an ideal society was not, as a literary form, fully exploited until this century, anticipations may be traced back at least to Swift's 'Laputa' in *Gulliver's Travels* and certainly to Samuel Butler's *Erewhon*. But satirists of the calibre of Swift and Butler used inversion of accepted moral and logical criteria in order to question social behaviour or trends, rather than to present in the manner of *Brave New World* or *1984* a complete picture of the ideally unpleasant society that not only satirizes but warns in a much more straightforward way. Thus Butler's brilliant discussion of machines tested accepted views and pushed new interpretations to their logical conclusion: they did not relate the evolution of machines to political control in the anti-Utopian fashion. The real father of the form was H. G. Wells who created a spectrum of Utopian novels and stories ranging from the most pessimistic in a novel such as *When the Sleeper Wakes* (1899) to the most optimistic in *Men Like Gods* (1923)—the latter being called, by Marie Louise Berneri, Wells's *News from Nowhere*.[23]

It has been customary to think of H. G. Wells as a socialist because of the humane and humorous sympathies revealed towards the 'little man' in such socially realistic novels as *Kipps* (1905), *Tono-Bungay* (1909) and *The History of Mr Polly* (1910). Yet Wells, like the Shaw of *Back To Methuselah* (1921), has received the taunt of being Fascist in his approval of man's will to evolve to a greater being. The title of *Men Like Gods* has a Nietzschean ring about it and, both in this novel and the serious discussion in *A Modern Utopia* (1905), Wells did not shrink from the question of eugenics. Always more dependent upon science than Shaw was in his hopes for the future, Wells created Utopias inconceivable without the kind of planning that only science and technology can facilitate. Yet Wells was not so naïve as Orwell claimed in his essay 'Wells, Hitler and the World State' (1941):

> In [Wells's] novels, Utopias, essays, films, pamphlets, the anti-thesis crops up, always more or less the same. On the one side science, order, progress, internationalism, aeroplanes, steel, concrete, hygiene: on the other side war, nationalism, religion, monarchy, peasants, Greek professors, poets, horses.[24]

Indeed Orwell himself had already called *When the Sleeper Wakes* and Jack London's *The Iron Heel* 'prophecies of Fascism'—and by saying this he indicated that such books anticipated *1984*.[25] Moreover the long tale called 'A Story of the Days to Come' contains virtually all the essential elements that constitute an anti-Utopia, including even the linguistic changes found in Huxley and Orwell.[26] The crucial difference between Wells and the pessimistic anti-Utopian writers who followed him was this: Wells believed that science could, not would, save man. The pessimists believed that man really no longer had a choice and that forces inherent in the modern world meant that willy-nilly a small oligarchy would always use the scientific method to enslave, or at the very least debase, mankind.

Wells did not, however, fully extend either the Utopia or the anti-Utopia as a literary form. He became increasingly a kind of journalist who wrote novels in which characters served the debate of ideas—especially ideas of federation and world government. A glance at *The New Machiavelli* (1911) is illuminating in this context since the points to be made sometimes obtrude so much that the prose degenerates into lists, particularly of book and magazine titles. It was left to Zamiatin, a Russian emigré and admirer of Wells, to create the first wholehearted anti-Utopian novel, *We* (first published in Paris as *Nous Autres*), a book which profoundly influenced *Brave New World* and *1984* and of which

Orwell provided the first English review in 1946.[27] What then are the essential qualities of the anti-Utopia and how does it differ from a pessimistic novel of ideas? Its crucial difference lies in its vision: all are subservient to it—character, plot, and even ideas, discussion, speculation. All these elements need to be arranged through the creative power of the imagination to serve the vision of an ideally unpleasant society. There also tends to be, in the Swiftian or Butlerian manner, a pushing of ideas or trends to their full extent, so that a black or bizarre humour can result. Thus in *We* the 'numbers'—citizens—are allowed to pull the curtains of their glass houses only during the 'sex-hour'. At other times their every movement is observed by hovering helicopters whose ultra-sensitive devices are watched by the 'Guardians' or secret police. (The ironical use of linguistic inversion is of course characteristic of this form.) Similarly in *Brave New World* the 'arch-chorister of Canterbury' is duty-bound to sleep with the nicely orthodox Lenina since 'Everyone belongs to everyone else'. What seems at times in these novels a joke has of course the serious purpose of showing the extent to which the State could strengthen its control of people by manipulating their sex-lives. These remarks are especially applicable to *1984* where 'sexual privation induced hysteria' which 'could be transformed into war-fever and leader-worship'.[28] Orwell's grim humour appears when a little sandy-haired woman (who works in the Ministry of Truth as a cataloguer of 'unpersons' and has had to include her husband's name on the list) worships Big Brother in a way that combines sex with religious mysticism:

> the face of Big Brother seemed to persist for several seconds on the screen . . . The little sandy-haired woman had flung herself forward over the back of the chair in front of her. With a tremulous murmur that sounded like 'My Saviour!' she extended her arms towards the screen. Then she buried her face in her hands. It was apparent that she was uttering a prayer. (pp. 16–17)

As Julia puts it: 'All this marching up and down and cheering and waving is simply sex gone sour' (p. 109). These examples show how a motif such as State control of sexual behaviour can be used in an anti-Utopia—or indeed in a Utopia such as More's work or Wells's *Men Like Gods*, where people are of course contented with the controls—and, by extending the implications of the ideas, reach a situation simultaneously bizarre and terrifying. Perhaps this is why so many 'sick' jokes are about concentration camps.

The anti-Utopia can, of course, have different textures. *We* is 'Futurist': the hero D. 503 is not sure whether or not to rebel because his love of machines is almost equal to the appeal of his rebellious, atavistic girl-friend I. 330 (the 'Julia' of this novel). *Brave New World* is really obsessed with the debasement of life in a society which controls through the perfected supply of scientifically stimulated pleasure: it raises questions at once moral and aesthetic. *1984* is the most political of the major anti-Utopias because its author has grasped the influential trends of modern mass society which, in his own experience, culminated in totalitarianism. All Orwell did was choose, order and extend political, social, linguistic, psychological and philosophical data, as he saw them, into a brilliantly cogent form instantly communicable even to minds normally closed to literature.

Despite their differences, however, what these novels share is perhaps even more significant. Although Dr Leavis would presumably allow Orwell no greater claim than H. G. Wells to membership of a 'great tradition',[29] it could well be argued that the anti-Utopian novel is 'psychological' in a sense different to that which is applicable to the work of Joyce, Woolf and D. H. Lawrence. For if the greatest modern novels owe a debt to Dostoievsky and Freud, they ought also to condemn all that Pavlov represents for the layman: the idea that man could be 'methodized', that he is 'infinitely malleable'. Although no doubt of less literary importance than those other psychologically orientated novels, the anti-Utopia (despite its reliance upon exaggeration, pessimism and satirical prediction) has an intellectual coherence and an historical justification which explains its frequent appearance in non-literary discussions of politics and society. The scenes of collective irrationalism that recur in these novels, and also in other novels which portray allegorically or directly the plight of the rebel in totalitarian society, have a passion and an insight that brings art to the world of science. Thus *We*, *Brave New World*, *1984*, *The Professor*, Ignazio Silone's *Bread and Wine* (1934) and even William Golding's *Lord of the Flies* (1954) all contain scenes in which a Leader credited with divine attributes manipulates a vast crowd of supporters by using all the colour and trickery available in the age of electronics and mass-communication.[30] (In Golding's novel thunder and lightning replace microphone and spotlight.) These scenes are of course observed by the rebel who tends simultaneously to be repelled and attracted by what he sees since his fear and loneliness have already been aggravated by life in an atomized society. And just as these events are presided over by a 'self-appointed god' or 'homo magus' so there has to be a 'devil' or 'beast' to be placated or 'destroyed'. In this century it is called the 'Enemy of the People'. The 'beast' can never die, or rather can never be allowed to die, since the collective fear provides a necessary social cohesion.

This vision of man's collective debasement in a totalitarian society where every aspect of life is inseparable from politics, or perhaps more accurately government, grew directly from the writers' observations of the world scene. Here is Orwell replying, as Literary Editor of *Tribune*, to a letter in 1944:

> All the national movements everywhere, even those that originate in resistance to German domination, seem to take non-democratic forms, to group themselves round some superhuman *fuehrer* (Hitler, Stalin, Salazar, Franco, Gandhi, De Valera are all varying examples) and to adopt the theory that the end justifies the means. Everywhere the world movement seems to be in the direction of centralized economies which can be made to 'work' in an economic sense but which are not democratically organized and which tend to establish a caste system. With this go the horrors of emotional nationalism and a tendency to disbelieve in the existence of objective truth because all the facts have to fit in with the words and prophesies of some infallible *fuehrer*.[31]

Thus the scenes of irrational behaviour put into visualizable form political and social tendencies recognized at the time by these novelists. Their exaggerated vision has, too, the advantage of being relevant in following years. It may be that the world in 1976 is not like *1984* or *Brave New World* but ongoing trends continue to exist from the time they were written. The problems that go with large economies, referred to in the previous quotation, are clearly found today in organizations like the Common Market, and, moreover, as such units grow so the individual may consider himself increasingly less of a participant in the running of his country. You might say that the anti-Utopian, and the pessimistic political novels of the thirties and forties showed once and for all that modern man is most of all characterized by such a non-human factor as governmental control. Herein lies the strength and weakness of most modern political novels—especially the anti-Utopian. As Saul Bellow has said: 'I do not believe that human capacity to feel or do can really have dwindled or that the quality of humanity has degenerated. I rather think that people appear smaller because society has become so immense.'[32] To the suggestion that such novels are social rather than political we must give the answer that for writers as for their fellow men the two adjectives have become virtually synonymous. Will the recent Olympic Games be remembered for their *non*-political events?

If, then, we accept *1984* and the other anti-Utopias as being terrifying visions of a potential and imaginable future, a heightening of observed and recorded history, a valid satirical exaggeration—where do we place *Animal Farm* (1945) and how do we judge it? Orwell called this book 'a little squib' and, despite an apparently concerted attempt by publishers to prevent its detonation, once let off glowing reports echoed. Laurence Brander said it was 'a little masterpiece', Tom Hopkinson called it 'By far Orwell's finest book' and Edward M. Thomas claimed it 'succeeded perfectly'. Even T. S. Eliot, while rejecting it on behalf of Faber (in view of the sensitive East–West alliance), described it as the finest satirical prose since Swift.[33] Others have suggested that its virtues are negative on the grounds that the form of a beast-fable avoids the difficulties and potentialities of proper characterization.[34] As we have seen, Orwell had a tendency to refer to stock types of person in a debasing society for reasons that are justifiable in logic, if not literature—and quite often the types are categorized as animals: 'For the vision of the totalitarian state there there is being substituted the vision of the totalitarian world . . . A world of rabbits ruled by stoats.'[35] But although *Animal Farm* 'solved' Orwell's problems of characterization, and enabled him to use his powers to simplify to its essence the outcome of revolution, the book's success had no real bearing on Orwell's work as a political novelist. Almost by definition a beast-fable cannot judge the demerits of politics and society in human terms. And by avoiding the recurrent self-dramatization of an 'egotistical' writer, *Animal Farm* had no place for the observer who watched events with a horrified fascination. Thus although 'perfect', *Animal Farm* is not characteristic of the writer and in only a limited sense prepares the way for what was to follow in *1984*, Napoleon anticipating Big Brother, and the alteration of the seven commandments looking forward to the verbal trickery of 'Newspeak'. Whatever else may be said about *Animal Farm*, it shares with *Gulliver's Travels* the rare merit of giving pleasure and instruction equally to politicians and children.

It could perhaps be argued that *Animal Farm* is an allegory, since it is 'narrative describing one subject under guise of another'. Such a technique was liable to attract writers of political literature, because they could use it to reduce implications to essentials: in this the method obviously has points of comparison with the anti-Utopia. But the allegory or fable could comment directly, if not precisely, since it could mirror actual events. Such a technique is used in Rex Warner's allegorical novel *The Professor* (1938), a work which characterizes the new dissociation from commitment which the writers of the Left were now displaying. Here, as in *Trial of a Judge*, no easy clear-cut answer can be given to the problem of how to succeed as a liberal in a world of extremist politics. This novel seems to be about Czechoslovakia at the time of the Munich crisis, but it tells how Professor A., a sane, learned classicist, who has been asked to become the Chancellor of his small country, fails to retain his control and his nation's sovereignty because he does not realize that in order to resist the giant Fascist neighbouring state he must use methods of which as a democrat he does not approve: control of the press, for example. He is doomed but he is civilized, and the novel is despairing because the only solution (to imitate your enemies) would negate the reason for struggle. The impossible situation of the Professor is communicated by a Kafkaesque atmosphere of loneliness and eventual nightmare. The debt to Kafka is obvious from the start: 'The last week enjoyed, or rather experienced, by Professor A. may be reconstructed with tolerable accuracy from two sources . . .' (p. 7). This debt was unfortunate since it caused Warner to be acclaimed as the 'English Kafka', compared with him, found wanting[36] and, as a novelist, until recently almost forgotten. The comparison was not entirely fair nor strictly relevant because Warner was only using a valid technique to explore in allegorical terms the vulnerability of the liberal in power whose opponents will use any method to destroy him. The total effect of the novel is a moral one and the work owes perhaps as much to Bunyan in its form and Thucydides in its thought as it does to any modern European literary or political influence.

An interesting comparison may be made between Warner's novels (such as *The Professor* and *The Aerodrome*) and Koestler's political novels—especially *Darkness at Noon* and *Arrival and Departure* (1943). Orwell said repeatedly that he admired political writers like Koestler and Silone because they really knew from experience what they were talking about:

> One development of the last ten years has been the appearance of the 'political book', a sort of enlarged pamphlet combining history with political criticism, as an important literary form. But the best

writers in this line—Trotsky, Rauschning, Rosenberg, Silone, Borkenau, Koestler and others—have none of them been Englishmen, and nearly all of them have been renegades from one or other extremist party, who have seen totalitarianism at close quarters and known the meaning of exile and persecution.[37]

We in England have received our political education chiefly from foreigners . . . there were voices . . . of anti-Fascist refugees, crying in the wilderness, and none, except perhaps Silone, cried more effectively than Arthur Koestler.[38]

Koestler may not have been English, but he settled in Britain and wrote a number of books in English which distilled to their essence the experiences referred to by Orwell, who in turn was undoubtedly influenced by them. *Darkness at Noon*, first published in German, provided the 'inspiration' for the Ministry of Truth and indeed much of the atmosphere of *1984*.[39] The betrayals, executions and prison sequences are conveyed with a harsh exactitude that in itself seems a necessary association of style and subject-matter in the writer's mind. It is as though the novelist were being a commentator who above all has to record with photographic accuracy. Indeed the uncompromising harshness and brutality seem even more pronounced in *Arrival and Departure* where the brilliant polyglot author relishes his choice of words as he describes an 'interrogation':

The man facing him again extended his arm and lifted Peter's face with his index-finger; he gave a belching noise, seemed to chew something in his mouth and then, with precision, spat into Peter's face. Peter stepped back; but the hooked index-finger once more caught him under the chin; his face, with one eye blinded by the slimy mass was thrust up, and in the next second the man's other fist, carrying his full weight from hip to shoulder, crashed against his nose. He staggered back, was caught by the man behind him, flung round to the next one, hit in the stomach, bent double, straightened by a kick against his shin, and sent reeling around and across the circle like a dance in a grotesque ballet. The saddle of his nose was broken by the first punch, his lips split and two teeth smashed by a later full hit . . . a strange, almost obscene ecstasy transformed his jumps and jerks in the circle of the sweating, snorting, hitting and kicking men into the performance of a ritual dance . . .[40]

Certain sports columnists would give their eye-teeth to be able to write like this and indeed Koestler and Orwell wrote in a kind of racy super-journalese singularly appropriate in an age where the mass-media were increasingly involved with political events and where such authors were at pains to present 'the facts' rather than distortions. (The interrogators become *really* unfriendly a couple of pages later.) And the overriding feeling is that the author himself has experienced what he describes. In Rex Warner's *The Professor* a comparable scene, in which the hero is beaten in his cell, is over very rapidly. It concludes:

> if anyone who had known him previously had looked at him after the four men had departed he would . . . have found it hard to recognize him. For he was lying huddled in a corner of the room, his spectacles broken and aslant his face, his lips curiously protruding, an effect which had been produced by the distortion of the plate which held his false teeth, some of which indeed had been knocked out and lay on the floor at his side. His forehead was cut and bruised: blood also disfigured the lower part of his face and chest. (p. 163)

Undoubtedly there is realism here but even in this scene it is as if we —author and reader—are observing from outside. Indeed in his other major allegorical novels, *The Wild Goose Chase* and *The Aerodrome*, an even greater 'distancing' from political events is successfully and, in my opinion, appropriately created.[41] The novelist is really interested in moral and philosophical implications which, in a sense, are outside time and place. Compare, for example, these passages:

> 'The trouble with you is that you are no psychologists, and that is why we shall smash you and your more dangerous allies, the Reds. For we appeal not to the intellect, or even to immediate self-interest, but to the dark, unsatisfied, and raging impulses of the real man. It is we who are, in a psychological sense, the liberators.'
>
> (*The Professor*, pp. 69–70)

> Then he explained to me where our theory had gone wrong. He quoted Luxemburg's polemics with Bucharin, spoke of the snags in the labour theory of value, of the over-simplification of mass-psychology in our theory of proletarian class-consciousness; of the Russian purges and Rubashov's trial. The terrible thing about Raditsch was that he knew our doctrine better than most of us.
>
> (*Arrival and Departure*, p. 101)

In the first passage the Fascist speaker presents academically his reasons for expected success. If it were not for the mention of 'Reds' and of psychology the points made would be relevant to any period of tyranny or revolution in which an emergent government used man's irrationality in its rise to power. In the second passage the Fascist is concerned with specific facts, events, theories identifiable in the relevant political textbooks.

To a considerable extent, therefore, our political literature and especially our political novels were taught by European influences: the creative writing of Zamiatin, Mayakovsky, Koestler, Silone; the thought of Marx, Freud, Trotsky; the lives of Stalin, Mussolini, Hitler, Franco. During the earlier part of the century, and in particular the late twenties and early thirties, writers had looked at Britain and looked to Britain with political hopes inspired by Soviet Russia. When such hopes were not only forgotten but invalidated by events, the tendency became, as we have seen, to look to the European political scene for the inspiration not of hope but of horror[42] or, perhaps worse, despair. This trend, which has a literary significance, is not of course unprecedented. The Jacobean dramatists often set their stories of political intrigue in foreign parts, in particular southern Europe—rather as Conrad and Greene, or to use a French example, Malraux, have often provided oriental or exotic settings for novels. This 'distancing', or recollecting in tranquillity, had the disadvantage of losing an immediacy which in our century a writer such as Koestler could help to replace. But the distancing had its advantages too: it allowed the writer to give greater shape, form and order to what he wanted to say and it allowed him to develop that intensity that creates a vision—especially a terrifying vision. Bamber Gascoigne has described the effect of such remoteness on American dramatists who observed Europe:

> Far from being isolationist, American authors were producing anti-Nazi plays before anyone else . . . they are in one sense very different from the equivalent plays written by authors who had lived under the Nazis. There is an element in the American plays of the horrified fascination which was later to move Orwell to write *1984*.[43]

An American who came to Europe and stayed here was Percy Wyndham Lewis. I have called him the Orwell of the Right because he came increasingly to despise political dogma and the extremes to which they led and to consider that nothing resembled the committed Communist so much as the committed Fascist: 'both Reds and Blackshirts were very gross material' for the civilized and tragic figure of Margot in *The Revenge For Love* (1937).[44] Although the love for her husband is inviolable it leads to both their deaths in a world of inhuman political intrigue and treachery set in Spain and London at the time of the Spanish Civil War. Like Orwell, Lewis learnt to feel politics as dirty and degrading; like Orwell, too, Lewis never lost his fascination with that dirty business; but unlike most political writers Lewis had an extraordinary talent for being witty, even genuinely funny (almost in the Amis and Wain situational manner) while punching home the most serious arguments. Here, with sublime bathos, Lewis describes the hierarchical seating arrangements at a party given in London by an Irish Communist in honour of a man recently wounded while escaping from a Spanish prison:

> A red patriarch, Percy Hardcaster reclined, propped by a plethora of red cushions, upon a wide reddish settee, in Red invalid magnificence. A red punkah should have been there to complete the picture. He was surrounded by men and women—by Red men and Red women. There were four women beside him upon the settee; in the place of honour Gillian Phipps, pressed up against his sick leg, which stuck straight out pointing at the assembly with all the declamatory force of Lord Kitchener's forefinger ('I want *you*') terminating in an ironshod stump, provided by the Lerroux administration.
>
> In the place of lesser honour, because leg to leg with his more ordinary and less dramatic limb, was Eilen Mulliner [the hostess] ...
>
> Before Percy Hardcaster, both upon the floor and upon chairs, was an impressive grouping of salon-Reds—of Oxford and Cambridge 'pinks'; the usual marxist don; the pimpled son of a Privy Councillor (who had *tovarish* painted all over him).
>
> (*The Revenge For Love*, pp. 144–5)

The contempt for the absurd pretensions of the 'politically initiated' Left is relaxed and good-humoured; it has not the fierce abuse of similar passages in Orwell's *The Road to Wigan Pier*, though its use of listed types is similar.[45] But the kinds of 'political animal' in *The Revenge For Love* are characterized with a depth and conviction quite beyond the scope of most political novels. If anything the power of characterization sharpens the satire so that political types can also be unique individuals caught in a degrading environment. For example

Gillian Phipps is seen first (by Margot) as a typical upper-class fellow-traveller using her Communist affiliations as a form of fashionably *chic* behaviour:

> the only way to keep this big proud girl in her place would have been to speak in the accents of Shoreditch to Notting Dale; to speak 'in character'—to allow that to be fastened on her, like the placards hung round the necks of offending Jews in the Reich. And even then Gillian would have merely mocked her only, instead of in the veiled way she was accustomed to do at present. Margot understood that no bridge existed across which she could pass to commune as an equal with this Communist 'lady'—living in a rat-infested cellar out of swank (as it appeared to her) from her painfully constructed gimcrack pagoda of gentility.
>
> (*The Revenge for Love*, p. 159)

This novel is really about falseness, especially 'false politics' and 'sham-underdogs athirst for power'. But Percy Hardcaster turns out to be the real thing: a genuine subversive who, without hypocrisy, uses the system for what he can achieve—and that includes Gillian. She loses interest in him when she discovers that her wounded hero bribed his way out of gaol, and so he tells her what he really thinks of upper-class 'Communists' who have joined for 'fun and excitement' and the 'romance of revolution':

> '. . . if it ever comes to a showdown and there's a bit of a shoot-up, it will be a matter of complete indifference to me *which* of you—whether you "Communist" intellectuals, you fancy *salon*-revolutionaries, you old-school-tie pinks, or on the other hand your fascist first-cousins—are wiped out'. (p. 209)

Although it is a political novel in the sense that it is about political behaviour, it is also a novel which enlarges our experience and not just our knowledge. Some of the characters, Jack Cruze is a good example, have a vitality of Dickensian dimensions, while others such as Margot possess a complete inner personality worthy of a creation by D. H. Lawrence or James Joyce. As in *Tarr* (1918) each character and situation is built up meticulously with minutely detailed descriptions, however minor the incident may be. This aspect of Lewis's technique is comparable to Isherwood's in *Mr Norris Changes Trains* (1935) and *Goodbye to Berlin* (1939) where the author has tried to record with the exactitude of the camera an unprecedented social and political scene. Alex Comfort, too, in *The Power House* (1944) uses description to the tiniest detail in his account of life in industrial France before and after Nazi occupation—though here the author writes with the eye of a surgeon:

> Uncle Pécquard was having a bath, standing upright in it, his whole remarkably deformed body exposed to view. His forearms were bent into semicircles, and his thighs bowed as if he had stood upon them when they were soft, and so bent them. His skin was surprisingly white, and his face, from the enlargement of his skull and his lower jaw, was concave and triangular. He held it on one side, so as to look out of the corner of his eyes, the other side being gradually obscured by a cloud which had come over it during the last six months . . . His face was black with coal dust, except for white circles where he had knuckled his eyes, and a black patch covered the part of his back that his deformity prevented him from reaching.[46]

This character, who has to work as a crane-operator, not only because of financial need at a time of growing unemployment, but because of intense pride, is in his misfortune a symbol of the callousness of capitalist industry which will use, ruin and then discard. When found to be unfit for work he is given a small pension:

> Old Pécquard bit his moustache and tried not to sob, since the dust from the ore and the rubbing of his eyes had made him tearless, so that all he could show of grief was a grimace. From then on he sat in his chair. When [his family] wanted him moved they pushed the chair with Uncle Pécquard in it. (p. 76)

Increasingly writers failed to distinguish between social and political matters because they could no longer be seen as separate. A character's treatment by society, even the psychology that explained his actions, were in a new sense political since the modern citizen who did not fit in could no longer be thought of as an isolated problem. 'Political' literature had indeed become, generally, *anti*-political and certainly uncommitted to any national or international political party: its concerns were increasingly moral and aesthetic. Here, I think, lies the reason for writers' return in the late 1930s and early 1940s to the personal and the psychological spurs that motivate behaviour. Yet the return was not to any *avant-garde* development of the 'stream of consciousness' technique nor was it unconnected with the world's political plight. The difficulties of a whole range of characters from the novels of the period

(Mr Norris, Peter Slavek, Fougueux, Percy Hardcaster, Professor A., even Winston Smith) are seen both as emotional ones, usually related to their childhood, and as social and political ones that affect and impinge upon everyone else. The Doctor in *The Power House* is sickened by the antics of political demonstrators during a May Day Rally who are supposed to be socialists but are really jockeying with each other for extra money. The activities of political parties no longer seemed to provide any real solution: 'Now politics made him weary. They had somehow lost their relevance. The real struggle was against Society' (p. 79).

Thus by 1945 a creative writer would have been unlikely to produce anything that could be considered specifically political. Even Orwell's post-war fiction was about government rather than politics. Yet the move away first from commitment to a party and then from specific concern with politics as a separate entity did not, as perhaps critics hoped, bring back loftiness and dispassion to literary creation. Not only were no names to emerge which might be placed beside Lawrence, Joyce, Yeats and Eliot (to limit ourselves to the earlier decades of this century) but few post-1945 writers would be able to offer the range or impact of even those political and social writers whom I have discussed. Nor has the move away from political commitment encouraged the evolution of new literary forms to the extent to which those who deplored 'le trahison des clercs' would presumably have wished. The 'academic-administrative' verse of the 'New Poetry' that appeared in the 1950s is characterized by its lack of experimentalism,[47] while for all their skill the 'Angry Young Men' can scarcely be said to have contributed more significantly to the form of the novel than Evelyn Waugh and P. G. Wodehouse before them. Indeed it is the drama of, among others, Osborne, Arden, Whiting, Wesker, Delaney, Pinter, Simpson—some of it savagely critical of society and the politics that perpetuate it—which has shown willingness to experiment and innovate. And if we take one post-1950 work which most critics agree is to be considered of high and permanent merit, William Golding's *Lord of the Flies*, we have a novel of original flavour which yet in its myth-making reminds us of D. H. Lawrence and, in its pessimistic portrayal of human types, of George Orwell. Perhaps it would be fair to conclude this chapter by saying that the flight from commitment left an inspirational vacuum which has been filled by uncertain views of the kind of society which comforts and titillates but does not civilize, and which menaces by its size and its systematization of mankind.

Chapter Four
Ars Longa, Vita Brevis?

> Works of art which lack artistic quality have no force, however progressive they are politically.
>
> Mao Tse-Tung

The literature that I have discussed has exhibited great variety: the range of verse, prose and drama—and the mixtures of these forms by individual writers, and by authors in collaboration—are undoubtedly impressive. Yet despite this variety one basic distinction seems to emerge, and it is a distinction relevant to form. There is at one extreme the kind of political literature which includes political ideas, events, discussions, even ideologies, rather as other works might include sport or farming or travel for the purpose of local colour and atmosphere. At the other extreme is the 'hard-core' political literature devoted to persuasion, to changing in some way the political views and convictions of the reader.

The first kind of political literature (which could, I suppose, be called 'uncommitted') will clearly allow the writer scope to produce whatever he likes or, at least, whatever he is capable of producing. Form will probably not be dependent upon content but independent of it. Thus the *literature* may be more impressive but the political content will tend to become subsidiary. Conrad's 'political' novels or Graham Greene's 'Entertainments' are examples of what I mean, as is Aldous Huxley's *Point Counter Point* (1928) which includes a character that anticipated Sir Oswald Mosley.[1] In 'hard-core' political literature, however, content will perhaps so far have influenced form, style, texture and technique that they are inseparable from what they are communicating—indeed they are part of the communication. Here the charge that the work is propaganda rather than literature is always possible. The 'New Country' group and their associates were obvious candidates for such accusations—or approval, according to your criteria. MacDiarmid, O'Casey and Roy Campbell would also qualify with some of their most characteristic writings. But I have pointed to extremes. Some writers have been quite capable of veering first to one end and then to the other of the politico-literary spectrum—though it is unlikely they would be 'party men'. Thus Shaw, Wells, Wyndham Lewis and Orwell can be satirical and politically aloof in one part of a work yet totally committed to a political view or judgement in another part: their commitment bringing with it the didacticism or dogmatism that is to be expected in a pamphlet or tract.

I have scarcely mentioned essays which discuss politics, or politics and literature, since, however important as they may have been, such politically orientated critical works as the Marxist *Studies in a Dying Culture* (1938) by Christopher Caudwell and the 'anarchist' *Art and Social Responsibility* (1947) by Alex Comfort have not contributed a new shaping influence upon the form of the essay. The technique admirably displayed by Aldous Huxley in, say, *Ends and Means* (1937) and Bertrand Russell in *Let the People Think* (1941) suggests that the essay was already developed to a pitch whereby it required no alteration of form to deal further with new political matters or to express politico-literary idealogies. Even Orwell did little more for the essay than write with clarity and common-sense while, for our purposes, his essays are a subsidiary reflection of matters projected in a more significantly literary manner in his fiction. Similarly *Journey to a War* (1939) by Auden and Isherwood illustrates a move into the established mode of travelogue and 'foreign correspondence' which, as we saw in the previous chapter, characterized certain 'journalistic' political novels of the time in which the writer emphasized the actuality of first-hand experience. Thus writing about or for politics modified the major literary forms but was unlikely to influence the perhaps already more ephemeral nature of the essay or the letter. Indeed for many critics it has been precisely in its bringing to the poem, the novel and the play the day-to-day considerations of the rapidly changing and deteriorating atmosphere of the *entre deux guerres* period, that political literature made its most notable contribution—though it is a contribution about whose aesthetic merit there have been inevitable differences of opinion.

Introducing his anthology of 'socialist verse' Alan Bold said that 'unless the political matter is humanized and transformed into poetry, it deserves to be forgotten'. And Bold quoted T. S. Eliot's dictum: 'A political association may help to give poetry immediate attention: it is in spite of this association that the poetry will be read, if it is read, tomorrow'.[2] These statements appear to agree with the view of Mao Tse-Tung quoted at the beginning of this chapter, and the agreement

93

is all the more remarkable when it is realized that Eliot was making a case for the verse of Rudyard Kipling. Is such a view correct? Will political literature succeed for all time only if it is 'good' literature? In one sense you have to agree because you are presented with a *fait accompli*: Kipling *must* have written well or he would not have survived because his views were so generally unacceptable. But in another sense such statements cloud the issue since judgement of political literature must rest upon differing and separate criteria. Certainly some politically committed works are of great artistic merit, but whether they are as effective *politically* as lesser, more propagandist, works is a question to be decided by other means than concern us here but which are the province of social scientists. What we can say is this: political literature that succeeds as *literature* does so, not despite its political content or commitment, but because of an aesthetic potency unassessable and unjustifiable in political science. If politics and literature are not incompatible they are, as human activities, essentially different in kind. And the difference will produce different and, sometimes, irreconcilable responses to that mixture called 'political literature'. Secular devils, too, of whatever shade or colour may well have the best tunes. What is more, one man's devil will be another's angel whose success as a harpist may, though it should not, depend on which orchestra pays him. Is there any political party that would not claim support in Shakespeare?

Notes

Introduction

1. John Galsworthy, *Loyalties, with two other plays* (Pan Books, London, 1953), p. 157; Arthur Koestler, *Darkness At Noon* (translated by Daphne Hardy, Penguin Books, Harmondsworth, 1964), pp. 180–1.

2. John Harrison, *The Reactionaries* (Gollancz, London, 1967).

3. *Ibid.* See also W. Y. Tindall, *Forces in Modern British Literature 1885–1956* (Vintage Books, New York, 1956), p. 84.

4. T. S. Eliot, *After Strange Gods* (Faber and Faber, London, 1934), p. 48.

5. George Orwell, *Collected Essays, Journalism and Letters*, ed. Sonia Orwell and Ian Angus (Penguin Books, Harmondsworth, 1970), vol. II, p. 311. (Hereafter referred to as *CEJL*.)

6. Harrison, *op. cit.*, p. 17.

7. See J. A. Morris, 'T. S. Eliot and Antisemitism', *Journal of European Studies* (1972), vol. II, No. 2, pp. 173–82.

8. *A New Anthology of Modern Verse 1920–1940* (Methuen, London, 1945), Introduction, p. xvii.

9. Orwell, *CEJL*, vol. IV, pp. 463–4.

10. *The Writer and Politics* (The Porcupine Press, London, 1948), p. 10.

11. See Michael MacLiammoir's Introduction to *J. M. Synge's Plays, Poems and Prose* (Dent, London, 1941), pp. vi–vii.

12. G. S. Fraser, *W. B. Yeats* (Longman, London, 1962), p. 5.

13. V. de S. Pinto, *Crisis in English Poetry 1880–1940* (Hutchinson, London, 1967), p. 108.

14. *Ibid.*, p. 153. Professor Pinto followed Dr Leavis in comparing Forster's echo with the 'fear in a handful of dust' of Eliot's *The Wasteland*, but a comparison with de la Mare's poem seems equally valid.

15. *The Trembling of the Veil* (1922); quoted in G. S. Fraser, *op. cit.*, p. 13.

16. E.g., see Bertrand Russell, *Philosophy and Politics* (Cambridge, 1946); Arthur Koestler, *The Invisible Writing* (London, 1954); George Orwell, *The Lion and the Unicorn* (London, 1941).

17. Louis MacNeice, *Modern Poetry* (London, 1938); quoted in Orwell's 'Inside the Whale', *CEJL*, vol. I, pp. 559–60.

18. Stephen Spender, *The Struggle of the Modern* (Methuen, London, 1965); see explanatory note at the front of the book.

19. MacNeice, *op. cit.* 'Yeats proposed to turn his back on desire and hatred; Eliot sat back and watched other people's emotions with *ennui* and an ironical self-pity.' The term 'New Country' is now used generally to indicate the early poetry of W. H. Auden, Cecil Day Lewis, Stephen Spender and others who contributed to a collection of poems, short stories and sketches edited and introduced by Michael Roberts and published under the title *New Country* in 1933. In the previous year Roberts had produced a collection called *New Signatures* which included work by these three poets (and Julian Bell, William Empson and John Lehmann) but which was less political and revolutionary in attitude and tone. John Lehmann distinguished in this way between the two books: 'The general tone of *New Country* was definitely political, impatient for radical social change, and while most of the *New Signatures* contributors who had little obvious connection with the political side of the movement had dropped out, two or three new poets were included, e.g. Charles Madge, Rex Warner and Richard Goodman, whose work owed a great deal to the pioneering of Auden, Day Lewis and Spender in technique and feeling and was even more bluntly revolutionary in attitude. Two new prose-writers also appear, Edward Upward and Christopher Isherwood, who were very closely connected with some of the poets personally and whose ideas had had considerable influence on them.' (J. Lehmann, *New Writing in Europe*, Penguin Books, Harmondsworth, 1940, p. 28.)

20. *Poetry of the Thirties*, introduced and edited by Robin Skelton (Penguin Books, Harmondsworth, 1964), p. 23. By 'the Left' I mean Auden, Day Lewis, Spender and other writers associated with them (see previous Note). Cf. Lehmann, *op cit.*, p. 26: '. . . the dominant trio among them, Auden, Day Lewis, Spender, soon came to be regarded as leaders of revolutionary writing, even communist writing; yet none of them was of anything approaching working-class origin.'

21. Lehmann, *op. cit.*, quoted pp. 23–4.

22. Woodcock, *op. cit.*, p. 12.

23. I am thinking of the later Wyndham Lewis who could write such a novel as *The Revenge for Love* (1937) and who expressed his admiration of Orwell's *Animal Farm* and *1984* in *The Writer and the Absolute* (London, 1952).

24. For the nineteenth-century tradition of cultural politics (Coleridge, Arnold, Dickens, George Eliot, etc.) see Raymond Williams, *Culture and Society 1780–1950* (Chatto and Windus, London, 1958). The disturbance to this tradition from the 1880s onwards and its subsequent effects, caused in particular by the secularization of thought, upon such writers as Hardy, Lawrence and Forster, are well discussed by Malcolm Bradbury in *The Social Context of Modern English Literature* (Blackwell, Oxford, 1971).

25. See Bradbury, *op. cit.*, Chapter III ('The Impress of the Moving Age') which considers *Howards End* (1910) as portraying the critical effects upon English culture of the new 'industrializing, centralizing and democratizing forces'. It is perhaps significant that the subject-matter and even the form of one of Forster's most famous short stories, 'The Machine Stops', was apparently the result of its being, in the author's words, 'a reaction to one of the earlier heavens of H. G. Wells'.

Chapter One

1. Holbrook Jackson, *The Eighteen Nineties* (Penguin Books, Harmondsworth, 1939), p. 17.

2. *Essays by Oscar Wilde*, ed. Hesketh Pearson (Methuen, London, 1950), Introduction, p. xi.

3. *Ibid.*, p. 244.

4. *Ibid.*, p. 245.

5. William Morris, *News from Nowhere* (Longman, London, 1891), pp. 107–8.

6. Edith C. Batho and Bonamy Dobrée, *The Victorians and After* (The Cresset Press, London), p. 23.

7. See also the remarkable poem 'Tom's Garland', whose sympathy with working men, those at the foot of the 'Commonwealth', is reminiscent of Shakespeare's Henry V in his attitude to the 'wretched slave . . . cramm'd with distressful bread'. The 'sprung rhythm' and idiosyncratic vocabulary of Hopkins's sonnet tend to hide the actual political views of the poet who, in a prose explanation, makes clear that the 'packs' who 'infest the age' are those whom society has made into 'Loafers, Tramps, Cornerboys, Roughs, Socialists and other pests of society'. See *Poems and Prose of Gerard Manley Hopkins*, ed. W. H. Gardner (Penguin Books, Harmondsworth, 1953), p. 236.

8. Pinto, *Crisis in English Poetry 1880–1940*, p. 144. In a sonnet called 'West London' Arnold had pictured the listlessness of the poverty-

stricken who would not beg from the rich but only from 'sharers in a common human fate', pointing 'to a better time than ours'.

9. T. S. Eliot, *Collected Poems 1909–1935* (Faber and Faber, London, 1958), pp. 11 and 21.

10. 'Modern Poetry: A Broadcast' from *Yeats: Selected Criticism*, ed. A. Norman Jeffares (Macmillan, London, 1964), p. 245.

11. Batho and Dobrée, *op. cit.*, p. 35.

12. Passages quoted in Pinto, *op. cit.*, pp. 11 and 142.

13. *Ibid.*, p. 142.

14. See 'The Burial of the Dead', ll. 60–8.

15. *The Secret Agent*, quoted in Pinto, *op. cit.*, p. 142.

16. *Mr Bennett and Mrs Brown* (The Hogarth Press, London, 1924), pp. 9–23.

17. *Under Western Eyes* (Penguin Books, Harmondsworth, 1957), pp. 117–18.

18. George Gissing, *Demos: A Story of English Socialism*, ed. Pierre Coustillas (The Harvester Press, Brighton, 1972), Introduction, p. xxv.

19. Although clearly a very different kind of novelist, Graham Greene was later to write with great realism about the intrigues of international spies. And here, too, in many 'literary thrillers' such as *Stamboul Train* (1932) and *The Confidential Agent* (1939) and also in *The Power and the Glory* (1940), violence and intrigue are really the setting rather than the substance of what the novelist is saying. *That* is, of course, of a religious or moral nature: any political atmosphere serves as a means whereby the novelist can portray spiritual crises. There is evidence, however, that Greene became more specifically political in *The Quiet American* (1955).

20. Robert Tressall, *The Ragged Trousered Philanthropists* (Penguin Books, Harmondsworth, 1940).

21. A. C. Ward, *Longman Companion to Twentieth Century Literature* (London, 1970), pp. 534–5.

22. Kingsley Amis, *New Maps of Hell* (Four Square Books, London, 1963), p. 111 (Note).

23. Tom Hopkinson, *George Orwell* (Longman, London, 1962), p. 20 (cf. R. H. Rovere, *The American Establishment and Other Reports, Opinions and Speculations* (New York, 1962), p. 174: '*The Road to Wigan Pier* is a masterpiece').

24. Cf. the contemplated suicide, in Wells's *The History of Mr Polly* (1910), which despite the real, and realistically portrayed, problems in the hero's life of deprivation, is almost a jolly affair.

25. Jackson, *The Eighteen Nineties*, p. 42. On p. 22 an account is given of the developing social consciousness of the press in such publications as Robert Blatchford's *Clarion* and W. T. Stead's *Review of Reviews*.

26. G. B. Shaw, *An Unsocial Socialist* (Phoenix Publishing Co., Berne and Paris, 1948), pp. 134–5.

27. G. B. Shaw, *Plays Unpleasant* (Penguin Books, Harmondsworth, 1946), p. 60.

28. W. Y. Tindall, *Forces in Modern British Literature 1885–1956* (Vintage Books, New York, 1956), p. 31.

29. *Major Barbara* (Penguin Books, Harmondsworth, 1945), pp. 156–7.

30. See Tindall, *op. cit.*, pp. 41–2.

31. G. K. Chesterton, *Heretics* (John Lane, New York and London, 1905), pp. 288–9.

32. *Ibid.* A point of view which C. Day Lewis came close to sharing; see above, p. 19.

33. A. E. Rodway, 'The Last Phase', *The Pelican Guide to English Literature* (ed. Boris Ford), vol. VI, pp. 385–405.

34. Pearson (ed.), *The Essays of Oscar Wilde*, p. 258.

35. Rodway, 'The Last Phase', p. 396.

36. E.g., see T. S. Eliot's introductory essay to *A Choice of Kipling's Verse* (Faber and Faber, London, 1941).

37. See *Language and Silence* (Faber and Faber, London, 1967) and *Extraterritorial* (Faber and Faber, London, 1972). Sartre's comment in *Qu'est-ce que la littérature?* (Chapter Two, note 3) that there can be no such thing as a good anti-Semitic or anti-Black or anti-worker novel, has stimulated discussion—not all of it in easy agreement; e.g., see David Caute, *The Illusion* (A. Deutsch, London, 1971), pp. 48–52, where the author comes near to apologizing for his appreciation of the artistry of Griffith's 'racist' film *The Birth of a Nation*.

38. George Orwell, 'Rudyard Kipling', *CEJL*, vol. II, p. 215.

39. 'The Man who would be King', *A Choice of Kipling's Prose* (Macmillan, London, 1952), p. 171.

40. Eliot had said (*A Choice of Kipling's Verse*, pp. 26–7) that he did not believe Kipling in 'Loot' was 'commending the rapacity and greed of such irregularities, or condoning rapine'.

41. Orwell, 'Inside the Whale', *CEJL*, vol. I, pp. 574–5. According to M. J. Garrety, Sassoon told Prof. V. de S. Pinto (Velmore in Sherston's Progress) 'here is a new poet you must read' and handed him a copy of 'Prufrock and Other Observations'.

Chapter Two

1. George Orwell, 'Inside the Whale', *CEJL*, vol. I, pp. 559–60.

2. W. Y. Tindall, *Forces in Modern British Literature 1885–1956*, p. 57. Further references to Tindall are placed in the text.

3. Pinto, *Crisis in English Poetry 1880–1940*, p. 29.

4. G. B. Shaw, *The Intelligent Woman's Guide to Socialism* (Penguin Books, Harmondsworth, 1937), vol. II, pp. 431–2.

5. Percy Wyndham Lewis, *The Art of Being Ruled* (Chatto and Windus, London, 1926), p. 370.

6. G. B. Shaw, *Everybody's Political What's What?* (Constable, London, 1944), p. 40.

7. See *Blasting and Bombardiering* (1937), especially Part III, Chapter I, on 'The Romance of War'.

8. *Blast*, No. I (June 1914). See William Gaunt, *The March of the Moderns* (Jonathan Cape, London, 1949), p. 148.

9. Stephen Spender, *World Within World* (Readers Union, London, 1953).

10. *Poetry of the Thirties*, Introduction, p. 18.

11. Spender, *op. cit.*, p. 215.

12. Tindall, *op. cit.*, p. 45: 'Following MacDiarmid's lead came younger poets—Auden, Day Lewis, Spender, and their chums'.

13. 'Second Hymn to Lenin', *Selected Poems*, edited by David Craig and John Manson (Penguin Books, Harmondsworth, 1970), p. 91.

14. *Selected Poems*, Introduction, p. 10.

15. 'First Hymn to Lenin', *ibid.*, pp. 53–4.

16. Originally the phrase was 'The conscious acceptance of the necessary murder' in the poem 'Spain' (1937), but Auden later changed the line to 'The conscious acceptance of guilt in the fact of murder' and, later still, dropped the poem completely. See John Fuller, *A Reader's Guide to W. H. Auden* (Thames and Hudson, London, 1970), pp. 258–9.

17. See 'Third Hymn to Lenin', *Selected Poems*, p. 110.

18. Tindall, *op. cit.*, p. 45: 'His "First Hymn to Lenin" . . . this muscular prayer . . . captures something of the grandeur of Yeats'.

19. 'Some Notes on Auden's Early Poetry', *Exhumations* (Methuen, London, 1966), p. 17.

20. *Poetry of the 1930s*, edited by Allan Rodway, Introduction, pp. 13–14.

21. *Southern Review*, vol. VI, Summer 1940; quoted in Fuller, *A Reader's Guide to W. H. Auden*, p. 47.

22. See Rodway, *op. cit.*, pp. 2–3, where he quotes Donald Davie's poem 'Remembering the Thirties', which describes the 'New Country' poets (and by implication their work) as 'impressive and absurd'.

23. Julian Symons, *The Thirties* The Cresset Press, London, 1960), pp. 17–18.

24. Orwell, 'Inside the Whale', *CEJL*, pp. 565–6.

25. Orwell, 'Why I Write', *CEJL*, p. 30.

26. 'Inside the Whale', p. 562.

27. Sigmund Freud, *Group Psychology and the Analysis of the Ego*, translated by James Strachey (London, 1922), p. 51.

28. *Poetry of the Thirties*, Introduction, p. 17.

29. 'Inside the Whale', p. 565: 'the "Communism" of the English intellectual is something explicable enough. It is the patriotism of the deracinated.'

30. 'Full Moon at Tierz: Before the Storming of Huesca', *Poetry of the Thirties*, pp. 137–9.

31. *Ibid.*

32. C. Day Lewis, 'The Magnetic Mountain (1933), *Collected Poems* (Jonathan Cape, London, 1954), p. 97. See also poem 27, pp. 109–10.

33. E.g., the half-rhymes 'heaven . . . haven' in poem 5 (p. 86) and the whole use of a kestrel as symbolic: 'My kestrel joy, O hoverer in wind' (poem 1, p. 81).

34. See above, Introduction, note 7.

35. 'Hymn', *Poetry of the Thirties*, pp. 59–61. D. E. S. Maxwell in *Poets of the Thirties* (Routledge and Kegan Paul, London, 1969) pp. 51–4, discusses the poetry of Charles Madge whose 'Letter to the Intelligentsia' (published in *The Disappearing Castle*, 1937) resembles Warner's 'Hymn'. Madge's most ambitious political verse, in *Delusions* I–VIII, expresses in poetic terms a Marxist analysis of modern history (cf. Cornford's 'Full Moon at Tierz' discussed in Chapter Two, pp. 57–8). In much of his verse Madge resembles other 'New Country' poets in communicating 'a disintegrating *bourgeois*-capitalist world and sensibility' by a poetry 'of flux, confusion' (Maxwell, *op. cit.*, p. 52). He also wrote prose fables, e.g., his 'Bourgeois News', which typifies the familiar 'intellectual slapstick' associated with the Auden of *The Dog Beneath the Skin*. Although Madge (who had not contributed to *New Signatures*, 1932) helped to make *New Country* (1933) more speci-

fically political, his technique as poet clearly depended enormously on the pioneering work of Auden, Day Lewis and Spender. (See John Lehmann, *New Writing in Europe*, Penguin Books, Harmondsworth, 1940, Chapter Two.) Maxwell, *op. cit.*, pp. 63–82, also gives an account of Christopher Caudwell's verse (published and unpublished) most of which was surprisingly unpolitical and that which was 'political' tending towards support for pacifism. Like William Empson, Caudwell seems rarely to have shrunk from being as learned and cerebral in verse as he was in prose.

36. Maxwell, p. 50, suggests that 'Hymn' contains 'prep-school abuse'.

37. See Symons, *op. cit.* Alan Bold in his Introduction to *The Penguin Book of Socialist Verse*, p. 45, quotes Day Lewis's retrospective poem 'An Italian Visit' (1953) where the poet admits 'we who "flowered" in the Thirties were an odd lot'. Bold suggests that 'a certain frivolity' characterized much 1930s' verse which 'displayed its political imagery like a trophy brought back from another country'.

38. In *The God that Failed: Six Studies in Communism* (Hamish Hamilton, London, 1950).

39. Spender, *op. cit.*, pp. 174–5.

40. Quoted in Lehmann, *op. cit.*, p. 109.

41. Though the poem beginning 'oh young men oh young comrades/it is too late now to stay in those houses/your fathers built' resembles Warner's 'Hymn'; see Stephen Spender, *Selected Poems* (Faber and Faber, London, 1940), p. 22.

42. See *World Within World*, pp. 181–213, and Spender's contribution to *The God that Failed*.

43. It is ironical that the title of Koestler's novel *Darkness at Noon* should suggest that a society founded on Marxism could produce irrationality which equalled the obscurantist dogmatism of any religion, whether Christian or otherwise. See John Strachey, 'The Strangled Cry', *Encounter* xv (November 1960), 8. Strachey took the novel's title to mean 'an eclipse of human reason, just when the enlightenment should have reached its noontide, in the coming to power of the first government to be consciously based upon rationalism'.

44. See H. G. Wells, *The Outlook for Homo Sapiens* (Readers Union, London, 1942), pp. 255–7.

45. See my discussion, above, in this chapter pp. 45–9, and specifically on Auden, pp. 54–5. A good foreign example (of how fascination with machine-power may simultaneously affect literary technique and

reflect an authoritarian view of man) is Antoine de Saint-Exupéry, whose machine is, significantly, the aeroplane.

46. Gaunt, *op. cit.*, p. 240: 'Marinetti had visited Moscow and St Petersburg before 1914 and had left behind some adherents of Futurism. It seemed in many ways a perfect theoretic basis for a proletarian state. It extolled action, energy. It praised the machine. It was opposed to art as a refinement which could distinguish one class from another. It was even possible to see as the means of making a new kind of man. No less was the ambitious programme of the Russians. To make a "collective man", completely absorbed in and identified with the mass, moving in harmony with the rest like a component of some vast mechanism.'

47. Stephen Spender, *The Struggle of the Modern*, p. 80. The poet uses the words 'future' and 'prophecy' in his poem 'The Pylons'.

48. Eugene Zamiatin, *We* (translated by Gregory Zilboorg, E. P. Dutton and Co., New York, 1952), p. 79.

49. C. B. Cox and A. E. Dyson, *Modern Poetry* (Arnold, London, 1963), p. 81: Spender 'was never a true Marxist but a romantic liberal longing for a new age of heroism'. The authors also draw attention to the Freudian interpretation which the reader can make of the poet's use of such symbols as express train, airliner and 'feminine land'.

50. Stephen Spender, *The Destructive Element* (Jonathan Cape, London, 1935), p. 234.

51. See Maxwell, pp. 199–200; cf. Edward Upward's 'Sketch for a Marxist Interpretation of Literature', in *The Mind in Chains* (1937), edited by C. Day Lewis (Muller, London, 1972), p. 41: '. . . literary criticism which aims at being Marxist . . . must proclaim that no book written *at the present time* can be "good" unless it is written from a Marxist or near-Marxist viewpoint'.

Chapter Three

1. Julian Symons, *The Thirties* (The Cresset Press, London, 1960), p. 162. The 1939 Nazi–Soviet non-aggression pact was for many writers of the Left the final proof that faith in Russian Communism had been betrayed and that to continue it would be stupid or even immoral. Koestler recalled 'the day when the swastika was hoisted on Moscow airport, in honour of Ribbentrop's arrival, and the Red Army band broke into the *Horst Wessel Lied*. That was the end; from then onward I no longer cared whether Hitler's allies called me a counter-revolutionary'. (*The God that Failed*, p. 81.) Orwell wrote: 'For several years the

coming war was a nightmare to me, and at times I even made speeches and wrote pamphlets against it. But the night before the Russo-German pact was announced I dreamed that the war had started ... It taught me ... that I ... would not sabotage or act against my own side, would support the war, would fight in it if possible. I came downstairs to find the newspaper announcing Ribbentrop's flight to Moscow.' ('My Country Right or Left', *Collected Essays, Journalism and Letters*, vol. I, pp. 590–1.)

2. Stephen Spender, *World Within World*, p. 219.

3. *On the Frontier* (published with *The Ascent of F.6*) (Faber and Faber, London), p. 190.

4. Rex Warner, *The Wild Goose Chase* (London, 1937), pp. 206–7.

5. John Lehmann, *New Writing in Europe*, p. 67.

6. Christopher Isherwood, *Lions and Shadows* (London, 1938); see pp. 294–303.

7. *The Dog Beneath the Skin* (Faber and Faber, London, 1935), p. 173.

8. *Trial of a Judge* (Faber and Faber, London, 1938), pp. 85–6.

9. *The Star Turns Red* (Macmillan, London, 1940), pp. 181–2.

10. See Spender's contribution to *The God that Failed* and Wyndham Lewis's discussion of Orwell's post-war fiction in *The Writer and the Absolute*.

11. In *Poetry of the 1930s*, Part One.

12. *The Ascent of F.6*, p. 17.

13. *Another Time* (New York, 1940), Part II, No. ii (2). The first line of the poem is 'James Honeyman was a silent child'.

14. See M. R. Hillegas, *The Future as Nightmare* (New York, 1967), p. 49. He sees Wells as seminal for anti-Utopian writing and describes 'A Story of the Days to Come' (1899) as 'rich in significance for later anti-Utopias'. (In this story a young couple try in vain to escape from a giant collectivist city of the future.)

15. See George Orwell, *Keep the Aspidistra Flying* (Penguin Books, Harmondsworth, 1962), p. 19.

16. 'My Country Right or Left', *CEJL*, vol. I, p. 591.

17. Letters dated 4 January and 5 March 1939, *CEJL*, pp. 414–16 and 424–6.

18. 14 June 1940, *CEJL*, vol. II, pp. 395–6.

19. *Coming Up for Air* (Penguin Books, Harmondsworth, 1962), pp. 25–7.

20. *Principles and Persuasions* (London, 1958), p. 158.

21. George Orwell, Review of *Russia under Soviet Rule* by N. de Basily, *CEJL*, vol. I, p. 419. See also the series of four essays called 'The Intellectual Revolt', *Manchester Evening News*, 24 January–14 February 1946, in which Orwell discusses the thought of Koestler, Russell, Silone, P. F. Drucker, Karl Popper, Michael Polanyi, F. A. Hayek and many others who feared the future consequences of collectivism.

22. See Irving Howe, 'The Fiction of Anti-Utopia', *New Republic* (23 April 1962).

23. *Journey Through Utopia* (Routledge and Kegan Paul, London), 1950), p. 303.

24. 'Wells, Hitler and the World State', Orwell, *CEJL*, vol. II, p. 169.

25. 'Prophecies of Fascism' (*ibid.*, pp. 45–9). Orwell used Wells's revised title of 1911: *The Sleeper Wakes*.

26. *The Short Stories of H. G. Wells* (Benn, London, 1927), pp. 796–897. His 'Hotel for Women' and 'General Intelligence Organisations' suggest the ambiguity of title to be developed in the anti-Utopian novel (for example, Zamatin's 'Guardians' and Orwell's 'Ministry of Love'). See Note 14 above.

27. 'Freedom and Happiness', *Tribune* (4 January 1946), Orwell, *CEJL*, vol IV, pp. 95–9.

28. George Orwell, *Nineteen Eighty-Four* (1949) (Penguin Books, Harmondsworth, 1954), p. 109.

29. See F. R. Leavis, *The Great Tradition* (1948) (Penguin Books, Harmondsworth, 1966), p. 16, where, having noticed that Lord David Cecil had mentioned Wells in the same breath as James and Conrad, Dr Leavis continues: 'I don't know what Wells is doing in that sentence; there is an elementary distinction to be made between the discussion of problems and ideas and what we find in the great novelists'. Dr Leavis seems never to have mentioned Orwell in print though his wife did say that 'nature didn't intend him [Orwell] to be a novelist'. (Q. D. Leavis, 'The Literary Life Respectable', *Scrutiny* IX, September 1940.)

30. See Zamiatin, *op. cit.*, pp. 43–7; Aldous Huxley, *Brave New World* (1932) (Penguin Books, Harmondsworth, 1955), pp. 69–73; George Orwell, *1984*, pp. 13–17 and 146–8; Rex Warner, *The Professor* (1938) (Penguin Books, Harmondsworth, 1945), pp. 149–51; Ignazio Silone, *Bread and Wine*, translated by G. D. and E. Mosbacher (Ace Books, London, 1959), pp. 159–61; William Golding, *Lord of the Flies* (Penguin Books, Harmondsworth, 1960), pp. 141–7.

31. Letter to H. J. Willmett, 18 May 1944, *CEJL*, vol. III, p. 177.

32. Quoted in Walter Allen, *Tradition and Dream* (Penguin Books, Harmondsworth, 1965), p. 342.

33. See Orwell's letter to Gleb Struve, 17 February 1944, *CEJL*, vol. III, pp. 118–19; Laurence Brander, *George Orwell* (London, 1954), p. 96; Tom Hopkinson, *George Orwell*, p. 28; Edward M. Thomas, *Orwell* (Oliver and Boyd, Edinburgh and London, 1965), p. 71; Frederic Warburg's letter in *Encounter* (February 1969), vol. XXXII, no. 2, 91.

34. E.g., Robert A. Lee, *Orwell's Fiction* (Notre Dame, 1969), p. 106; John Wain, *Essays on Literature and Ideas* (London, 1963), p. 201.

35. *The Road to Wigan Pier* (1937) (Penguin Books, Harmondsworth, 1962), p. 189.

36. See the symposium on Kafka and Rex Warner in *Focus One*, ed. B. Rajan and Andrew Pearse (Dennis Dobson, London, 1945), pp. 7–65.

37. 'Wells, Hitler and the World State', *CEJL*, vol. II, p. 169.

38. 'Freud or Marx', review of Koestler's *Arrival and Departure*, *Manchester Evening News* (9 December 1943).

39. Arthur Koestler has written: 'I cannot recall having given him [Orwell] information in technical terms on the psychology of brain-washing—except perhaps indirectly through my writings (he reviewed *Darkness at Noon* for the *New Statesman*). Incidentally, you will find the seminal idea of the 'Ministry of Truth' in that book, page 117.' (Letter to me of 26 October 1966.)

40. *Arrival and Departure* (1943) (Arrow Books, London, 1962), pp. 106–7.

41. Neither parallels the course of particular historical events, though both satirize, through parody, authoritarian government—especially the authoritarianism of the Third Reich. Indeed the 'distancing' achieved by placing the 'new order' of the Air Force in a recognizably English setting caused Rex Warner to preface *The Aerodrome* with a note affirming his 'utmost affection and respect' for 'the Air Force and for the villages of my own country'.

42. J. Walsh in 'George Orwell', *Marxist Quarterly*, vol. 3, no. 1 (January 1956), pp. 35–6, wrote: '[Orwell] runs shrieking into the arms of the capitalist publishers with a couple of horror comics which bring him fame and fortune'. Raymond Williams replied that such a comment was 'arrogant and crass' (*Culture and Society 1780–1950* (Penguin Books, Harmondsworth), p. 284).

43. *Twentieth Century Drama* (Hutchinson, London, 1962), p. 29.

44. *The Revenge for Love* (Methuen, London, 1952), p. 71 (cf. *Coming Up for Air*, Penguin Books, p. 149: 'Gang up, choose your Leader. Hitler's black and Stalin's white. But it might just as well be the other way about . . .').

45. E.g., see the list of 'Socialists' in *The Road to Wigan Pier* (p. 190): 'a picture of vegetarians with wilting beards, of Bolshevik commissars (half gangster, half gramophone), of earnest ladies in sandals, shock-headed Marxists chewing polysyllables, escaped Quakers . . .' etc.

46. *The Power House* (Readers Union, London, 1945), p. 8.

47. See A. Alvarez (ed.), *The New Poetry* (Revised Edition) (Penguin Books, Harmondsworth), Introduction, pp. 21-4.

Chapter Four

1. Everard Webley is founder and head of the B.B.F. (Brotherhood of British Freemen). Sir Oswald Mosley considered calling his organization the U.B.F. (Union of British Fascists) but later changed it to the B.U.F. on realizing that the original order of the initials, though effective mnemonically, was unfortunate in its possible interpretation.

2. *The Penguin Book of Socialist Verse*, Introduction, p. 40. Eliot's statement is from 'A Choice of Kipling's Verse' (Faber and Faber, London, 1963), p. 7.

Acknowledgments

Thanks are due to the following for permission to reproduce copyright material:

Methuen & Co. Ltd: ed. C. Day Lewis and L. A. G. Strong (*Modern Verse 1920–1940: A New Anthology*), Percy Wyndham Lewis (*The Revenge for Love*); Jonathan Cape Ltd. and the Estate of John Cornford: ed. Pat Sloan ('Full Moon at Tierz: Before the Storming of Huesca' in *John Cornford: A Memoir*); Jonathan Cape Ltd, the Hogarth Press and the Executors of the Estate of C. Day Lewis ('The Magnetic Mountain' and 'The Nabara' in *Collected Poems 1954*); Victor Gollancz Ltd: John Harrison (*The Reactionaries*); The Bodley Head: Rex Warner ('Hymn' in *Poems, The Wild Goose Chase* and *The Professor*), G. K. Chesterton (*Heretics*); The Society of Authors on behalf of the Bernard Shaw Estate (*Major Barbara, An Unsocial Socialist* and *Widowers' Houses*); The Society of Authors as the literary representative of the Estate of John Galsworthy (*The Skin Game*); the Literary Trustees of Walter de la Mare and the Society of Authors as their representative ('The Old Angler' and 'Echo' in *The Complete Poems of Walter de la Mare 1969*); Lawrence & Wishart Ltd: Robert Tressall (*The Ragged Trousered Philanthropists*); A. D. Peters & Co. Ltd: Arthur Koestler (*Darkness at Noon* and *Arrival and Departure*), Stephen Spender (*World Within World*); William Empson and Chatto & Windus Ltd: William Empson ('Just a Smack at Auden' in *Collected Poems*); The Owen Estate and Chatto & Windus Ltd ('Strange Meeting' in *The Collected Poems of Wilfrid Owen*); Curtis Brown Ltd on behalf of Julian Symons (*The Thirties*); Curtis Brown Ltd on behalf of the Estate of Roy Campbell ('A Song for the People' in *Adamastor*); Faber & Faber Ltd: W. H. Auden ('Petition' and '1st September 1939' in *Collected Shorter Poems 1930–1944*, 'Let History be my Judge', 'Consider', 'In Memory of W. B. Yeats' and 'Miss Gee' in *Collected Shorter Poems 1927–1957*), W. H. Auden and Christopher Isherwood (*The Ascent of F6* and *On the Frontier*), T. S. Eliot ('The Love Song of J. Alfred Prufrock' and 'A Cooking Egg' in *Collected Poems 1909–1962*), Louis Macneice ('Jigsaw

II' in *Collected Poems of Louis Macneice*), Stephen Spender ('The Pylons', 'The Landscape near an Aerodrome', 'The Express' and 'Vienna' in *Collected Poems of Stephen Spender*, and *Trial of a Judge*); Macmillan, London and Basingstoke: W. E. Henley ('A Song of Speed' in *Poems by W. E. Henley*), Sean O'Casey (*The Star Turns Red*); Hugh MacDiarmid and Macmillan, London and Basingstoke: Hugh MacDiarmid ('First Hymn to Lenin', 'Second Hymn to Lenin' and 'Third Hymn to Lenin'); M. B. Yeats, Miss Anne Yeats and the Macmillan Company of London and Basingstoke ('The Song of Wandering Aengus', 'The Second Coming' and 'Easter 1916' in *The Collected Works of W. B. Yeats*, and *Yeats: Selected Criticism* edited by A. Norman Jeffares); Mrs George Bambridge and the Macmillan Company of London and Basingstoke: Rudyard Kipling ('The Man who would be King' in *Wee Willie Winkie*, and 'That Day'); Laurence Pollinger Ltd., the Estate of the late Mrs Frieda Lawrence and William Heinemann Ltd: D. H. Lawrence ('Mountain Lion' in *The Complete Poems of D. H. Lawrence*); Dr Alexander Comfort (*The Power House*); Mrs Sonia Brownell Orwell and Secker & Warburg Ltd: George Orwell (*Keep the Aspidistra Flying* and *Collected Essays, Journalism and Letters*, vols. I, II and III); Mr George Woodcock (*The Writer and Politics*); and Oxford University Press: ed. W. H. Gardner and N. H. MacKenzie (*The Poems of Gerard Manley Hopkins 1967*, published by arrangement with the Society of Jesus).

WRITERS AND POLITICS
IN MODERN FRANCE

Foreword

The term 'political literature' like 'committed literature' with which it is frequently associated has become an accepted part of the language of literary history. Yet however convenient, it is, on examination, surprisingly imprecise and misleading. The whole area of the interaction between politics and literature is a vast and complex one which has yet, especially on a European scale, to be fully and comprehensively charted. Certainly invaluable contributions do already exist: Jean-Paul Sartre's *Qu'est-ce que la littérature?* (1947), George Woodcock's *The Writer and Politics* (1948), Jürgen Rühle's *Literatur und Revolution* (1960), Irving Howe's *Politics and the Novel* (1961), John Mander's *The Writer and Commitment* (1961) for example. There are too, as the bibliographical information contained in the individual essays in this series will reveal, a number of equally important books which deal with the issue in purely national terms. With few exceptions, however, these, like many of the more general studies, suffer from the same defects resulting in the main from a failure to distinguish adequately between 'political literature' and what might be termed 'social literature', and from an incomplete assessment of changes both in political climates and in the writer's relationship to society as a whole. Yet, even when the area of investigation and terminology has been more carefully ascertained, we often find that these books are principally concerned either with an examination of the political ideas *per se* contained in various works of literature, or with an assessment of the ways in which parties and movements have controlled and used to best advantage writers and intellectuals who claim political allegiance. More recently Roland Barthes in *Le Degré Zéro de l'écriture* (1967), George Steiner in *Language and Silence* (1967) and David Caute in *Illusion* (1971) have suggested a wider perspective, outlining some of the problems of style and form which an imaginative writer has to face when he offers his pen to a political (or social) cause. On the whole, however, it is fair to say that the majority of critics have concentrated more on *what* ideas are expressed than on *how* they have been. In addition therefore to attempting to define the concept of political literature more precisely and to exploring such issues as the suitability of imaginative literature as a vehicle for political ideas or the effect such literature

can have on the public for example, one of the principal concerns of these essays is to attempt to examine ways in which an author's political sympathy or affiliation can be seen to affect or even dictate the way in which he writes. In some countries—in Russia, France or Spain, for example—direct influence of this kind is more apparent than in others. Elsewhere, notably in Britain, where political directives concerning art and literature have not been the rule, the problem is in some ways more difficult to assess. Indeed national variation of this kind is one of the principal contributory factors to the complex nature of the whole question. Thus while the subject is best illustrated and examined in the literature of France and Germany during the interwar years, it is after the Second World War that it fully emerges in the works of Italian and Scandinavian writers. Furthermore literary experiment seen and approved in some countries as an expression of a progressive, even revolutionary, political position is considered in others to be characteristic of subversion and decadence.

Given such problems as these and given too the amount of space available, these seven small volumes can do little more than hope to encourage a new approach to political literature. While free to explore the subject in the way they believe to be most useful within the context of the literary history of their particular countries, contributors have been encouraged to balance general comment with examination of specific examples. Inevitably therefore the essays appear arbitrarily selective. But like the literature which they choose to examine it is hoped that they will be judged not only for what they contain but also for the ways in which they deal with it.

John Flower

General Bibliography

The following are a selection of those books which discuss some of the general problems associated with this subject. Suggestions for further reading are contained in the notes to individual essays.

BARTHES, Roland, *Le Degré Zéro de l'écriture*, Editions du Seuil, Paris, 1953 (Translated: *Writing Degree Zero*, Cape, London, 1967).

CAUTE, David, *Illusion: An Essay on Politics, Theatre and the Novel*, Deutsch, London, 1971.

CROSSMAN, Richard, *The God that Failed: Six Studies in Communism*, Hamish Hamilton, London, 1950.

HOWE, Irving, *Politics and the Novel*, Horizon Press, New York, 1955.

MANDER, John, *The Writer and Commitment*, Secker & Warburg, London, 1961.

MUIR, Edwin, *Essays on Literature and Society*, Hogarth Press, London, 1965.

PANICHAS, George, A. (ed.), *The Politics of Twentieth-Century Novelists*. Crowell, New York, 1974.

RÜHLE, Jürgen, *Literatur und Revolution*, Kiepenheuer & Witsch, 1960. (Translated: *Literature and Revolution*, Pall Mall, London, 1969).

SARTRE, Jean-Paul, *Qu'est-ce que la littérature?* Gallimard, Paris, 1948 (Translated: *What is Literature?* Methuen, London, 1951).

STEINER, George, *Language and Silence: Essays and Notes, 1958–66*, Faber, London, 1967.

TROTSKY, Leon, *Literature and Revolution*, University of Michigan Press, Ann Arbor, 1960.

WINEGARTEN, Renee, *Writers and Revolution: the fatal lure of action*, Franklin Watts, New York, 1974.

WOODCOCK, George, *The Writer and Politics*, The Porcupine Press, London, 1948.

Contents

Introduction

Almost without exception, critics who have been concerned with political literature in France have turned with some regularity to Stendhal. With his views that personal relationships—love, hate, ambition, revenge and so on—were basically motivated by social and political considerations of the most general kind, and that the novelist's duty should be to reflect such tensions in his work as accurately as possible, Stendhal is generally considered, especially in *La Chartreuse de Parme*, to have produced a political novel in its most polished and complete form. Yet Stendhal is equally remembered for his remark that politics in the novel are as incongruous as a pistol shot in a concert-hall. These two views are not quite so paradoxical as they might at first appear to be, however. The first relates to a total view of life in which political motivation is closely related to psychological development and clash; the second to the introduction of arid ideological or political debate. Although political debate (as in *Le Rouge et le Noir*) may be occasioned naturally enough by the fictive situation which the author has created, and indeed may endow the fiction with a certain authenticity, it none the less threatens to lead the reader away on a tangent into a world of irrelevant detail.

Yet while Stendhal's view of the way politics may be integrated in literature does have a relevance for a large body of work produced some hundred years after he was writing, it is essentially one which belongs very much to a nineteenth-century tradition. His portrayal of a particular political regime or figure may indeed indicate his personal preferences concerning government or statesmanship, but he is primarily concerned not with the need to persuade or to convince his reader of the justness of his opinions, but rather to strike a balance. He sets out to describe situations in which the personal and the political harmonize, in which there is no fragmentation, no discontinuity but rather something similar to what Benjamin described as an 'aura'.[1] In a similar, though perhaps less complete and less successful way, Balzac in, for example, *Une Ténébreuse Affaire* may show the political intrigues of the Republicans to be utterly odious with virtue belonging entirely to

3

the monarchist cause, but he makes no *overt* attempt to draw his reader actively into the debate in order to persuade him to take sides. (It may be of course that the reader does so in the same way that in Stendhal's work he will disapprove of M. de Rênal or approve of Mosca, for example, but in no way is it intended that he should carry his sympathies beyond the private experience of reading the novel.)

However, just as the character of political literature—or perhaps as it would be more accurate at this point to say 'the depiction of political matters in literature'—was to change radically in France within the next hundred years, so, too, should we remember that it had already enjoyed a different role before the early nineteenth century. It would hardly be unreasonable, for example, to consider the medieval epic *La Chanson de Roland* as having a strong nationalistic tone to it. In the sixteenth century with his mixture of satire, humour and the grotesque, Rabelais in a more specific fashion had both ridiculed the political, social, religious and educational systems of his day and pleaded for their reform. In the eighteenth century Voltaire was personally involved in cases of social and political injustice and sought, especially in his *contes* (and as indeed Rabelais had done in, for example, his attacks on the Sorbonne) a form and a style which would be most apt to draw the attention of a fast-increasing reading public to the need for change. The examples are various and not difficult to find, and participation of this kind by the artist in the arena of political and social debate certainly continued in the nineteenth century when people like Constant, Lamartine and Hugo all played important political roles. Yet, in the main, political activity and art were kept apart, and by the second half of the century the idea of an art free from any form of overt political, social or moral comment gradually came to the fore. As Flaubert (who with Gautier is usually held up to be the chief exponent of this theory of 'l'art pour l'art' as it became known) once wrote in words that have long since assumed almost the status of a slogan: 'un romancier n'a pas le droit d'exprimer son opinion sur quoi que ce soit'. Since then the same sentiments have been echoed by writers like Gide[2] and above all by Robbe-Grillet: 'Dès qu'apparaît le souci de signifier quelque chose (quelque chose d'extérieur à l'art) la littérature commence à reculer, à disparaître.'[3] Yet in the main, until very recent years at least, this has been the attitude of a minority, attacked in particular by Sartre who considers it to amount to no less than a refusal by the writer to face up to his responsibilities, a form of 'mauvaise foi'.[4] Already in the last part of the nineteenth century, however, there were signs that the climate

4

was changing. Zola, for example, in novels like *L'Assommoir* (1877) or *Germinal* (1885) was allowing the kind of concern for justice he was to display at the time of the Dreyfus trial in the 1890s to colour his imaginative writing. Description for its own sake was disappearing and was instead beginning to carry perceptible social or political implications, however general these may have been. Even more noticeably, by the 1890s Barrès had expanded the 'culte du moi' philosophy of the 'trois romans idéologiques' of his first trilogy *Sous l'œil des barbares*, *Un Homme libre* and *Le Jardin de Bérénice* (1888–91) into the beginnings of a political creed based on tradition and conservative nationalism which was to permeate a whole range of novels extending beyond the end of the First World War. Unlike Flaubert, Barrès, admittedly in retrospect, saw the need to adapt style to content, 'cadences' to 'doctrine': 'l'art pour nous, ce serait d'exciter, d'émouvoir l'être profond par la justesse des cadences, mais en même temps de le persuader par la force de la doctrine'.[5]

While not quite so aware, perhaps, of the persuasive potential of his style, another influential figure for whom the Dreyfus Affair brought about a significant change both in his personal political attitude and in his work was Anatole France. Conservative and choosing to remain somewhat apart from social and political events in his early years, France was moved to defend Dreyfus staunchly in the name of justice. Subsequently his work assumed a new politically and socially conscious dimension and France himself moved, largely through the influence of Jaurès, through socialism and, towards the end of his life, tentatively towards Communism. Yet, despite this development, his work does not become programmed or schematized in the way that much subsequent left-wing writing was to be. France's targets are large. Works like the four volumes of his *Histoire contemporaine* (*L'Orme du Mail*, 1897; *Le Mannequin d'osier*, 1897; *L'Anneau d'améthyste*, 1899; *Monsieur Bergeret à Paris*, 1901) contain sharply observed satirical portraits of various aspects of French political and social life. *Les Dieux ont soif* (1912), set at the time of the Revolution, contains a strikingly prophetic attack on the effects of ideological excess. But for all that they reflect a growing awareness on his part that as a writer he had a certain social and political responsibility towards his public, such works as these lack the firm proselytizing element of many that were to appear in the years following.

Works like these already provide evidence, however general, of the beginnings of a shift in emphasis and concern that was to become even more marked. That this was so was due in no small measure both to changes in the political and social pressures to which French society was being subjected, and to the growing importance given to the intellectual or *clerc* as he was known. Defeat at the hands of the Prussians in 1870–1, the declining influence of the Church and of the conservative Right, the new emergent nationalism of Maurras' extra-parliamentary movement the Action Française, the growth of syndicalism and of socialism, the Dreyfus Affair, all contributed during the late nineteenth and early twentieth centuries to create within France a climate which, in spite of the gloss and apparent security of the 'belle époque', was potentially changeable.[6] When the War came it was welcomed almost unanimously by intellectuals and artists who, as in other European countries, believed that it would both be short-lived and provide the means by which France could cleanse her national soul (Claudel talked of 'le salut et la régénération de notre pauvre pays')[7] and subsequently re-establish herself as a leading European nation. In the end, having had part of her countryside totally ravaged and her adult male population cut by over one and a half million, France did emerge on the winning side. But the aftermath of war offered little relief. As the War had progressed so had collective attitudes towards it. While the naïve chauvinism of the first months—so much deplored by Romain Rolland in his essay *Au-dessus de la mêlée* (1914)—had provided for many 'the sense of belonging to a splendid fraternity',[8] it had soon paled as the situation became static and as the prospect of the War's ending receded. For some, indeed the majority, this rapidly encouraged the development of a supra-national feeling of victimization and waste, contemporaneously expressed in novels like Barbusse's *Le Feu* (1916) or in the English war poetry of 1916–18, and later in Dorgelès' *Les Croix de bois* (1919) or Remarque's *Im Westen nichts Neues* (1928); for others the delight in the crusading spirit and in the struggle for survival remained and gave rise in Germany to Jünger's *In Stahlgewittern* (1920) and in France to some of Drieu la Rochelle's writing. But most important of all is the fact that the War had been a hot-bed in which the seeds of the extreme left- and right-wing ideologies of the twenties and thirties had already begun to develop. As their shadow spread across Europe, as collective issues increasingly eclipsed private, individual concerns, intellectuals and writers found themselves with roles and responsibilities that were quite different from those of their predecessors. To borrow the words from Orwell's essay *Writers and Leviathan* (1948) in which he discusses English literature after the Second World War, this was a new political age in which 'the invasion of literature by politics was bound to happen'.[9]

The response of French intellectuals to the social, political and economic turmoil into which their country, along with the rest of Western Europe, had been plunged was almost unanimous. Emmanuel Mounier, for example, referred to '[une] crise totale de la civilisation'; Raymond Lefebvre to '[une] génération de débris, génération de décadence'; Ernst Curtius to 'notre existence nationale brisée et mise en question'.[10] For many, of course, much of the trouble lay in the very real threat of future German expansion, while Russia, in a period of post-Revolutionary enthusiasm, was seen to be insidiously extending her influence westwards in ever increasing proportions. Henri Massis' reaction in 1919 was typical: 'l'univers est à nouveau plastique entre les mains des hommes et ceux-ci [Russians and Germans] peuvent désormais faire de lui ce qu'ils veulent';[11] Drieu la Rochelle (for whom Germany represented much more to be admired) predicted with rather more accuracy that the long-term struggle for the soul of Europe would ultimately be decided between Russia and America. Yet, whatever their reactions to external forces or to attempts to find a political antidote, more significant is the way in which writers and intellectuals focused their attention of what they unanimously agreed was the real *internal* weakness of France, her physical and moral decadence nowhere better exemplified than by the 'bourgeoisie', a term which became used with an ever-increasing degree of contempt. For those whose political sympathies took them towards the Right, an answer lay in the re-establishment of authority and discipline. Maurras' Action Française tempted many, as did the various quasi-fascist groups like Valois' Le Faisceau or Taittinger's Jeunesses Patriotes in the late twenties.[12] For some, like Bernanos or Maritain, what was needed above all was a spiritual regeneration which only the Church could provide, and they idealistically pleaded for a return to what the latter defined as the 'sacral civilization' of the Middle Ages, a period when in their view Church and State had co-existed in perfect harmony.

For those on the Left, however, such views as these were themselves seen to be 'bourgeois', albeit expressed in an extreme and aggressive manner. Simone de Beauvoir, writing about her own family in the first volume of her autobiography, *Mémoires d'une jeune fille rangée*, catches their attitude perfectly:

Par ses opinions, mon père appartenait à son époque et à sa classe. Il tenait pour utopique l'idée d'un rétablissement de la royauté;

mais la République ne lui inspirait que du dégoût. Sans être affilié à *l'Action française*, il avait des amis parmi les 'Camelots du Roi' et il admirait Maurras et Daudet. Il interdisait qu'on mît en question les principes du nationalisme; si quelqu'un de malavisé prétendait en discuter, il s'y refusait avec un grand rire: son amour de la Patrie se situait au-delà des arguments et des mots: 'C'est ma seule religion', disait-il [. . .] Sa morale privée était axée sur le culte de la famille; la femme en tant que mère, lui était sacrée; il exigeait des épouses la fidelité, des jeunes filles l'innocence, mais consentait aux hommes de grandes libertés, ce qui l'amenait à considérer avec indulgence les femmes qu'on dit légères. Comme il est classique, l'idéalisme s'alliait chez lui à un scepticisme qui frôlait le cynisme.[13]

Such condemnation was not limited to and voiced only in works such as this, however. No matter what their ideological sympathies, intellectuals actively attempted in a more positive way through reviews, books and pamphlets to exert an influence. Indeed the names alone of many of the reviews and journals which proliferated at this time are enough to indicate their intention—*Ordre nouveau, Nouvel Age, Nouvelles Equipes, Clarté, Réaction, Combat, L'Homme nouveau, Esprit*, for example.[14] Among books and essays the difference in tone was considerable: the measured analysis of Aron and Dandieu's *La Décadence de la Nation française* (1931); Nizan's revolutionary and at times almost hysterical *Aden Arabie* (1931); Massis' conservative and patriotic *La Défense de L'Occident* (1927); Bernanos' onslaught on bourgeois hypocrisy and complacency in *La Grande peur des bien-pensants* (1931); Malraux's plea for virile action in *La Tentation de L'Occident* (1926). The list is potentially endless. It is arguable perhaps that much of this activity was self-indulgent or, as Malraux put it, narcissistic, yet its force and effectiveness cannot be denied. In the 1880s and 1890s both Barrès and Béranger had used the word 'intellectual' disparagingly.[15] It is well known that for Barrès, in particular, at the time of the Dreyfus affair the intellectual was considered to be the upholder of abstract and universal Kantian values like Justice and Truth, and as such represented a real threat to the immediate political and social stability of France enshrined as it was in the Army, the Church and the Judicial system. Now, nearly half a century later, attitudes had turned nearly full circle: the intellectual was involved. While some, like Julien Benda, remained true to the kind of role the intellectual had fitted some thirty or forty years earlier, and therefore deplored the situation, an increasingly large proportion of writers and intellectuals saw it their duty to take sides in the socio-political debate which raged about them. *Engagement* was fast becoming fashionable.

As we have already noted, writers and intellectuals generally during the post-war years expressed deep concern at their country's decadence. Such a concern provided a common focus for intellectuals whose attitudes otherwise to their role in and responsibility towards society were completely antithetical to one another and, moreover, indicative of the generation to which they belonged. A useful illustration of this is to be found in a group of essays written between 1927 and 1932 by Julien Benda, *La Trahison des clercs* (1927), Emmanuel Berl, *Mort de la pensée bourgeoise* and *Mort de la morale bourgeoise* (1929), and Paul Nizan, *Aden Arabie* (1931) and *Les Chiens de garde* (1932).

Predictably, the form taken by their attempt to destroy what they repeatedly decried as the 'mystique bourgeois' is a verbal onslaught on a self-perpetuating and exclusive system based primarily on exploitation and supported by a firm belief that material gain should be the just and natural reward for certain moral and social attitudes. Berl and Nizan, in particular, argue that the bourgeoisie has developed into a form of caste with its own rites and style; its members indulge in a series of 'mascarades, cortèges et cérémonies',[16] 'ils taillent des vêtements pour leur corps en imitant, comme malgré eux, le vêtement et le masque de leurs prédécesseurs'.[17] Furthermore, they have their own language, a series of passwords which set a seal on their identity and ensure their insulation from the outside world. It is at this point, however, that the difference in generation between Benda (born in 1867) and his younger colleagues (Berl born in 1898, Nizan born in 1907) can be seen to be relevant to the shift in attitude towards the intellectuals which we have already noted. (Barrès we should remember was born in 1862.)

For Benda this new assertiveness of the bourgeois class[18] has resulted both in the dignifying of certain issues like patriotism and class distinction, which in his view should remain subsidiary to absolute, eternal values, and also in the seduction of the artist and intellectual from his responsibility to act as a guardian for such values, stand apart from and be a guide for the rest of mankind. Translated into the Platonic philosophy which underpins much of *La Trahison des clercs*, attention has been directed at the particular expense of the universal; the *clerc* has failed precisely because he has allowed the mundane, local and, above all, the political to dictate the criteria by which his actions are governed. But Benda's view rests on the assumption that the *clerc* is a creature apart, a mysteriously endowed higher being who has what amounts to a divine right of pronouncement. For Berl and Nizan he has no such status: he is for them the archetypal representative of the very elitist educational system of the Ecole Normale[19] which has been guilty of perpetuating the bourgeois caste, of encouraging it to believe in its own values and to refrain both from questioning such values and from acknowledging the political and social realities of the world outside. The title of Nizan's second essay is apt; the intellectuals are the watchdogs who not only repel intruders but actively prevent any inclinations to rebel. They and those in their charge 'n'éprouvent jamais le besoin de marcher parmi les hommes'.[20] Yet there is no small degree of irony, of course, in the fact that the style (the wide-ranging vocabulary and the involved syntax, for example), the rhetoric and use of learned allusion which both Berl and Nizan employ in order to express their indignation are those which they have been taught by the very system which they now decry. Indeed, this failure to escape entirely from their intellectual and cultural heritage constitutes a problem which has important repercussions for the kind of political literature which was developing at this time. For the moment, however, it is enough to note that it is the attitude of Berl and Nizan which is the dominant one during these years. Benda, for all that he ultimately aligned himself closely with the Communist Party, was at this time considered conservative and reactionary, out of touch with reality. The prevailing climate on both the Right and the Left was one of action, and it was in this climate that a literature developed which, to quote Nizan, should have a positive effect on its readers: '[qui] s'occuperait plutôt d'accroître leur conscience d'eux-mêmes que de leur procurer des plaisirs'.[21] While by 1935 Nizan was a fully committed and active member of the Communist Party, with the result that such words inevitably have a very special ring to them, taken out of context they none the less crystallize the aims of a whole range of writers, whatever their political sympathies. In view of such intellectual activity, it is in many ways surprising that there was no extensive examination of the whole idea of what Nizan called 'une littérature responsable' and of its attendant problems. Indeed, it is not until 1948 when Sartre published his influential essay *Qu'est-ce que la littérature?* that the subject is given anything like a thorough examination.

Despite the fact that in more recent years Sartre has considerably modified his views on the political effectiveness of literature, notably at the end of the first part of his autobiography, *Les Mots* (1964), and in a handful of articles and interviews,[22] no discussion of the subject can afford to ignore this earlier essay. Yet, however important it may be, it is in many ways a misleading work. Basically *Qu'est-ce que la littérature?* is theoretical discussion illustrated by a partial and selective analysis of French literary history. From the theoretical sections of the book a number of interesting and valid points emerge. For Sartre the act of writing is one of exposure (*dévoilement*),[23] though this, he argues, can only be achieved by the language of prose, in which words are indicative of a situation, they are 'signs': 'il ne s'agit pas d'abord de savoir s'ils plaisent ou déplaisent en eux-mêmes, mais s'ils indiquent correctement une certaine chose du monde ou une certaine notion' (p. 26). It will follow, he maintains, that if a writer can achieve this his reader will be made equally aware and in consequence be moved to act. Following Marx's views on the function of literature Sartre sees the duty of the writer to be to place himself on the side of the oppressed against the oppressor, yet, as he readily acknowledges, the writer is ironically—and here we may recall Nizan and Berl—a member of that very bourgeois class which he should be setting out to attack. The writer is, therefore, faced with a dilemma. He *should*—and Sartre here identifies himself with the writer—ally himself with members of the working class ('Nous avons en commun avec [eux] le devoir de contester et de construire' p. 303), yet works already produced by Communist writers show the dangers of such an allegiance only too clearly and Sartre characteristically rejects the idea that literature can be produced to order. All he can hope for consequently is that writers will continue to prompt an awareness in their readers, to assist the movement to destroy oppression in any form whatsoever, and above all to reflect what he calls 'la subjectivité d'une société en révolution permanente' (p. 195). Sartre's arguments and expositions are persuasive, yet in the final analysis what he is really concerned with is the perennial Sartrean question of freedom (here the writer's) and how to explore it through literature. It is also important of course to remember that *Qu'est-ce que la littérature?* was written at a time when Sartre was experiencing some of the most severe pressures of his love–hate relationship both with the French Communist Party and with the Communist dominated *Comité nationale des Ecrivains*, and that the kind of dilemma he is discussing is in many ways a very personal one. While that is unquestionably relevant to an understanding of the essay, it cannot disguise the fact that in it

Sartre is only very marginally concerned with the effect that political (for him left-wing) allegiance or even mere sympathy can have on the actual processes of writing. In his brief discussion of socialist realism he does, to be sure, show himself to be alert to the dangers of schematization, yet he fails in a wider context to consider such matters as character portrayal, narrative method, imagery, the problems of conveying positive values and so on.[24] Moreover, and this perhaps is where the real limitations of *Qu'est-ce que la littérature?* become noticeable, he begs a number of questions of a more general nature that are directly relevant to any discussion of political literature. Will all readers respond in the way he predicts? How can the impact and effect of a book be measured? Is there a general acceptance and understanding of key words? How effective can purely destructive description be? What role should be played by 'party' critics?[25] Is it not possible to have political literature that is right-wing in inspiration?[26] To what extent does political literature overlap with social literature? What do we make of those who claim that all literature is political or that the absence of political issues or views from a work itself implies a political position? What relationship is there, if any, between a writer's public statements about his political sympathies and the way in which he projects them into his imaginative work? When does political literature become propaganda? How appropriate are different forms and styles of writing like allegory, fable or satire? To be fair to Sartre, some of these questions would seem to be unanswerable at least with any degree of real accuracy. While it may be possible to assess a particular book's sales success and hence try, as Raymond Escarpit has done, to obtain some idea of its popularity, it is surely not possible to estimate the *extent* to which it causes its readers' political outlook to change. (Though there are cases of religious conversion having occurred in similar circumstances.) Perhaps, too, Sartre's refusal to consider the whole issue in any detail in recent years acknowledges the futility of the exercise as much as a lack of interest on his part. Yet there are areas where a closer examination can yield results. Barthes, for example, in his *Degré zéro de l'écriture* (1953) has indicated the kind of linguistic limitation—what he defines as a 'closed sphere of language'—which would seem to be one of the inevitable concomitants of works of socialist realism. It might be equally fruitful to extend his method to works of fascist or more moderate right-wing inspiration. And what of religious literature? Similarly, while many critics have acknowledged that in view of its intended revolutionary nature, left-wing literature can only *anticipate* a new society or political system, it would seem reasonable to suppose that right-wing literature with its tendency to refer to tradition and to the past should not have the same problems.

To examine and answer the wide variety of questions raised by the interaction of politics and literature would require far more space than is presently available. All the more reason, therefore, that an attempt should be made to indicate what particular aspects of the subject this essay sets out to explore, and to justify (or to defend) both the method employed and the texts selected for more detailed analysis. One immediate objection might be that to divide literature quite so neatly between Left and Right is a gross oversimplification of an issue that is clearly extremely complex; a second might be that the texts chosen are less representative than ones by Malraux, Camus, Sartre, Céline or Simone de Beauvoir, for example. Yet if I have not chosen, say, *La Condition humaine* (1933), *Les Chemins de la liberté* (1945–9), *La Peste* (1947) or *Les Justes* (1950), it is precisely because I see them as belonging essentially to that tradition which stems from Stendhal and as such fall outside the purview of this essay.[27] This is not to say, of course, that such works are not political; indeed, they may appear in conjunction with certain moments and developments in history to be acutely so—the rise of Communism in France in the early thirties or the Resistance, for example—but they are also more.

In his Nobel Prize speech in 1957 Camus remarked that for a revolutionary work to be successful it required '[la] grandeur artistique'.[28] In his short story 'Jonas ou l'artiste au travail' (*L'Exil et le Royaume*, 1957) he presented and illustrated the dilemma of the committed and even controlled artist, and it is here that the key to the problem as I have chosen to interpret it is to be found. The writers whose works are discussed in this essay have all at one time or another actually belonged to a specific party or political group, and have consciously and actively sought through their imaginative writing to promote a particular ideology; more significantly, in so doing they have frequently been prepared (and this is particularly true of those on the Left) to write in accordance with a set of 'official' directives. For Camus, Sartre and others, however, political sympathy and even on occasions party membership have never been allowed to influence or restrict them in their roles as creative artists. Thus, while Malraux's tacit approval for international Communism in *La Condition humaine* or *L'Espoir* (1937) may be readily apparent, ultimately it is subordinate to his exploration of human dignity and suffering. Sartre's analysis of the problems surrounding political choice in *Les Chemins de la liberté* is only one part of his exploration of the existentialist dilemma as he sees it, and even in a play like *Les Séquestrés d'Altona* (1959) his violent attack on capitalism must eventually be subordinate to the much more complex matter of man's responsibility towards and place in history. Yet it should not follow that the books discussed in the next chapters are *necessarily* inferior to these. It may of course be true that in some cases they have less chance of enduring since they are often dated works relating in a very specific way to certain events and issues,[29] and, what is more, have been written with a view to convince the reader of the validity of a particular political solution. They are works in which, as Irving Howe has aptly observed, attempts have been made to absorb the 'hard and perhaps insoluble pellets of modern ideology'[30] and as such they are interesting and worthy of our attention. In periods when political attitudes to art and literature have on occasions been extreme and uncompromising the results, it is true, may not always be entirely happy, the pellets remain undissolved and the works amount to little more than caricatures of what they aim to be or pieces of thinly disguised propaganda. This is particularly true of much left-wing literature which, as has already been mentioned, tends to become increasingly schematic, tendentious and doctrinaire. And while on the Right the problem is less immediately noticeable, largely due to the simple fact that in France at least no similar policy for the control or direction of art and writing was evolved or adopted, it none the less does exist.

One further prefatory remark is also needed. The majority of texts used as the principal illustrations in the following chapters will be found to be novels. While it is true that neither plays nor poetry fall entirely outside this debate, in France at least it is to the novel that those who concerned themselves with the debate constantly returned as the most appropriate form. Certainly, few would deny that much of the work of Péguy, for example, or of the Resistance poets would not be without relevance, but with few exceptions the issues with which such writing deals have an import which stretches beyond the context of an immediate reality, however poignantly this may be expressed. What follows is an introduction to and illustration of some of the ways in which a number of writers have attempted to come to terms with pressures and demands, which by their very nature immediately threaten to stifle creative inspiration.

Chapter One

The Appeal to Tradition and Authority

During the last twenty years or so in particular, right-wing movements have been a popular subject for students of French political and social history.[1] Certainly the topic is a fruitful one if only because of the virtual impossibility of establishing a set of definitions which could apply with some degree of relevance to a wide range of political attitudes varying from nineteenth-century conservatism through the often militant, though ultimately ineffective, nationalism and monarchism of the Action Française, to the so-called fascist groups of the late twenties and thirties, some of which, like Georges Valois' Le Faisceau or Marcel Bucard's Le Francisme, were largely inspired by the examples of Italian and German fascism abroad. This is not the place—nor indeed is there the space—even to chart the developments of such a wide variety of right-wing attitudes and movements. Suffice it to say that *politically*, at least, the Right is characterized above all by its fragmentation, by what Robert Soucy has called 'a great deal of variety, contradiction and sheer ideological confusion'.[2] No single group or party emerged which promised the same degree of unity and cohesion of the kind that the Communist Party provided for the Left, whatever its many setbacks and disputes both internally and with Moscow may have been. More significant, too, as far as the principal consideration of this essay is concerned, is the fact that there was no concerted attempt on the Right to establish any form of clearly defined literary or cultural programme of the kind which, as we shall see, developed on the Left particularly during the late twenties and early thirties, and again after the Second World War. There was no equivalent of the Kharkov conference, nor of the *Association des Ecrivains et Artistes révolutionnaires,* nor even in a more general way of the theory of socialist realism. The nearest approximation to such a programme came, as Stephen Wilson has shown,[3] in the extremely active attempts made by the Action Française to infiltrate its doctrine through its newspaper, journal and reviews. At the height of its popularity the daily *Action Française* had a circulation of about 90,000[4] (and a reading public of more); important and influential literary reviews like the *Revue critique des idées et des livres*, the *Revue du siècle* and the *Revue hebdomadaire* possessed editorial boards which often comprised a large number of Action Française members, even though they were not under their direct control: others like the *Revue de Paris* or the *Revue des deux mondes* readily made their pages available for articles by Action Française writers.

Saturation of this kind must have had its effect, as did the fact that the movement also enjoyed at various moments in its development the sympathy and in some cases even the membership of such disparate but highly influential figures as Georges Bernanos, Jacques Maritain and André Malraux. Yet influence, however strong, does not create a programme, and despite the fact that certain right-wing writers and intellectuals like Barrès, Drieu la Rochelle, Céline, Brasillach, Rebatet or Châteaubriant, for example, came increasingly to the fore, it was soon evident that no common policy was being formulated. Indeed, given this situation, it would appear that if not entirely meaningless the terms 'fascist' or even 'right-wing' literature are less helpful than their left-wing equivalents. (It is worth noting that those who were principally responsible for establishing a left-wing programme for literature and the arts in France belonged on the whole to a much narrower age band: inevitably, therefore, they at least appeared to be a much more unified group.)

This is not to say, however, that right-wing literature is free either of political elements or argument, or that its authors were apolitical creatures who spent their lives nostalgically recalling better times or creating situations quite without relevance for the modern world in which they lived. Some, notably Brasillach, did tend to remain apart; others were more active: for example, Barrès whose career was as much marked by his political activities as by his literary pursuits, and a generation later Drieu la Rochelle, who at one point became an active member of Jacques Doriot's *Parti populaire français*. There is much evidence to show that Drieu's awareness of the national and European situations was much more acute than that of most of his immediate contemporaries and he had no hesitation in stating his beliefs in the political and economic benefits to be gained from an openly fascist regime:

> le fascisme est une étape nécessaire à la destruction du capitalisme [. . .] le fascisme crée une civilisation de transition, dans laquelle

le capitalisme tel qu'il a existé dans sa période de grande prospérité est amené à une destruction rapide.[5]

Yet among right-wing writers and intellectuals generally such direct political involvement as his was relatively rare. More usually, those who shared his sympathies contented themselves with violent outbursts of dissatisfaction and criticism of the kind that Berl and Nizan also produced. Much of the blame for the present state of French society was placed on members of the older generation (that of Benda) who were seen to be physically[6] and spiritually sick, while those of the younger were in danger of becoming either mere pawns in a society increasingly dominated by the machine and impersonal capitalist exploitation, or the dupes of the Marxist creed of equality. Encouraged by the philosophies of Nietzsche and Sorel, right-wing intellectuals appealed instead for discipline and authority, for a society in which the individual could by his own efforts determine the shape of history. More immediately such attitudes also found encouragement in the example of Germany. Already in his early collection of poems *Interrogation*, Drieu had paid tribute to the virility and military efficiency of the German soldiers. In the late thirties, he, Brasillach and Châteaubriant all reported with enthusiasm—in Châteaubriant's case somewhat excessive[7]—on the Nuremberg rallies and on the spirit of corporate effort and comradeship (what Brasillach referred to as 'le sens du gang') that they believed to be essential for France were she to recover her morale and status. Yet, above all, it was the romantic, essentially youthful aspects of German national socialism which captured their imaginations, together with what Brasillach again in *Notre avant-guerre* described as '[une] religion nouvelle' and 'une poésie'. At once it can be seen that what they found in fascism was far less a positive political programme than a means of expressing what Jean Turlais once defined as 'une conception subjective du monde [. . .] surtout une esthétique'.[8]

It is not surprising, therefore, that their imaginative writing should concern itself in the main less with political issues as such than with a number of more general values in which they personally believed: a rejection of all that is rational, intellectual and materialistic, with instead a firm reliance on the instinctive and the natural, a call for the need for struggle whether in sport, war or sexual relationships, and an appeal to tradition, emotion and a christo–pagan sense of religion. As these themes and ideas emerge, so it becomes possible to draw the works in which they appear together and place them under a common head.

Quite clearly a grouping of this kind is not specifically political in inspiration, yet that is not to say that these works are entirely devoid of political argument or of demonstrations of the need for or validity of certain kinds of political activity. Indeed, as the later work of Drieu la Rochelle in particular shows, such aims are very much to the fore, firmly situating it like that of his contemporaries in the context of political literature as it developed in the inter-war years. Yet it also remains true that there is very little that is programmatic about this literature. While many of these writers publicly subscribed to or sympathized with various forms of right-wing political movements, their imaginative writing has a much more personal quality about it. Admiration for a collective activity is not allowed to shroud an account of what is essentially a private experience. And although a personal conviction may be presented to us as unchallengeably correct, these works have neither the sense of urgency about them nor, ostensibly at least, the same educative intention as many of the left-wing works produced during the same period.

1. Maurice Barrès: *Colette Baudoche* (1909)

As Frédéric Grover has attempted to demonstrate, Barrès' influence upon the interwar generation of writers was considerable.[9] Indeed, in his double role of politician and writer (his works total over a hundred volumes) Barrès has a claim to be considered the most influential figure of his kind to emerge in France during the last fifteen years or so of the nineteenth century and the first twenty of the present.

Barrès began his political career as a Boulangist deputy for Nancy in 1889. Soon, however, he formulated his policy of national socialism for which he became best known and which he outlined in *Scènes et doctrines du nationalisme* (1902). In spite of the later emotive overtones to be associated with such a programme, Barrès' nationalism was, as political commentators frequently remind us, conservative. ('Le nationalisme est un protectionisme.') He firmly believed in those guardians of national stability, the Church, the Army and the Judicial System. Over Dreyfus he was adamant. In spite of some grudging admission in later years that Dreyfus had perhaps been innocent and wrongly treated, he considered abstract Kantian values like Truth and Justice to be merely an escape, a way of avoiding the need to face up to all important national interests. Given such views, Barrès would seem to be a natural ally of Maurras and the Action Française yet, in spite of some shared opinions, Barrès really found the monarchist movement unacceptable. Unlike Maurras (whom he accused of lacking in sensitivity)[10] Barrès, like Péguy, believed both in the Revolution and in the idea that the true soul of the French nation lay with 'le peuple'. Already in *boulangisme* he had found what he retrospectively called in 1923 'de la fantaisie, de l'allégresse de jeunesse'.[11] Moreover, his belief in the irrational and the unconscious in man[12] received an important boost when he attended the lectures of Jules Soury at the *Ecoles des Hautes Etudes* in which the biologist outlined his theory of the way in which characteristics are transmitted from one generation to another subconsciously. For Barrès this was most convincingly exemplified by his own province of Lorraine. His childhood memories of German soldiers not only occupying his native region, but entering his house as well affected him deeply, and throughout his life he continued to believe that in the inhabitants of Lorraine would be found the true spirit of French nationalism: the progression from the local and provincial to the national was, for him at least, a logical one. It is, of course, arguable that there was very little evolution in Barrès' thinking, yet such criticism is hardly likely to have concerned him very much. Barrès was a self-acknowledged traditionalist, who belonged more to a line of nineteenth-century conservative thinkers like de Maistre and Taine than to any reactionary movement which developed out of the more aggressive nationalism of the Action Française. His favourite theory of the influence of 'la terre et les morts' remained constant throughout his life and, together with his belief in the instinctive and the subconscious, characterized much of his work and also looked forward—though it is dangerous to overstate the case—to some of the themes to emerge from the works of the more openly fascist writers in later years.

Barrès first made his mark as an imaginative writer with his *culte du moi* trilogy, *Sous l'œil des Barbares*, *Un Homme libre* and *Le Jardin de Bérénice* (1888–91). Within the space of these volumes Barrès moved from an unashamed defence of individual sensitivity to a statement, albeit in a somewhat romantic and sentimental form, of what was to be the basis of his nationalism. In the third volume Bérénice is made to incarnate the essential spirit of Provence. Contrasted with Martin the engineer ('cet esprit sec') she is shown to be wholly animal and instinctive in her responses; she has a feeling for her native region which no amount of rational thinking can destroy. In *Les Déracinés* (1897) the same thesis is elaborated on a larger scale. Seven young men from Lorraine are taken from the protective atmosphere of their local region and thrust into the totally foreign environment of Paris. Here they are subjected to the influence of a philosophy teacher Bouteiller (a fictionalized version of Barrès' own teacher at Nancy, Burdeau) who preaches the virtues of the universal values of Kant. As we might expect the results are, for some at least, disastrous with only Sturel, who is most akin to Barrès himself, fully realizing the dangers and being able to resist. In *Le Jardin de Bérénice* there is an air of unreality, Barrès' philosophy is carried by his descriptions of the Provençal landscape or of Bérénice herself, by key words like *inconscient* or *divin*; in *Les Déracinés* we have exposition and demonstration. In *Colette Baudoche* we find a mixture of the two and a good example of the way in which Barrès attempted to construct a novel in which the stylistic features are used to reinforce the traditionalism of its political message.

Colette Baudoche[13] is the account of a young girl's (and by implication of a whole people's) reaction to the German occupation of Alsace-Lorraine after the French defeat of 1870-1. Like Vercors' *Le Silence de la Mer* with which in terms of style it is worth comparing, *Colette Baudoche* is the story of passive resistance. It is a didactic, moralizing tale, ideologically naïve yet bearing clear indications of Barrès' concern for its style and form.

Basically *Colette Baudoche* depends on a system of contrasts and oppositions which serves in various ways to illustrate the political message of the book, though it should be noted that nowhere is there any suggestion of aggression or violence. The two sides are presented factually—even though Barrès does himself intervene on occasions to express approval or praise—with a 'correct' interpretation being implied by description. Thus in the opening pages, for example, and at the risk of caricature, we are shown the contrast between what remains of the original Lorraine architecture of Metz ('partout droiture et simplicité, netteté des frontons sculptés, aspect rectiligne de l'ensemble', pp. 12, 13) and the new German buildings ('d'énormes caravansérails et des villas bourgeoises, encombrés de sculptures économiques et tapageuses', p. 18). Not only is there this architectural debasement but in it is reflected the difference between the essential spiritual and moral qualities of the two peoples. The old Metz symbolizes the purity and simplicity of its founders ('Ce pays était épuré, décanté, je voudrais dire spiritualisé', p. 22); the new Metz, the banal materialism and pretentiousness of the invaders. Into this context comes Frédéric Asmus, a German schoolteacher who lodges with Colette and her grandmother (Barrès deliberately omitting a generation in order to substantiate his theory of heredity).[14] Again Barrès' descriptions of him ('un puissant garçon, mais informe', p. 26) are such that the moral implications are obvious: he is authoritarian in manner, self-centred, pedantic, intellectual and, initially at least, staunchly patriotic. And as we might expect while Asmus is stiff and formal, Colette is a fresh, natural creature: 'Elle était assise au bord de sa chaise, et, penché sur la table, tout son jeune corps souple dessinait une courbe. [. . .] elle semblait avoir une sorte d'oubli animal de soi-même' (p. 89). Yet we should not neglect Barrès' initial description of Asmus as *informe*. Gradually under the influence of Lorraine generally and of the Baudoche household in particular he begins unwittingly ('à son insu', p. 61) to change, to soften, a process reflected in Barrès' account of his reactions to the countryside of the Moselle valley: 'il se plaisait à la *douceur* de l'eau bruissante et des voix *traînantes* qui parlent français, il écoutait *glisser* le son des cloches catholiques sur les longues prairies, il voyait au loin les villages se *noyer* dans la *brume*, et *se laissait amollir* par ces *vagues* beautés' (p. 65. My italics). Elsewhere Barrès is less subtle, openly using his omniscience as narrator to inform us that Asmus is changing or deliberately contrasting his increasingly 'reasonable' manner with that of his colleagues in Metz or of the mixed marriage of the Krauss family in the neighbouring apartment. Asmus also defends the French language, refuses to subscribe to the official German view of Napoleon[15] and, perhaps most significantly of all, protects the old Frenchman against two young Germans in the presence of Colette and her grandmother. Yet, however much he may appear to be moving away from his own German traditions and culture and to be accepting and being accepted by those of Lorraine, complete assimilation is ultimately impossible. The test comes in the form of his proposal of marriage to Colette; significantly he still judges her by his own German standards: 'Son esprit est plus *ferme* que celui d'une jeune allemande et surtout plus *clair*. [. . .] Mariée avec un officier, elle le conduirait certainement au grade de général' (pp. 185–6. My italics). Asmus leaves Metz with his proposal unanswered; we know that on his return it will be refused. For Barrès, however, Colette's refusal is more than a personal matter; it becomes as well the symbolic rejection of an alien culture and a final reaffirmation of all those traditional Lorraine values which Barrès has applauded throughout the book. Asmus is given his answer after the traditional 'messe des morts' at which the people of Metz come together in a mystical union: 'Ils forment une communauté, liée par ses souvenirs et par ses plaintes, et chacun d'eux sent qu'il s'augmente de l'agrandissement de tous'. The spirit of the dead and of Lorraine combine to form the 'sentiment religieux' which in turn inspires in Colette a new sense of strength and makes her feel *instinctively* what her duty should be: 'Elle se sent chargée d'une grande dignité, soulevée vers quelque chose de plus vaste, de plus haut et de plus constant que sa modeste personne' (p. 254). Asmus, significantly redefined in the last pages as a Prussian, is allowed no appeal, nor indeed much sympathy.

For all that Barrès does inject some degree of human interest into his book, the outcome of the situation is never in doubt, the simple duality which we noted in the opening pages remaining ever present. Had Barrès left matters in this state *Colette Baudoche* could have been said to enjoy a curious fable-like quality: weighted descriptions of both Asmus and Colette, of the Lorraine countryside, the use of the central theme of the teacher being taught by his new environment would, for all that they are obvious techniques, have formed a unified if somewhat simplistic illustration for Barrès' political message. But Barrès allows his own partiality to express itself in other ways all too readily: the use of Colette's grandmother as a vehicle for undiluted statements of his own philosophy; his frequent intrusions into the narrative in order to direct our attention or shape our responses more forcefully; his omniscience which affords him the privilege of knowing more than his character and thereby the ability to interpret the latter's actions differently; his rhetorical appeals to the people of France to heed his message and act accordingly. But what emerges most noticeably from *Colette Baudoche* is Barrès' confident assumption that *his* attitude alone is the right one. There is no attempt to persuade by argument or by intellectual rationalization; Barrès' response is instinctive and intuitive, and he expects other peoples' to be the same. What is offered is a programme of stoic resistance[16] not just to an occupying force but by implication to the whole idea of change in any form. It is a conservative, and, in the way in which it constantly appeals to the past at the expense of the future, even regressive philosophy and one which in varying degree was to continue to be characteristic of much of the right-wing literature that would appear in the next twenty or thirty years.

2. Pierre Drieu la Rochelle: *La Comédie de Charleroi* (1934); *Gilles* (1939)

In spite of a number of attempts to reassess Drieu and his work and to present a more balanced picture of him than that created during the years immediately following his death, the label of fascist has been a difficult one to dislodge.[17] Politically essays like *Mesure de la France* (1922), *Le Jeune Européen* (1927), *Genève ou Moscou* (1928) and *Socialisme fasciste* (1934) provide more than enough evidence to encourage such a view. His concern for his country's low birth-rate and for the position of France in Europe, his intense opposition to capitalism, his hatred of the machine age and technology, were, as has already been noted, shared by many who allied themselves with one or other of the various right-wing groups which developed in the twenties and thirties. In particular his admiration for Germany, which was an extension of his belief that only by forming a federation of states could Europe withstand the inevitable power struggle that would develop between Russia and America,[18] caused him to be placed on the extreme edge of such groups. Yet before she was ready to participate in such a federation France had first to create the right climate internally. Politically he saw the answer to lie in a programme of national socialism which would both destroy the exploitation inherent in capitalism and preserve a sense of equality through subordination to the state. At the same time influenced by Nietzsche and by Sorel he also believed in the need for an elite, what he called 'une jeune aristocratie [. . .] fondée [. . .] sur le mérite',[19] from which in turn a leader—and not a dictator who is sought by a weak people only—would emerge to direct France to her new European destiny. Yet according to Drieu, France was by no means ready for such developments, a view he later considered to have been justified by defeat and Occupation. For him as for so many others France was crippled by mediocrity, compromise and decadence. Certainly he had his own theories as to how the situation might be overcome. He never tired of extolling the virtues of sport and of military training, for example,[20] yet these, like the sense of fraternity inspired among all Europeans by religious faith which he (like Bernanos and Maritain for example) maintained had been best exemplified in the thirteenth century, are ideals and not to be instantly realized in the modern world. Indeed, personal experience had taught him otherwise. Communism, the Action Française, Gustave Bergery's left-wing Front Commun and Jacques Doriot's Parti populaire français[21] had all at different times attracted him only to disappoint. So too had the Surrealists whom he ultimately accused of being 'les plus décadents des écrivains bourgeois'.[22] Always, it seemed, he found it impossible in the final analysis to reconcile personal values with those of a collective enterprise, however single-minded it appeared to be.

On his own admission Drieu saw the efficacy of his novels to lie principally in their exposure of the decadence of contemporary society; only Céline, he maintained, could claim a similar success:

> Je me suis trouvé comme tous les autres écrivains contemporains devant un fait écrasant: la décadence. Tous ont dû se défendre et réagir, chacun à sa manière, contre ce fait. Mais aucun comme moi—sauf Céline—n'en a eu la conscience claire. Les uns s'en sont tirés par l'évasion, le dépaysement, diverses formes de refus, de fuite ou d'exil: moi, presque seul, par l'observation systématique et par la satire.[23]

Certainly in early works like *L'homme couvert de femmes* (1925) or *Le Feu follet* (1931) his exposure was thorough if somewhat monotonous; in *Blèche* (1928) or *Une femme à sa fenêtre* (1930) he explored reactions to a political solution, Communism, though again with an emphasis on description rather than on any attempt to preach its positive values. In later years the exposure continues, the best example perhaps occurring in *Rêveuse bourgeoisie* (1937) which with its prominent theme of inherited weakness in the Le Plesnel family is reminiscent of Zola.

While he was totally opposed to the idea of didactic or moralizing literature (perhaps the example of Aragon was still too fresh in his mind), Drieu's view of literature as a means by which he could express positively those values he believed to be crucial for a revitalization of society emerge more clearly in the thirties. In 1934 he published *La Comédie de Charleroi*, a collection of interrelated short stories recalling his experiences of the First World War. Already in his two early collections of poems, *Interrogation* (written 1915–17, published 1917 and later defined by him as 'une effusion lyrique')[24] and *Fond de cantine* (written 1915–19, published 1920) we find him enthusing about the virility and excitement of combat, and speaking of war as an experience which will provide the opportunity of total self-expression: 'là-bas je vais chercher ma vie, la vie de ma pensée' ('Paroles au départ', *Interrogation*, p. 9). Later in the same poem he attempts to give military service a special quality by implicitly comparing it to the challenge of a religious vocation:

> Entre dans les ordres—infanterie, artillerie, génie, aviation.
> Prends cellule dans le poste d'écoute ou la sape—là
> tu es en présence de la mort, là menace l'abominable souffrance liminaire.

Ou élève-toi, si tu en es digne, dans l'avion
Au sommet du champ de bataille, à la clef de la voûte
sonore, au comble du son humain.

Such a concept of war also, and more significantly, transcends national differences. In 'Caserne haïe' he acknowledges the role played by the Germans as worthy opponents, a view which he re-emphasizes in what for the time is a remarkably unpatriotic poem, 'A vous, Allemands'. ('Hommes, par toute la terre réjouissons-nous de la / force des Allemands'.) As we might expect, given this idealized view of war as an epic and, in his opinion, noble struggle between men—close, of course, to Freud's theory that war liberated man's most primitive instincts— Drieu has only scorn for modern military devices:

Machines, esclaves brutaux, mauvais servi-
teurs sourdement hostiles, inhumains.
Ils trahissent l'homme. ('Atlantide', *Fond de cantine*)

In *La Comédie de Charleroi*[25] the same themes reappear and, largely due to a combination of the density of the short story and to the use of the first person narrative, are conveyed with the same degree of poetical intensity.

Ostensibly *La Comédie de Charleroi* is the account of the narrator's return to a scene of battle in the company of Mme Pragen, the mother of one of his fellow soldiers who was killed there. Certainly this provides some material for the kind of satire Drieu enjoyed. Mme Pragen is shown to be playing the part of the proud mother, seeking the merit which should by right belong to her son. Like so many of her social class she is pretending ('Sa vie avait été remplie de velléités et de faux-semblants', p. 13). But it soon becomes evident that the journey is a mere framework for a reflection on war and on a response to it. Here again, in view of Drieu's belief in the need for virile combat, much is predictable. The French army is shown to be inefficient and controlled by men wholly unsuited to be leaders (a regular theme of the earlier poems). More important still is the same denunciation of modern warfare: 'La guerre aujourd'hui, c'est d'être couché, vautré, aplati. [. . .] La guerre d'aujourd'hui, ce sont les postures de la honte' (p. 31). Surrounded on all sides by 'des inconnus médiocres' (p. 68) the narrator scorns the anonymity and dullness of the modern war which, as the title suggests, is like a play, a pretence. For one who had dreamed of heroics ('mes rêves d'enfance où j'étais un chef', p. 32) and of war

25

as a liberating process, reality is disillusioning. Yet *La Comédie de Charleroi* also describes a moment of total self-fulfilment. From the time when he is tempted by the thought of suicide the narrator suddenly becomes aware of his true potential; only God can judge him: 'Dieu allait reconnaître les siens; cette plaine c'était le champ du jugement. La guerre m'intéressait parce que j'allais me faire capitaine, colonel—bien mieux que cela, chef' (p. 69). In an eight-page (pp. 70–7) section Drieu's prose attains the kind of lyrical intensity that had marked *Interrogation*. Short paragraphs, sentences often reduced to no more than a single line, repetition of phrases and a careful use of images and individual words (especially of *je*) create a sense of drive and urgency which perfectly matches the ideas he intends to convey. Whereas modern war had earlier been described as dull and shameful in words denoting inaction, we now find a vocabulary of upward movement and growth (e.g., *lever, bouillonnement, élan, s'élancer*) coupled with a thinly disguised symbol of phallic erection and ejaculation:

> Je gesticulais, je craillais.
> Je trébuchais, je tombais.
> [. . .]
> Il y a eu un élan dans cette guerre, mais il a été tout de
> suite brisé. (p. 77)

As he describes it the whole experience is a primitive, elemental one, a rite that is later given its ultimate expression when the narrator is wounded: 'Mon sang coulait. Je me rappelle ma fierté. J'étais un homme, mon sang avait coulé' (p. 108). But it also remains an individual, private experience. Unlike Barrès, who projected his personal convictions through his descriptions or who openly and unashamedly preached the virtues of Colette's resistance, Drieu could only romanticize. Yet, as he became increasingly concerned with the idea of the political effectiveness of literature, the more he realized the danger of didacticism. It was one thing to expose the decadence of French society about him; it was entirely another to project a solution in any convincing manner. Despite the unquestionable sincerity of his views, the lyrical descriptions in *La Comédie de Charleroi* take us into a realm of private fantasy divorced from the political and social realities of life. In view of the restrospective nature of the story this might in a sense be allowable: in *Gilles*,[26] however, which is intended to have a much more direct relevance to the contemporary political situation, we find the same pattern recurring.

The very size of *Gilles* precludes an extensive analysis of all the many aspects of what is a remarkably thorough and informative panoramic survey of the interwar years. Throughout Drieu's attention rarely wanders from his principal target—decadence. The novel traces the fortunes of Gilles Gambier who, returning from the war, has a large number of sexual, political and even cultural adventures before finally settling for a career in the international fascist brigade in the Spanish Civil War. In spite of Drieu's claim in the 1942 Preface to *Gilles* that the novel should not be read as a veiled autobiography, there is clearly much in it that relates to his personal experience. Characters are projections of people he knew intimately—Galant (Aragon), Caël (Breton), Clérences (Bergery), Preuss (Berl), for example—even though the intention is to draw attention to types rather than to individuals. But most striking of all in his exposure of contemporary decadence is the manner in which Drieu through Gilles himself acknowledges his own complicity. He is, as Frédéric Grover observes, 'the decadent enveloped in the ambient decadence',[27] his body, half healthy, half scarred and withered[28] symbolically testifying to such involvement. As an orphan he is rootless and the novel traces what might have been an educative process, but one which in fact, rather like Frédéric Moreau's in Flaubert's *L'Education sentimentale*, proves to be wholly inadequate. What is more, Gilles' true mentor, Carentan ('Je suis ton père spirituel' p. 108), lives in the country in self-imposed exile. His existence is a primitive one and the elemental, natural world about him is masked by a permanent Darwinian struggle for existence (pp. 100–1). With his emphasis on the need for virility, purity and for an intimate (*barrésien*) contact with the land (p. 107 and p. 357), Carentan is clearly intended to voice Drieu's own beliefs, but he significantly remains apart. Drieu's problem in *Gilles* is to convert the ideal into the practical, to demonstrate how such beliefs can be given positive expression. In all of his projects and activities described in the first three sections of the novel, Gilles may be said to have betrayed Carentan and what he represents. None the less Gilles does gradually become aware that the only solution lies in fascism, and in the 'Epilogue' we find him masquerading under the name of Paul Walter (and thereby dissociating himself from his previous existence), participating in the Spanish Civil War. Here, as we might expect, he experiences the kind of primitive bond ('une espèce de sincérité animale' p. 463) in which Carentan believes; he also expresses a faith in a discipline based on a supra-national religion (again the influence of Barrès is evident) and secular harmony:

> Pour moi, je me suis retiré d'entre les nations. J'appartiens à un nouvel ordre militaire et religieux qui s'est fondé quelque part dans le monde et poursuit, envers et contre tout, la conciliation de l'Eglise et du fascisme et leur double triomphe sur l'Europe. (p. 492)

In the closing section of the novel Gilles is both theorist and man of action, a role which in terms of style Drieu acknowledges by making of him what Sartre would call both the 'il objet' and the 'il sujet' of the narrative.[29] And in so doing Drieu is able to a certain extent to move from the somewhat unreal presentation of ideas in the Carentan episodes to a more immediately acceptable one. Yet, in spite of the change of name and of the emphasis on the internationalism of Gilles' fascist group, there is no sense of collective relevance. As a political novel *Gilles*' principal strength lies—as indeed Drieu himself claimed —in its exposure of contemporary decadence in its various forms. But while the political solution which Gilles discovers emerges logically enough from the situation in which he finds himself and as it is presented to us, it does so only in an incidental way. Like *La Comédie de Charleroi*, albeit on a much grander and more ambitious scale, *Gilles* is in the final analysis the case-book of an individual and of a series of his personal experiences.

3. Robert Brasillach: *Les Sept Couleurs* (1939)

In spite of a number of eloquent appeals made on his behalf—notably one by François Mauriac—Brasillach was executed on 6 February 1945, having been arrested five months earlier and accused of collaboration with the Nazis. Today the political stain remains. For the majority of people the name of Brasillach evokes the man who unashamedly admired fascism as it manifested itself in both Italy and Germany, and who openly voiced his opinions in papers and journals like *L'Emancipation nationale* and above all in *Je suis partout*.[30] Yet, while in the main he shared the view that only in fascism could a solution be found to the problem of the spiritual and physical decadence from which France was suffering, Brasillach was not a man of action who enjoyed or even sought a political role; nor did he indulge to anything like the same extent in the kind of political essay-writing which so occupied Drieu la Rochelle, for example. He was a much more private person (photographs of him suggest real shyness) whose formative influences were literature (especially the Classics), the theatre and the cinema, and who, as William Tucker has observed,[31] was more at home in small, self-contained groups of intellectuals or journalists, for example, than in larger movements. Indeed when Brasillach first made his mark as a public figure, it was as a literary critic with his articles for the *Action Française* in 1930–1, and with his study of Virgil, *Présence de Virgile* (1932) and as a novelist with *Le Voleur d'étincelles* (1932) and *L'Enfant de la nuit* (1934). His early fictional writing and indeed some of the poems in the posthumously published collection *Poèmes de Fresnes* are characterized by a lyricism and by an emphasis, reminiscent of the early Gide, on the importance of sense impressions before intellectual satisfaction. Childhood, always a key theme of his work, is portrayed as an idyllic, dream-like period of one's life followed by the vital years of adolescence. Indeed the age of thirty marks the threshold of the inevitable general physiological and mental deterioration to which all must eventually come! In spite of his admiration for classical order, however, his works tend to be loosely structured with particular themes and ideas—that of perfect love being realized once in a lifetime only, for example—and recurring figures, barely compensating for a lack of creative stamina. But in October 1937 Brasillach attended the Nuremberg rallies: the experience was a vital one. Here for the first time he personally discovered a means of expression on a large scale of those ideals which he valued so highly and which already permeated his work albeit in a non-political manner. Fascism became for him what, viewed from afar, it had always promised to be, a religion in which he could immerse himself completely, an extension in real terms of those fantasy escapist worlds which he so admired of some of Giraudoux's plays or Alain-Fournier's *Le Grand Meaulnes*. While, unlike Drieu, Brasillach appears not to have been concerned with the political effectiveness of literature, this new experience led him directly to write *Les Sept Couleurs*. In it through both form and style he attempts to provide the most effective means of expression for what was now both a personal philosophy and a political creed.

The basic theme of *Les Sept Couleurs*[32] is simple in the extreme—the movement towards fascism of three characters: Patrice who on numerous occasions closely resembles Brasillach himself, François who abandons Communism, and Catherine who moves from Patrice and his world of youthful fantasy to François with his security and reliability. The events in the book cover approximately a dozen years, by the end of which all three characters have passed the magical age of thirty; as

Catherine remarks in the closing pages: 'Ainsi se ferme le cercle de l'adolescence' (p. 253). Despite its linear movement, therefore, the book does have a self-contained quality with a single point of focus to which everything is directed.

As its title suggests, *Les Sept Couleurs* is divided into seven sections, each one written in a distinctive and appropriate (if not always successful) manner. In Part I, a third person narrative describing the lives of Patrice and Catherine as students in Paris, it is possible to see the early Brasillach. The usual themes are easily discernible: youth (Patrice and Catherine are 'deux instants de la jeunesse incarnée' (p. 47)), isolation (the boat excursion on the lake in the Bois de Boulogne or the day spent in St-Germain), a sense of permanence (the two small children symbolically named Patrice and Catherine) and a *barrésien* concern for historical influences (the cemetery of St-Germain). There is also a dated atmosphere which pervades this first section (the people in Patrice's *pension* constantly recall their past while he expresses a taste for pre-war literature) and a lyrical sentimentality developed through long sentences and resonant and often nearly synonymous phrases reminiscent of Brasillach's earlier writing. In Part II, a series of letters between Patrice and Catherine after the former has left for Italy, much of the same lyrical enthusiasm is retained, Patrice finding in Italian fascism the first large-scale expression of those qualities he values so highly (p. 65). Physical separation from Catherine, however, now becomes spiritual as well, the tone of their letters nicely catching the sense of growing alienation. While therefore Patrice remains essentially the same, his ties with the past are broken and he is ready to move forward to the full experience of national socialism. Consequently, in Parts III and IV Brasillach is able to allow his protagonist full personal expression, first in the form of a diary in which he records his impressions of Germany, and subsequently in a collection of philosophical and political reflections. In his diary Patrice's record is a mixture of the journalist's impressions (e.g., pp. 109–10) and enthusiastic admiration which reaches its climax in the account of the Nazi congress (pp. 110–28) where the language becomes increasingly lyrical and intense as it is required to convey the sense of magic and religion ('la semaine sainte du Reichsparteitag' p. 111; 'cette religion nouvelle' p. 121) which Patrice experiences.[33] Sense impressions, particularly those of sight and hearing, are frequent; so too are references to Patrice's feelings of youthful comradeship. From this it is an easy stage to the barely disguised reflections by Brasillach himself in Part IV which culminate in his apotheosis of the new European man, the ' "uomo fascista" [. . .] qui peut réclamer [. . .] la désignation universelle de l'entomologie' (p. 156). Patrice himself has now reached this stage and his name, containing as it does the notion of *patrie* (unlike the narrowly national François) assumes its full significance. Like Drieu who exalts the noble struggle of the natural world, Brasillach finds an elemental bond between men which transcends national limits and which they now recognize:

> Ils aiment souvent à vivre ensemble, dans ces immenses réunions d'hommes où les mouvements rhythmés des armées et des foules semblent les pulsations d'un vaste cœur. [. . .] ils appellent la justice qui règne par la force. Et ils savent que de cette force pourra naître la joie. (p. 157)

Essentially this is the climax of the book and, having brought Patrice who was always predisposed to such ideas to this position, Brasillach turns in the final sections to show the effect fascism has on the more cautious Catherine and François, even though we have learned by now that the latter has abandoned Communism for some form of primitive fascism. The result, particularly in Part v where the dialogue does occasionally have a Claudelian ring to it,[34] is artificial. Only Catherine's refusal to leave with Patrice (even though it reflects Brasillach's basic view that fascism was for men)[35] is momentarily unexpected. Elsewhere the debate is a simple one: security and reliability symbolized by François' set-square (we may recall that Martin in *Le Jardin de Bérénice* was an engineer) and seen by Patrice to be totally worthless (p. 184), against his own newly realized values. For Catherine the first is reality, the second no matter how attractive, fantasy. Even so, when he believes that she has left with Patrice it is enough to convince François that his earlier values were wrong and that there is still some hope. He leaves for Spain to join the fascist forces and in Part vi, through a variety of documents, we are provided with what, ostensibly, is an objective account of his progress in the Civil War. Once again Brasillach resorts to the religious vocabulary and imagery that had characterized his descriptions of the Nazi rallies in Part iii. The War is considered (as it was by so many who were opposed to Communism) as a crusade, and François' part in it as an initiation: the words in the doctor's report after he has been wounded and hospitalized are surely significant: 'Son état n'est pas désespéré et nous formerons sa guérison' (p. 234).[36] François has successfully completed his journey. Finally in Part vii, which is in the form of an interior monologue, Catherine leaves Paris to join François. Her journey, too, is now drawing to a close as she comes finally to accept a mature though inevitably dull version of what Patrice had originally represented, and in the final lines of the book the dominant images of sexual submission (pp. 243–5) and travelling give way to the less striking one of the breaking dawn.

Despite Brasillach's use of a much wider variety of narrative technique, when compared to *Gilles, Les Sept Couleurs* at once strikes us as being a much more tightly constructed book. Certainly Brasillach's canvas is much smaller, incidents and characters are fewer, but there is a level of language and a use of image and motif which maintain the kind of lyrical intensity that is characteristic of his earlier work even though it has here been given a specific ideological gloss. Thus, for example, an image like that of 'light' (*lumière, clarté*) subsumes the notions of spirituality, joy, friendship and so on which constantly recur in the descriptions of the fascist meetings and rallies where they are seen to find their most complete expression. By contrast, France and the whole theme of bourgeois concern for security are frequently referred to as 'dark' (e.g., Catherine: 'Je déteste la clarté' p. 175).

In his *Lettre à un soldat de la classe 60*, written while he was awaiting trial, Brasillach, attempting to justify his collaborationist attitude, recalls how he had been attracted by pre-war Germany: 'J'ai été d'abord un simple curieux de l'Allemagne d'avant-guerre, de sa renaissance, de ses mythes, de la poésie national-socialiste avec ses fêtes géantes et son romantisme wagnérien'.[37] As we have seen *Les Sept Couleurs* perfectly catches this atmosphere and Brasillach's response to it. Like so many other fascist works it also carries in it the suggestion that fascism alone can offer a political solution to the problems faced by Europe as a whole and by France in particular. Once more, however, the enshrining of the ideological elements of the book in a much more general and lyrical account of private beliefs and obsessions forces us to admit that any political effectiveness it may have had is inevitably reduced.

Chapter Two
The Progressive Way

To turn from right-wing and especially from such so-called fascist literature in France to its political counterpart on the Left is to move into an entirely different sphere in the whole question of political literature. The former is characterized as we have seen by highly personalized responses to political developments, by a number of general and for the most part non-political themes, and by an absence of any form of imposed programme or attempted schematization. Certainly it is arguable that many of the works which have been referred to regularly by critics as 'left-wing' are only so in a very general way on account of their portrayal of liberal, humanitarian ideals and concern for the individual. But the kind of literature with which we are concerned here and to which Sartre alludes in *Qu'est-ce que la littérature?* is that which developed under the direct control of a politically inspired programme and became known as populist, proletarian and socialist realist literature.

That this rigid control of art and writing should have evolved to the extent it did was due directly to the political growth and success of the French Communist Party (*PCF*).[1] It should not be assumed, however, that writers and intellectuals whether members or fellow travellers always accepted without question or criticism Moscow's directives concerning the role of literature and art in society. Certainly there were some occasions when slavish acceptance was more pronounced than others. Some writers—Henri Barbusse, Louis Aragon or André Stil, for example—allowed themselves to be won over almost entirely: others like Paul Nizan or Roger Vailland, for all their official membership of the Party, retained a much higher degree of independence both in their political attitudes and in their writing. Again, others, fellow travellers like André Gide or André Malraux for all their support and enthusiasm for communism as an ideology, were ultimately too individual in their responses ever to submit entirely or for long to any imposed discipline.

During the early twenties after the foundation of the *PCF* in 1920, left-wing literature tended still to echo the pacifism and socialist humanitarian principles that had been characteristic of works like Rolland's essay *Au-dessus de la mêlée* or Barbusse's novel *Le Feu* (a passionate outcry against the aggressive nationalism which he held to have been responsible for the war). Yet as the Communist Party soon made clear, however praiseworthy such works may have been, they failed to convey a sufficiently clear Marxist doctrine. At the second International Congress of the party held in the summer of 1920 representatives from European countries were encouraged to see art and literature as potential propaganda weapons. Unfortunately Raymond Lefebvre, the French representative, was drowned on his way back to France, though whether or not the Congress's advice would have had much immediate effect is unlikely. Certainly by the mid- and even late twenties there was nothing like the large scale organization of proletarian writers (literary study circles, collective writing experiments, for example) that there was in Russia. Nor indeed was there any systematic attempt to develop a popular theatre as there was in Germany. Yet through Barbusse (who officially joined the Party in 1923) and his *Clarté* group with its 'volonté d'arracher le communisme au ronron de l'humanisme et du pacifisme internationaliste,'[2] some progress was made. There were attempts to create a genuine proletarian literature in which the class struggle would emerge powerfully and unequivocally, yet much of what was written was no more than descriptive. Indeed the populists, as writers like André Thérive and Léon Lemonnier were known, were quite clear about their intentions: 'Nous prenons le peuple tel qu'il est, nous le peignons tel qu'il vit, nous l'aimons en lui-même et pour lui-même.'[3] Not surprisingly such mildness was unacceptable to the hard-line Marxists and at a conference held at Kharkov in 1930 it was condemned. In France Henry Poulaille, for whom writers supporting Lemonnier's populist school were dilettantes, attempted to formulate a more aggressive policy: literature, he argued, should make a positive contribution to revolutionary action: 'Elle est l'expression d'une classe et dit les aspirations, les volontés de cette classe souvent, car la plupart de ses manifestations sont des œuvres de combat.'[4]

But the impact of Kharkov was short-lived. In the spring of 1932 the Russian Association of Proletarian writers (*RAPP*) was disbanded and the strict doctrinaire line which it had attempted to impose was replaced by a much more flexible policy of what in France became known as *rassemblement* and was articulated by the *Association des Ecrivains et Artistes révolutionnaires* (*AEAR*) founded in December of the same year, and whose official publication was the review *Commune*. And while Poulaille and his colleagues were ever ready with their accusations that the *AEAR* was little more than a bourgeois stronghold, it is barely an exaggeration to say that since 1920 no work of the kind they had in mind inspired by Marxism in however mild a form and of real literary merit had been produced in France. As Bernard has pointed out, political action and literary activity during the twenties were for the most part separate issues; moreover the political figures within the *PCF*, unlike their counterparts in Russia, were little concerned with literary and artistic developments. During the years up to and including the Front Populaire in 1936, however, the climate was to change radically. The *PCF* realized what it could gain in prestige (and strength) by encouraging its fellow travellers: indeed within four years from the end of 1932 membership of the party increased tenfold to approximately 300,000.[5]

While no single outstanding Marxist inspired work may have appeared before 1932, a significant episode for the whole issue of the relationship between literature and left-wing politics had occurred in the growing association between the Communists and the Surrealists.[6] In the early twenties (André Breton's first *Manifeste du surréalisme* appeared in 1924) the aim of the Surrealists was revolution in all aspects of life, a complete freeing of man from the stifling conditions imposed by civilization and society: 'La réalité immédiate de la révolution surréaliste n'est pas tellement de changer quoique ce soit à l'ordre physique et apparent des choses que de créer un mouvement dans les esprits.'[7] Art should be an expression of such release. While the Surrealists in no way set out to establish a political system of their own making, they did gradually come to realize that political revolution could provide the right context within which such ambitions might flourish, and early scorn for the Communist Party (voiced for example by Aragon in *Clarté* in December 1924),[8] began to change to anticipated collaboration. In 1925 the war in Morocco between the Riffs and the French forces under Pétain brought the *Clarté* group, the Surrealists and a band of intellectuals (including Politzer, Morhange, Friedmann and Guterman) known as the 'philosophie' group together. This union, which hoped to replace *Clarté* by *La Guerre civile*, based as its name suggests on a much more determinedly revolutionary spirit than that behind Barbusse's journal, failed, however—a fact recorded several years later by Nizan in *La Conspiration* (1938). Moreover Breton was already showing himself to be uneasy about such collaboration which he saw as a threat to the artistic integrity of his movement. Even so in

35

1927 he, together with Aragon, Eluard, Peret and Unik, applied for membership of the Communist Party. Not surprisingly in this immediate pre-Kharkov era they were viewed with some suspicion even though in the *Second manifeste du surréalisme* (1930) Breton re-emphasized their good intentions. Aragon and Sadoul attended the conference as spokesmen. Although on his return he claimed to have spoken strongly in favour of Surrealism, Aragon had, so it transpired in 1932, actually betrayed or at best denied it. Here in miniature was the moment of choice which they were all sooner or later to have to take. Aragon became the centre of a controversy. Based on the experience of his trip to Russia he wrote a number of poems of which one, *Le Front Rouge*, was violently critical of established French (Western) society with its sacred idols and its complacent attitude towards both material possession and political security. Faced with prosecution Aragon found himself supported by the Surrealists (and by Breton in particular) on the grounds that the artist should be free to write how he chose. But the distinction between 'how' and 'why' or 'for whom' is blurred. Much of *Le Front Rouge* is blatant, uncompromising propaganda[9] albeit expressed in verse which moves at times effectively from flowing lines to brutal interjection with a motif based on the initials *URSS* emerging towards the end like a cry of triumph:

> Ce qui grandit comme un cri dans les montagnes
> Quand l'aigle frappé relâche soudainement ses serres
> SSSR SSSR SSSR
> C'est le chant de l'homme et son rire
> C'est le train de l'étoile rouge
> qui brûle les gares les signaux les airs
> SSSR octobre octobre c'est l'express
> octobre à travers l'univers SS
> SR SSSR SSSR
> SSSR SSSR

Aragon was forced to choose his allegiance: he opted for the Communist Party. For a while, until the summer of 1933, Breton, Eluard, Crevel and Alquié remained members of the Party as well. Then, faced with Alquié's review of a Russian film *The Way of Life* in which he wrote of 'le vent de crétinisation systématique qui souffle de l'*URSS*',[10] the Party excommunicated them. Yet put in perspective this was a minor issue. Essentially the difference between the Communists and the Surrealists was one that had always threatened to make itself felt:

on the one hand the acceptance not just of a political ideology but of Party discipline, and on the other the need to preserve artistic integrity and freedom. Stubbornness could be mutual. Furthermore with the development of the policy of *rassemblement*, albeit in face of threats of both Fascism and war, the Surrealists also accused the Communist Party of diluting its basic ideological tenets. Certainly they continued in a relatively minor, disruptive way to be active, but the idea of a collaboration which might have led to politically oriented Surrealist writing was short lived. For this kind of fruitful interaction to take place on a large scale required the continuation of the proletarian literature of the late twenties by the method which rapidly became known as socialist realism, a 'truthful, historically concrete representation of reality in its revolutionary development'.[11]

While in Russia, after the dissolution in April 1932 of the association of proletarian writers, a new emphasis—for which Gorki and Bukharin were early spokesmen—was given to the idea of socialist realism, in France it had much less immediate influence. While Malraux, Bloch (neither of whom was a Party member), Nizan and Aragon did attend the first congress of Soviet writers in Moscow in August 1932, it was not to be until after the Second World War that the full effects of socialist realism were to be felt. During the mid- and late thirties in France the most immediately noticeable effect that the atmosphere of *détente* had was to bring a wide-ranging body of writers and intellectuals together under a banner of general sympathy for the Left. Hence we find people as disparate in their political outlook as Mauriac, Gide, Géhenno and Malraux, for example, aligning themselves with regular members of the Party. Yet it was not to last. Some like Gide became disillusioned and from being for many Communists a prestige figure he quickly became one of scorn. But the real blow for the majority was delivered in 1939 with the signing on 23 August of the Nazi–Soviet pact. Some like Nizan resigned; others like Aragon wrote countless pages of attempted justification. For many writers and intellectuals this was the first significant test of political allegiance; one of the consequences was the development of a left-wing literature which became increasingly overtly ideological, partisan and tendentious in tone and which was to reach its peak in the post-liberation years of the Cold War.

1. Henri Barbusse: *Le Feu* (1916)

Few works capture the tone of late nineteenth- and early twentieth-century socialist humanitarianism quite so successfully as Barbusse's novel of the First World War which, written when he was forty-three, emerged upon the literary scene with a force which made him something of an overnight success. Barbusse's early literary exploits had been relatively slight, limited in the main to a collection of symbolist inspired poems *Les Pleureuses*, (1885), and two novels *Les Suppliants* (1903) and *L'Enfer* (1908) the second of which contested unsuccessfully for the Prix Goncourt. Yet his early pacifist tendencies and above all his concern for his fellow men, which led him ultimately to join the Communist Party in 1923, were already noticeable and had occasioned his collaboration with both *La Revue de la Paix* and *La Paix par le Droit*. In spite of the fact that he had for some while suffered from tuberculosis, Barbusse volunteered for active service and had twenty-two months at the front as a stretcher bearer. While he may not have shared the view that the war offered an opportunity for glorious and heroic exploits he did come to see it as a necessary evil and believed like so many that it would be short-lived.

Le Feu originated in the diary accounts Barbusse kept of his experiences and sent home to his wife.[12] Between August and November 1916 it was serialized in *L'Œuvre*, the only major cut made by the censor being that of Chapter XII, 'Le Portique', in which a French soldier is taken behind the lines by German soldiers and sees his wife openly flirting with German officers. In December of the same year it appeared in book form[13] with this Chapter included; Barbusse also added the opening Chapter 'La Vision' and a number of politically loaded statements to the final one. The only alterations made without his approval were a number of petty cuts and an attempt (which Barbusse found intensely annoying) to make the soldiers' language less crude.

Essentially *Le Feu* is an anti-war novel and in writing it Barbusse is faced with the problem not simply of destroying the prevalent contemporary notion of war as a romantic and colourful episode, but of presenting an experience with which the large majority of the public have no direct contact and of rendering his soldier characters credible: 'Je me débats dans la difficulté de mettre debout la mentalité du soldat, du simple soldat actuel et de peindre son existence par des tableaux et des conversations . . .'.[14] Subtitled the 'Journal d'un Escouade' it is not surprising to find that much of *Le Feu* reads like an impressionistic account of war based on direct experience. Indeed Barbusse rarely lets up. We are bombarded with horrific details in the same way as the soldiers are by enemy bullets. His sentences often have the staccato tempo of machine gun fire.[15] Occasionally an incident will strike home more than others—Caron's boots which, when he pulled them off a dead German, came away filled with the rotting flesh of the man's legs (p. 14); Godefroy who when hit by a piece of shell 's'est vidé de sang sur place, en un instant comme un baquet qu'on renverse' (p. 45); Poterloo who is blown up by a mine: 'j'ai vu son corps monter, debout, noir, les deux bras étendus de toute leur envergure, et une flamme à la place de la tête' (p. 167). And perhaps most horrific of all, the slow-motion gestures of the soldiers at the end as they struggle to escape from the sea of mud. Ultimately of course, soldiers (Barbusse included) became anaesthetized to such occurrences, a fact conveyed by Barbusse's flat, unemotional descriptions of them. Yet in view of his intended aim, he has as an author somehow to induce in us a sense of horror and outrage, and, if possible, bring us to the point whereby we will then naturally accept the basically socialist and humanitarian message he wishes also to convey.

In addition to the welter of horror, Barbusse's method in *Le Feu* can be observed working in and at various ways and levels. Most obvious of all perhaps is the contrast—common to almost all anti-war novels—between the action, the front-line and the officialdom and bureaucracy of the government administrators, the public whose picture of war has been created for them by misleading press accounts and those who for one reason or another have managed to escape conscription. But the novel owes its real power to a number of themes and motifs which are constantly emerging. Through his emphasis on the elements (not only the fire of the title but land and water as well) Barbusse endows his book with an almost epic quality. Rain, mentioned literally hundreds of times and matched by a constant repetition of adjectives like *gris, noir* and *froid*, accompanies the soldiers' every move. Only occasionally, as when they go to Paris (Chapter XXII) on leave, or in the final paragraphs does it give way to brighter weather and then with a clear and irritating symbolic significance. Men are absorbed in a system of such vastness that they struggle wildly to preserve their identity as thinking beings ('Nous ne sommes pas des soldats, nous, nous sommes des hommes' p. 45) yet ultimately their efforts are of little use. Throughout the novel—and in spite of what Barbusse may be urging us to understand—they are shown to be basic, primitive creatures, reacting like animals

39

during the journalists' visit for example (p. 35), charging like demented beings in the attack in Chapter XX or frequently alluded to as actors (clowns and puppets) in a theatre of war. (Note for example the use Barbusse makes throughout of the contrast between light and dark, or the careful description of the total desolation of a war-scape on the opening page of Chapter II.) Within such a situation of enforced anonymity the mundane and the trivial often assume an importance normally quite foreign to them. A dog (Chapter XI), an egg (Chapter XV) and matches (Chapter XVIII) provoke reactions both physical and emotional which are quite out of proportion to their normal worth. But this is an abnormal world through which men move towards the promise of better things and it is here, of course, that Barbusse's problems begin.

Basically Barbusse attempts with varying degrees of success to convey his message in three ways: the first by the self-evident use of the opening chapter ('La Vision'), in which from the setting of a sanatorium a group of convalescing soldiers reflect in pompous terms on the War, and of the discussion of equality and of the symbolism of the breaking dawn at the close of the book; the second by the inclusion of a number of episodes meant to illustrate values which war cannot destroy; the third by various stylistic devices through which he aims to infiltrate his personal views in the guise of those of a common soldier or at least without their becoming too obvious. Of these three the first is clearly the least successful, yet presumably Barbusse must have felt that in spite of the relentless indictment of war and its horror which he had provided, the humanitarian and pacifist values in which he so passionately believed had to be still more heavily underlined. It is perhaps arguable that the tone of the closing lines is not all that far removed from a sentimentality that threatens to break through on earlier occasions: 'Entre deux masses de nuées ténébreuses, un éclair tranquille en sort et cette ligne de lumière, si resserrée, si endeuillée, si pauvre, qu'elle a l'air pensante, apporte tout de même la preuve que le soleil existe' (p. 349). But it is the way in which the exhausted soldiers, French and German alike, are subjected to the narrator's homily on 'égalité [. . .] la grande formule des hommes' (p. 341) that is so unacceptable. Elsewhere in the novel individual incidents like the one when two soldiers exchange identity cards so that the one who is not mortally wounded can forget his criminal past or the execution of a soldier more on account of his prewar civilian record than of his attempted desertion are left successfully without the intrusion of obvious authorial comment. Yet such examples as these are too rare. More typical are the airman's account of the religious services, the absurd description of the horses which regard another camouflaged war horse with suspicion, and above all the depiction of the usually taciturn Bertrand who, the attack over, calls on Liebknecht (the Reichstag deputy who had refused to vote war credits) and delivers a short but highly rhetorical statement of his belief in the future. In this last instance in particular not only does the change in the register of the language jar, it is also, in terms of the novel's reality, quite out of place.

It is clear from Chapter XIII, 'Les Gros Mots', that Barbusse was aware of at least one kind of linguistic problem that faced him. The group of men depicted by him are all from the working class: 'Pas de profession libérale parmi ceux qui m'entourent' (p. 17);[16] moreover they are from a wide variety of regions and hence are collectively intended to represent the French nation as a whole. Only Barbusse himself is different. His problem then is to convey a working class language of the trenches that is authentic and acceptable both to the censor and to general reader. In spite of various dilutions and alterations Barbusse is at this level generally successful, but it is when he attempts to use this more general context to bear his message that certain weaknesses begin to appear. His methods for conveying his message are various—from the unashamed interventions at the close to the discussion of German officers which takes place quite naturally between the group of common soldiers (p. 32). He attempts early in the book to identify himself with his fellow soldiers: '*Je* vois des ombres émerger [. . .] C'est *nous*' (p. 6, my italics); he frequently uses the pronoun *on* in order to create the illusion of objective observation; we discover passages of apparently impersonal though loaded reflection in the middle of conversations or descriptions:

—Allons, dépêchez-vous! Allons, allons qu'est-ce que vous foutez! Voulez-vous vous dépêcher, oui ou non?

Un détachement de soldats portant comme insigne des haches croisées sur la manche, se frayent passage et, rapidement, creusent des trous dans la paroi de la tranchée. On les regarde de côté en achevant de s'équiper.

—Qu'est-ce qu'ils font, ceux-là?

—C'est pour monter.

On est prêt. Les hommes se rangent, toujours en silence, avec leur couverture en sautoir, la jugulaire du casque au menton, appuyés sur leurs fusils. Je regarde leurs faces crispées, pâlies, profondes.

> Ce ne sont pas des soldats: ce sont des hommes. Ce ne sont pas des aventuriers, des guerriers, faits pour la boucherie humaine—bouchers ou bétail. Ce sont des laboureurs et des ouvriers qu'on reconnaît dans leurs uniformes. Ce sont des civils déracinés. Ils sont prêts. (p. 243)

And most subtle of all is the shift of pronoun in the space of a single paragraph in order to involve the reader's emotion. Thus, for example, during the attack we read:

> A un coup, *je* lâche mon fusil, tellement le souffle d'une explosion *m*'a brûlé les mains. *Je* le ramasse en chancelant [. . .] Les stridences des éclats qui passent *vous* font mal aux oreilles [. . .] et *on* ne peut retenir un cri lorsqu'*on* les subit. [. . .] Les souffles de la mort *nous* poussent, *nous* soulèvent, *nous* balancent. (pp. 246–7. My italics).

Of these various techniques the last is by far the most successful, since, once he has engaged his reader's sympathy for the soldiers' plight, Barbusse has a ready audience for comments of a more philosophical or political nature. Yet although except in the very last Chapter *Le Feu* rarely suffers from the kind of tendentious statements that were to mar much subsequent Communist-inspired writing, it does illustrate the potential dangers. By the time Barbusse came to publish his next novel, *Clarté*, in 1919 he was in all but name a member of the Communist Party. It is not surprising therefore that this book, which describes a lower middle-class worker's gradual realization of the essential unity of the working class and the justness of its demands, should have its narrative qualities almost completely hidden by the moralizing and often sententious tone of Barbusse's frequent interventions. By these standards there is no doubt that *Le Feu* is a much more successful book; indeed it is a good example of what in 1925 Barbusse, acting as spokesman for Moscow, claimed should be the aim of all writers—'faire entrer le collectif dans l'art'.[17] There can be little doubt that the combination of time, subject and treatment was a guarantee of *Le Feu*'s success. Barbusse's subsequent attempts to arouse enthusiasm for revolutionary socialism, however, pushed him more and more towards the kind of polemical writing that was being demanded of left-wing writers in France by Moscow and towards undisguised sentimentality. (This was also exacerbated by a growing obsession in his later years with religion.) Ultimately Barbusse's techniques as a novelist failed him and it was left to others who as imaginative writers were more gifted than he was to attempt to put into practice those directives which were being eagerly absorbed by both members and fellow travellers of the Communist inspired cultural left wing.

2. Louis Aragon: *Les Cloches de Bâle* (1934)

As we have already noted the Kharkov conference was for Aragon a moment of truth not only for him personally but for his work as well: 'à mon retour je n'étais plus le même, plus l'auteur du *Paysan de Paris*, mais de *Front Rouge*'.[18] From now on the features of his poem—its rhetorical style, its blatant anti-capitalist propaganda and support for the workers' struggle—were to become with ever-increasing intensity the hallmarks of his work as a whole and in particular of his novels. For him the new socialist realism offered a means of salvation for a *genre* that had been rapidly becoming fossilized and degraded. As he was to remark in 1959: 'Le réalisme socialiste est la conception organisatrice des *faits* en littérature, du *détail* de l'art, qui interprète ce détail, lui donne sens et force, l'intègre dans le mouvement de l'humanité, au-delà de l'individualisme des écrivains'.[19] Aragon set about putting his new views on literature into practice with *Les Cloches de Bâle*, the first in a series of six novels entitled *Le Monde réel* of which the last section, *Les Communistes*, written between 1949 and 1951, has remained without sequel.

When it was published *Les Cloches de Bâle* was greeted, not entirely surprisingly, by Georges Sadoul (Aragon's *Commune* colleague) as a milestone in the history of French literature. It was, he said, one of the first works to which the term 'socialist realism' could be properly applied: 'En ce sens, ce livre n'est pas seulement un livre décisif dans l'œuvre d'Aragon, il est aussi une date de notre histoire littéraire'.[20] For Sadoul—and indeed for Aragon too—the novel both described society (that of the immediate pre-First World War years) and indicated the ways in which social change should come about. Critics sympathetic to Aragon are inclined, though with the benefit of hindsight, to emphasize that *Les Cloches de Bâle* was the first of a series, an instalment almost, and as such should be approached leniently. Yet Aragon himself seems to have had less conviction about this and certainly some difficulty in writing the novel as he conceived it. When, for example, he showed the first section, 'Diane', to Elsa Triolet she immediately raised the question of its relevance, (for *whom* was it written?) and it was in an attempt to answer this question that Aragon wrote the remaining parts. Even so it is, as he himself has subsequently admitted in *J'abats mon jeu* (1959), an uneven, poorly structured novel which for all that it undoubtedly does have some of those qualities which Bukharin believed belonged to socialist realism, indicates at the same time some of the inherent dangers.

The novel has four parts.[21] Almost without exception critics have acknowledged that of these 'Diane' is the most successful. In it—and in a style which frequently recalls the satire and irony of his own *Traité du style* (1928) as well as much of the work of Drieu with whom Aragon was friendly in the early twenties—Aragon exposes the bourgeois world with what he considers to be its overriding concern for material gain and appearances. Only as the characters reveal themselves by their actions do we begin to glimpse their superficiality and duplicity towards one another. Brunel, who initially appears affable and generous, proves to be nothing more than a money lender who eventually 'sells' his wife to the industrialist Wisner and himself ends as a police informant. Diane gives herself to a succession of men in her craving for social advancement while, as Garaudy has justly pointed out, her ability to act the part that is required of her is nowhere better illustrated than in her interview with Jacques de Sabran. All in all Aragon's characters in this first section of the novel become willing victims of the parts they play (Brunel: 'Le parasitisme est une forme supérieure de la sociabilité, et l'avenir est au parasitisme' p. 89); like many of Bernanos' characters they live out a lie only to discover ultimately that the values of plain human decency have escaped them for good.

However brilliant this opening section is as a kind of expanded image, Elsa Triolet's criticism is valid. Aragon in his role as omniscient author may well intervene—for example on the question of credit (p. 44) or of colonialism (p. 87)—but never so forcefully and at such length as to disturb the general tone or to appear irrelevant. Nor indeed does the brief skirmish between Guy and the working-class boy carry much weight. In a sense therefore the rest of the novel has to be read *against* the opening section, as a positive response to a situation presented negatively, a corrective. The two central episodes, 'Catherine' and 'Victor', describe the growing political awareness of a young Russian immigrant Catherine Simonidzé. She, like Diane de Nettencourt, moves through a series of love affairs, not like the latter for payment but in order to prove her equality with men and to reject quite openly conventional bourgeois morality. In this way Aragon attempts and indeed succeeds in integrating the private with the public, the individual with the historical. Catherine's moment of truth comes when she witnesses the workers' revolt at Cluses and its brutal repression by the police (Part II Chapter 10). The oppression and suffering of the working class are brought home to her by the young boy who is shot and whose body she mourns with the mother. His eyes ('Les yeux ne voulaient absolument pas se fermer' p. 184) symbolize his class's refusal to submit, and the incident looks forward to the workers' growing solidarity in the following section. Yet conversion to a cause, however poignantly experienced, is not quite so straightforward. From this point on Catherine oscillates between sharing in the struggle of the working class and experiencing a sense of guilt about her own bourgeois background. On her return to Paris she becomes for a while involved with the anarchists whose attitude is immediately more satisfying than that of the socialists, with their simplistic Marxism 'qui coupe le monde en deux comme une pomme, avec d'un côté les exploités, de l'autre les exploiteurs' (p. 211). Yet the attraction is short-lived and a growing sense of waste and of the reality of death drives her eventually almost to suicide. She is rescued by Victor Dehaynin through whom she is introduced to the real socialist world of Paris and to what Aragon clearly believes are the true values of comradeship and solidarity. Yet even when she becomes involved, to the extent of acting as secretary for the group organizing the taxi-drivers' strike, she has moments of guilt. Put in simple terms, as long as she continues to receive her allowance from her father Catherine is not nor can she ever be a worker: 'Tant qu'elle n'aurait pas accepté sa part du travail commun, elle ne pouvait qu'être une étrangère dans le monde où chacun gagne sa vie' (p. 376).

Given the way Aragon presents it, the dilemma which Catherine illustrates in *Les Cloches de Bâle* is without solution. After continuing to float in this way she is eventually left in a hotel bedroom in Brussels ironically owing her freedom to her first lover Jean Thiébault, now a high-ranking army officer. Clearly such an inconclusive ending was insufficient, and Aragon, apologizing as he does so, offers in the final and much more lyrical[22] section 'Clara', the brief portrait of the ideal 'femme de demain, ou mieux, osons le dire: [. . .] la femme d'aujourd'hui [. . .] dont l'esprit s'est formé dans les conditions de l'oppression, au milieu de sa classe opprimée' (p. 437). Clara Zetkin makes her appearance at the socialist peace conference held at Bâle on the eve of the First World War. In no normal sense can she be considered the heroine of *Les Cloches de Bâle*, yet as the incarnation of an ideological ideal Aragon

45

is asking her *as a character* to bear far too much weight, and in terms of the novel it is not enough, as Garaudy argues it is,[23] to see in her the logical if symbolic expression of a stage in an historical process.

Les Cloches de Bâle is a long book; necessarily, therefore, this outline is both oversimplified and selective. Yet it should be enough to indicate the book's principal quality which is the way in which, with the exception of Clara, Aragon succeeds in interweaving individual destinies with the much broader context of historical development in a true Marxist tradition. Moreover, unlike *Les Communistes*, in which as Catharine Savage has rightly pointed out Communism is ever present as an ideology against which all others by definition fail,[24] *Les Cloches de Bâle* succeeds by disclosure. (What Sartre in *Qu'est-ce que la littérature?* was to term *dévoilement*.) Only gradually do we learn that the self-seeking, materialist bourgeois world in the first section will destroy itself, or that anarchy is potentially and indeed ultimately less politically effective than socialism. As we have noted, Aragon's omniscience in the opening section allows him to intervene and pass comment: later too we find him addressing the reader directly, commenting from his present position in the 1930s on police activities, implicitly criticizing certain anarchists or using that device, so frequently used about this time by Mauriac, of the future tense to indicate his total control. Yet for the most part these more obvious weaknesses of a literature which aims in certain ways to edify are relatively infrequent, and certainly less marked than in much of Aragon's subsequent writing. It is arguable of course that Aragon had yet fully to find his way in socialist realism even, as Garaudy suggests, that his earlier experience of the Surrealist movement ensured that his awareness of devices which made for successful imaginative literature had not yet been fully shaped. Yet already the signs are present. His experience as a journalist gave him the taste for historical accuracy (his reporting for *L'Humanité* of a taxi drivers' strike in 1934 provided him with the details for Part III); historical figures—Jaurès, Cailloux, Bataille are introduced to add authenticity; he has an ear for language so that we find representatives of different social classes speaking in an appropriate fashion; and above all, like Barbusse, he effectively uses incident and detail (often in contrast) to point up a general effect: Catherine's meeting with Henry Bataille (Part II Chapters XIX and XX), Judith's death after her abortion (Part II Chapter XXIII) or Jeanette's miscarriage, for example.

Ultimately, however, we are obliged to return to Elsa Triolet's question concerning the novel's relevance. While unlike *Le Feu*, *Les*

Cloches de Bâle is a much more discursive and less immediate work, from his vantage point of the thirties Aragon none the less succeeds in shaping his historical material and in creating a sense of evolution. In face of the growing threat of fascism and even, especially for those of the Left, that of another war, *Les Cloches de Bâle* clearly had much to offer. In spite of the idealistically portrayed Clara in the final section, there does emerge from the novel in general a sense of the need for solidarity and at the same time an important criticism (much of which can be read as self-directed) of any attempt to remain apart or uncommitted. In October 1963 Aragon remarked in an interview with Francis Crémieux that writing for him was both the acquisition and communication of knowledge ('écrire pour connaître, et par là communiquer à autrui ce que j'ai appris').[25] In this context *Les Cloches de Bâle* might well be considered as the first and, not insignificantly, one of the more successful of Aragon's achievements.

3. Paul Nizan: *Le Cheval de Troie* (1935)

When at the age of twenty-eight Nizan published his second novel, *Le Cheval de Troie*, he had, as was acknowledged, an already well established reputation as an incisive even acerbic essayist with *Aden Arabie* and *Les Chiens de Garde*, as a critic, and, with *Antoine Bloyé* (1933), as a novelist. In this first fictional work, a thinly disguised biography of his own father, Nizan traces and explores the sense of alienation which develops in a railway worker as he slowly improves his position and in so doing betrays the class to which he properly belongs. The result is a book which has both a sociological and a psychological perspective and which also throws up issues to which Nizan returned almost obsessively—man's purpose in life and the problem of death. In many ways with its detailed and knowledgeable descriptions of the world of the railway worker *Antoine Bloyé* belongs, as both Bernard[26] and Jacqueline Leiner (not to mention a number of contemporary reviewers) have remarked, to the naturalist tradition as exemplified in particular by the later works of Zola. One consequence of this is that while it clearly does have (if only by implication) a relevance for the developing class struggle in France in the late twenties and early thirties, and also contains various features which relate it to the debate concerning populist and proletarian literature at this time, it is not an overtly militant book. As Nizan himself remarked: 'Je n'ai pas voulu faire de la politique dans mon roman. Mais s'il y a des conclusions

47

politiques à en tirer, c'est le sujet qui le veut.'[27] In January 1933, however, Nizan had joined the *AEAR* and in June had become a member of the editorial board of *Commune* ('un organe assez violent de contre-attaque'). More significantly we may recall that he spent 1934 in Russia and in August attended the congress of Soviet writers at which the principles of socialist realism were first formulated. It is against this experience and against Bukharin's assertion that the *imaginative* writer should both depict the present and outline a future based on suitable left-wing principles that *Le Cheval de Troie* should be read.[28]

As the title of the book suggests, this is a story of invasion. Furthermore it is presumably intended that the classical reference should lend a certain grandeur to the efforts of Bloyé (who appears in all Nizan's published novels) and his friends. The action, which lasts precisely a week, occurs in the town of Villefranche, not only an amalgam of these provincial centres where Nizan worked and was politically active (Villefranche-sur-Saône, Bourg and Vienne) but, with the figurative meaning of *franche* in mind ('true', 'loyal'), symbolic as well. We learn in the first part of the novel that for some time the Communists have been attempting to focus elements of political unrest more sharply, to give shape and purpose to what before was *mou*, as Philippe describes pre-war socialism (p. 36). Hitherto, however, the opportunity has come only in the form of strikes which seem to have made little real impact on the town and in the distribution of their political newspaper *Le Tréfileur Rouge*. Now the announcement of the projected visit of a fascist speaker galvanizes them into concerted preparation (reflected in the much shorter and tenser Chapter III), and the novel traces the effect which this new political urgency has both on a large scale—the general issue of the emergent Left culminating in Part II in direct confrontation with the fascists—and at an individual, private level.

Le Cheval de Troie opens, as Walter Redfern has remarked, with 'a breathing space'.[29] Bloyé and his companions have left the town for the country; they are ostensibly free from the pressures of their normal working lives and enjoy like children (p. 26) the intoxicating effect of fresh air and outdoor activities. Yet the signs of their real life are ever present. As Bloyé watches his companions asleep in the grass he sees not release on their faces but the marks of care and strain. The women in particular, Berthe with her swollen stomach, Catherine with her empty breasts (a premonition of her later abortion and death) have had their fertility sterilized prematurely. The only exception is Marie-Louise whose youth, confidence and natural inclination to happiness make her a complementary figure to Bloyé whom she will rejoin at the very end of the novel. And as Jacqueline Leiner has pointed out, the factory chimneys, church spires and the roof of the law courts which they can see in the distance are reminders (symbols even) of those elements of society against which they are struggling.

After this opening Nizan moves into the town where his descriptions of the school or the church, for example, recall the hostility of his remarks in his earlier *Les Chiens de Garde*. As we have already noted, Part I describes the growing political awareness of the working-class elements of the town largely, it is implied, under the guiding inspiration of Bloyé. ('Qu'est-ce que tu veux faire?—Changer le monde, dit Bloyé' p. 53). At once it is obvious that Bloyé and Nizan are virtually synonymous, and furthermore, the narrative method on which the latter finally settled—once again that of the omniscient author—allows him to be at once both inside and outside his characters, and also to treat the general situation in a descriptive but deliberately selective way. Given his aim to provide a general perspective in Part I, the method is undoubtedly successful. We do to be sure have the impression that Nizan overplays his hand and intervenes—rather in the manner of Barbusse at the end of *Le Feu*—to point a moral or to make a general statement which invites us into a world of theoretical speculation beyond the immediate context of the novel's action. For example, the description of Bloyé and his colleagues painting slogans:

> Faire des inscriptions sur les murs, au petit commencement de l'aube, dans une ville de province, ça n'a pas l'air d'une action capitale, c'est une entreprise qui n'ébranle pas l'ordre du monde, et le lendemain les trains arriveront à l'heure, les gens iront tous à leur travail, il n'y aura peut-être que le commissaire de police pour s'en émouvoir parce qu'elle a un nom dans le Code pénal et que le Code pénal, c'est toute sa tête. Ce n'est pas une entreprise bien dangereuse, on ne risque pas encore d'être tué, on ne risque pas beaucoup de prison pour dégradation des monuments publics ou de la propriété privée . . . Mais c'est une entreprise qui a plus de sens que les plus grandes œuvres des ennemis: elle fait partie d'un mouvement qui accuse le monde et délibère de le changer.
> (pp. 118, 19)

Inevitably too perhaps, the picture we are given of Villefranche is one-sided and precisely because it is so, our reaction to any alternative is conditioned in advance. While therefore the prefect's dinner party may be described in a completely objective fashion, and while Voirin's descriptions of nascent fascism ('une renaissance de l'honneur' p. 98) sounds neither more nor less glib and complacent than some of the statements concerning the plight of the workers or the virtues of left-wing unity ('c'était une machine de révolte, mais c'était aussi une machine d'amitié' p. 117), we automatically find it objectionable. The same result is experienced at the beginning of Part II where Nizan's description of the Sunday morning and of Villefranche's bourgeoisie is in appearance at least quite straightforward, yet we again find ourselves reading it as a piece of criticism.

Having captured our sympathy in this way, however, Nizan then regrettably allows himself to be seduced by the need to make the political message of the novel more explicit, with the result that we have a series of weighted contrasts and the use of a naïve symbolism: the growing sense of communion of the left is greeted by the sun and by the warm red of the unfurled flags (p. 136); the left-wing meeting takes place in the open air while that of the fascists is held in a disused cinema ('la salle était obscure et froide et la réunion avait d'abord ressemblé à une descente dans un monde sous-marin' p. 139); the left-wing speakers may lack organization but they have warmth and life; by contrast 'l'homme de Paris avait un veston noir et un visage immobile et coupant' (pp. 139–40); the elements of the left have come together spontaneously (and will remain united); the sense of collectivity which the fascists believe they have is as superficial as the uniform they aspire to wear. The tone continues to the end. The workers are happy (p. 174); the fascists fearful. The riot squad called in to break up the demonstrators appears to wear armoured clothing and fight with guns; the workers have no protection, only stones as weapons, and at no time are they the aggressors. Finally, when the riot police have driven the workers back into their part of the town they are met with total resistance (pp. 194–6). It is a final symbolic statement of where true values and comradeship are to be found. Yet there is more, for in the two final chapters Nizan allows himself to sink to the kind of sententious moralizing which marked the closing pages of both *Le Feu* and *Les Cloches de Bâle* and which continues to be a feature of later pieces of socialist realist writing. The repeated emphasis on the workers' dignity ('Ils avançaient pourtant avec une allure d'hommes qui ont achevé leur journée, une journée qui a été pleine et digne de l'homme' p. 187); on their sense of martyrdom ('Un jour pareil [. . .] suffit pour tout changer' p. 191) and the description of the final dawn, however chilly, witnessed by Bloyé and Marie-Louise, are all examples of this style of writing at its worst.

Yet to reduce *Le Cheval de Troie* to these features alone would be to ignore much that is to be admired. With no little justification is it considered one of the more successful novels of its kind. Nizan's sense of dialogue and proportion (the novel neatly spans a week), his use of imagery, his constant shifts of focus from the group to the individual and back again all deserve attention. Within the space available here a few words should be said about what is undoubtedly one of Nizan's principal qualities, namely the manner in which he explores and illustrates the political implications of the novel through various individual characters and private dilemmas.

Le Cheval de Troie has three main characters: Louis the worker who arrives from Lyon and who, killed by the police, becomes an innocent victim of events and thereby a martyr for the workers' cause; Albert whose concern about his wife's abortion drives him into a world of private despair; and Lange. Of these by far the most complex is Lange, a curious figure who looks forward to Sartre's Roquentin in *La Nausée* (and to a lesser extent to Lucien Fleurier in 'L'Enfance d'un Chef') and who seems, according to Simone de Beauvoir, to have been based on a mixture of Sartre, Nizan himself, their friend Brice Parain and Drieu la Rochelle. It is significant that when he appears for the first time Lange should turn his back on Bloyé; he is totally uncommitted, apolitical. Fascinated (like Nizan) by death, Lange's conception of life as a series of struggles whether political, sporting or sexual has a strong fascist ring about it. He is a solitary person preferring to live by night, a *voyeur* (p. 108), passive.[30] When he goes to the political meetings, therefore, he does so as a cynical observer ready to criticize and sneer, yet before long and in spite of himself he is subject to a shift of position reflected in Nizan's description. At first resistant and therefore active in a positive, thinking way, he soon becomes passive: 'il s'éloigna d'un pas ordonné [. . .] Mais la fuite des vaincus l'enveloppa, le contraignait' (p. 168), 'Lange fut entraîné dans le mouvement du monde' (p. 174). Ultimately, having become completely passive, entranced even ('son exaltation était aussi forte qu'une satisfaction sexuelle' p. 175), it is Lange who fires upon the workers first and precipitates the confrontation with its bloody consequences.

The advantages of exploring such distinct individual responses as these to political situations and attitudes are twofold. In terms of the novel's intended political impact such examples of failure to act responsibly (or at best of a confusion of priorities) can be as effective as any demonstration of exemplary action—indeed the obsession with the ideal bolshevik figure in later pieces of socialist realism would create its own special problems. More importantly such fragmentation ensures that the human interest of the novel is not lost. As we have already seen, there is no doubt that the Soviet Writers' congress in 1935 had a marked effect upon him. Nizan was quite convinced that the purpose of literature was to awaken his readers' awareness and to lead them to revolutionary action. Not surprisingly, therefore, *Le Cheval de Troie* is a much more schematic novel than *La Conspiration* published three years later, by which time it is generally agreed that his allegiance to the Communist Party was beginning to weaken.[31] Yet even so he does show in the earlier novel that he had sufficient ability as an imaginative writer to come to terms with Party directives and to blend the personal and the political persuasively together.

The Second Phase of Socialist Realism

The kind of programmed, schematic political literature that was beginning to emerge during the 1930s largely, though not entirely, came to a halt with the War. Certainly it is true that much, indeed nearly all, of the literature inspired by the War years and in particular by the Resistance dealt in a general Stendhalian way with politics. Eluard's poetry, Vercors' *Silence de la mer* (1942) Anouilh's *Antigone* (1944), Sartre's *Les Chemins de la liberté* and his play *Les Mouches* (1943), Camus' *La Peste* or *Les Justes* to name but a handful of the most obvious examples, all relate to or draw on recent political events. As was suggested in the Introduction, while purely sectarian politics are not entirely ignored, the overriding concern of such books is more a philosophical one. Brunet, Mathieu, Kaliayev and others clearly debate political questions but do so in the wider context of such issues as patriotism, freedom or individual moral responsibility and in this sense the works in which they appear relate much more directly to earlier works like, say, *La Condition humaine* than to *Les Cloches de Bâle* or *Le Cheval de Troie*. Even so particularly among those who remained stubbornly faithful to the Party in spite of the Nazi–Soviet pact (soon to be rendered meaningless much to their smug delight when Russia entered the war by invading the Baltic states), the heritage of socialist realism could be seen. In Elsa Triolet's short story, for example, 'Les Amants d'Avignon' (1943), the heroine Juliette Noël is shown to be a paragon of both political integrity and physical beauty. It was not to be long, however, before the spectre of socialist realism as it had appeared in the thirties began to have more substance. In spite of their supreme Resistance record and of the myths which had grown up around them, politically the Communists were, by their own pre-war standards at least, relatively ineffective. A need was felt to exert a more positive influence and it is in no way surprising that in what David Caute has described as the 'bitter, post-Republican mood of 1947–8'[1] the development of the anti-Western attitudes of the freeze and the new

53

Stalinist orthodoxy concerning the arts should have been particularly welcome.

While there was obviously no state machinery like that which existed in Russia to enforce any strict control over art or literature, there none the less rapidly developed in France a body of hard-line Communist intellectuals for whom Jean Kanapa and Laurent Casanova became the principal spokesmen with the review *La Nouvelle Critique* (founded in 1948) as the main source of information and instruction. To Casanova and his supporters, who included Aragon, Garaudy, Stil and Courtade, Zhdanov, who had been responsible for the official Party line on culture since the early thirties and the official source of the new orthodoxy, was both saviour and guide. (Casanova describes him as the incarnation of 'la Volonté tranquille et ferme de Staline'.)[2] For them the Trotskyist view that there was after all much that was good in the bourgeois literature of the past and that the proletariat should be instructed in how to evaluate it, was clearly a retrograde one. Rather the function of literature should be much more positive; its aim should be to instruct the public in the principles of Stalinist political truth. Not surprisingly therefore the literature of this second wave of socialist realism returns obsessively to a number of standard themes—the virtues of the Soviet State, Stalin himself (the *vrai bolchevik* as Vailland liked to describe him), and even Maurice Thorez as an ideal authoritarian figure, the French Communist Party as the only saving organization in France, violent opposition both to any form of American interference in national affairs and to all manifestations of what were considered to be the natural repressive tendencies of a bourgeois government and society. Laurent Casanova defined the qualities of this literature in the following way:

> la volonté d'aider à la prise de conscience du peuple et le désir de l'aider à atteindre les buts qu'il se propose [. . .] l'honnêteté dans la recherche des valeurs culturelles, propres à notre temps et à notre pays [. . .] l'esprit de responsabilité personnelle devant le peuple.[3]

Unfortunately (though not surprisingly) what he did not consider was the means of expression and the effect that such aims would have. As we shall see such a view tended (even after 1956) to encourage the production of a series of stereotyped and repetitive works in which political propaganda was now much more discernible than ever before.

Yet it should not be assumed that there was ready or total submission and acceptance of any directives among the Communist writers and intellectuals. During the late forties and early fifties the stability of the Communist Parties outside Russia was deeply disturbed by a number of events: the attacks on Yugoslavia and Tito, the trials and executions of Rajk and Kostov, the revelation of the existence of Soviet labour camps, the Korean War and the invasion of Hungary, for example. Together with these the orthodoxy of the Zdhanov doctrine was for many a further strain, a new tension between unquestioning or even blind obedience to the Party line and a sense of individual responsibility and integrity. Defections occurred at fairly regular intervals; for example, Vercors in 1957, Roy in 1958, Vailland in 1959, even though he had effectively 'lost faith' three years earlier. Furthermore Stalin's death in 1953 and more importantly the Kruschev revelations in 1956 of the atrocities and persecutions carried out during his predecessor's regime, inevitably had a diluting effect on the political orthodoxy which had prevailed since the late forties.

Predictably, perhaps, the effect of changes that were made was more noticeable in Russia than in France, where many hard-liners retained an unshakeable faith in a large number of the values established during the Stalinist era and where Stalin himself continued to be viewed as a justifiable (because inevitable) link in the historical process which would lead to an ideal revolutionary society. Inevitably, too, such ideological inflexibility was also expressed in a literature which all too frequently tended to become in consequence increasingly monotonous and sterile. Certainly there were exceptions. Aragon, for example, in *La Semaine sainte* (1958), considered by many to be one of his best works, 'renounced' socialist realism and turned to historical fiction. In this novel, set in 1815 at the time of the exile of Louis XVIII and the return to power of Napoleon, Aragon focuses his attention on a crucial moment in history—a theme already present of course in *Les Communistes*. But he also explores through his protagonist the dual tensions of betrayal and loyalty, a theme not all that remote from his personal preoccupations at this time. In this way *La Semaine sainte* offers, in addition to its colourful evocation of a particular and carefully defined historical moment, a confessional perspective that is new in Aragon's work. There is little doubt that this successfully lifts the book out of a socialist-realist mould, but it also takes it outside the kind of politically inspired literature with which Aragon's name is normally so readily associated. Yet Aragon's reaction to recent circumstances and developments was by no means widely shared. More usually writers whose allegiance to the old orthodoxy had never wavered, believed it their duty to continue to write much in the same vein. The result was inevitable: socialist realism ran itself into an impasse.

1. Roger Vailland: *Le Colonel Foster Plaidera Coupable* (1952)

After 1947 and Zdhanov's violent attacks on American expansionist policy, anti-Americanism featured as a principal theme in a number of works. In essays both Garaudy (*L'Eglise, Le Communisme et les Chrétiens,* 1949) and Vailland (*Le Vatican contre la paix,* unpublished) accused the Americans of being in league with the Catholic Church in France and of attempting to make of Europe generally a federal state economically and politically dependent on their support. Pierre Courtade who had been *L'Humanité*'s American correspondent in 1950 attacked American aggression in his novel *Jimmy* (1951), but of the various works to have been inspired by this particular theme one of the more successful was Vailland's play centred on the Korean War, *Le Colonel Foster plaidera coupable.*

Vailland's attitude to the war was that of the majority of Communists for whom responsibility was seen to lie entirely with President Rhee and the South Korean forces, who with American aid were threatening not just another people, but the whole notion of democratic government and freedom. Although not yet officially a member of it, Vailland had been courting the Communist Party for ten years. His record as a Resistance worker (related in his thinly disguised auto-biographical novel *Drôle de jeu,* 1945) and the positions he had adopted after the liberation towards such issues as the role of the church or American influence in Europe would seem to have made him entirely acceptable. Yet Vailland had always been too much of an individualist, too much, as he liked to put it, of an 'intellectuel petit bourgeois' ever to have been readily accepted by the Party—indeed a first application for membership made in late 1942 was left unanswered. Moreover a background of drugs and a broken marriage hardly argued for a stable character. By 1950 however, Vailland's personal life was much more settled, while politically he had moved unambiguously towards a much more orthodox left-wing position. It is not surprising therefore to find him expressing an optimism in the ultimate outcome of the war: 'La Corée peut être vaincue, provisoirement, mais l'ensemble des pays communistes ne peut plus être "mis à genoux" même provisoirement, et il est assez fort pour ne plus connaître que des échecs locaux.'[4]

Vailland's play was originally intended to have been called *Le major Brown est porté disparu*. Brown himself was to be shown as someone who was genuinely convinced that he was fighting in the cause of freedom, and who was only to realize his mistake when it was too late. The conflict, both ideological and psychological, was promising. After a few weeks Vailland changed the play's title to its present one— possibly in order to associate the name of the protagonist with that of John Foster Dulles, the American Foreign Secretary—and completed it on a wave of sustained enthusiasm between 14 August and 28 September 1950.

Basically the theme he had originally set out to explore remained the same and in its final form the play shows only a number of relatively minor alterations or modifications made either to trim its physical, dramatic shape or to reinforce its ideological message. Foster remains the liberal at heart whose 'idéaux humanitaires' and 'convictions progressistes'[5] are eventually only overcome by his military training and conditioning ('Citoyen, j'ai le droit de n'être pas d'accord avec le politique de mon gouvernement. Soldat, j'exécute les ordres que je reçois' p. 292); Paganel, whose Catholic formation causes him to regard the war as a crusade, none the less also admits to similar feelings but is at once suspected of betraying the section's instructions to the partisan forces; Jimmy McAllen represents the archetypal young American soldier full of racial and political prejudice. Of the local population Cho is the collaborator—as long as the American forces seem likely to provide the best protection for his business concerns; his daughter Lya, who has been a Communist for some years, plays the dangerous and difficult game of betrayal inside the American Command Post, and Masan, the Communist, who is captured and finally executed, is clearly intended to go unflinching to his death (not unlike Katow in Malraux's *La Condition humaine*) with the message for all mankind to hear on his lips.

In spite of the undoubted promise of Vailland's original design and intention, the result is disappointing. However oversimplified such observations as these may be, there can be no disregarding the fact that *Le Colonel Foster plaidera coupable* has few redeeming features and is essentially a loaded and simplistic dialogue between American (Western) imperialism and Communism. The most obvious manner in which Vailland uses his stage directions in the last act reinforces this impression. Victory for the partisan forces is accompanied by that well-worn image, the dawning of a new day; the American prisoners now stand in the places formerly occupied by Masan and the two thieves. Perhaps most artificial of all, however, is the conversation which Lya and Masan have immediately before the latter's execution and which is punctuated by such statements as 'Dans l'instant même où ils nous tuent, ils ont honte de n'être pas communistes' (p. 298) or 'C'est parce que nous sommes les plus humaines que nous sommes communistes' (p. 299–30). They also share a vision of the promised city in which Communists from all over the world will unite in peace. To be fair to Vailland, *Le Colonel Foster plaidera coupable* is not composed entirely of such ideologically pregnant statements. The fact that Cho is allowed (presumably at least) to escape remains an enigma: either it indicates a token attempt by Vailland to introduce an element of balance into the play, or it suggests a more sinister degree of sympathy between author and character, or it has simply been overlooked. The last, I suspect, is most likely, though the same kind of ambiguity is to be found again in *La Condition humaine* where it is the master of disguise and opportunist, Clappique, who is allowed to find his way to safety. The question of the extent to which Lya allows her ideals to become compromised through her complicity with the American forces, and Foster's inner struggle between his humanitarian ideals and his belief that American forces are fighting in the cause of freedom, do give them each some psychological depth. Similarly the final scene is interestingly ambiguous. Does Foster plead guilty to having been responsible for certain atrocities against the local native population or on a much grander scale to having perpetrated imperialist aggression against his better and more humane judgments? The second interpretation is temptingly and no doubt intentionally present. Yet in spite of such interesting possibilities which promise to lift the play out of a clearly defined ideological pigeon-hole, it remains a weighted and predictable piece. As in *Les Communistes*, the premises from which Vailland is arguing are there before the play begins. As propaganda it may well have been effective; as a piece of dramatic literature it does not rate very highly. Instead it was in his novels of the fifties that Vailland was to prove himself superior to the majority of his fellow Communist novelists both in his demonstration of the key theses and also—albeit unbeknown to himself—in his tacit admission of their debilitating effect on his art.

2. Roger Vailland: *Beau Masque* (1954); Pierre Courtade: *La Place rouge* (1961)

In terms both of content and of presentation these two novels are nicely representative of the kind of fiction that was produced during this period. In a way, too, they may be seen to reflect two essentially different attitudes towards the Communist Party and towards any form of programmed writing. *Beau Masque* is complex, balanced and with the exception of its Epilogue relatively free from too much moralizing; *La Place rouge* is narrow in focus, sentimentally as well as ideologically weighted, with Courtade increasingly identifying himself with his protagonist Simon Bordes as he moves towards political maturity.

As we have already noted, Vailland's official membership of the Party dated from 1952. In 1953 he wrote a short essay on the theatre entitled *Expérience du drame* in which he argued for a literature and in particular for a novel 'dont la lecture se précipite comme une action et qui provoque à l'action'.[6] When *Beau Masque* appeared the Communist critic André Wurmser reviewed it in *Les Lettres françaises*, describing it as being 'humaine dans sa totalité' and strikingly free from schematization. Ostensibly the novel is an orthodox exploration of the exploiter-exploited theme illustrated at a local level by the struggle between the management of a silk factory (*FETA, Filatures et Tissages Anonymes*) and their employees, and with national implications introduced through the investment in the enterprise of American money. The workers' leader is a young divorcée, Pierrette Amable, who finally succeeds in bringing together those who are less totally committed or simply more cautious than herself in the organization of a strike and massive demonstration at the time of the visit paid by Johnston the American shareholders' delegate. At the same time Vailland also analyses for us the struggle for power that is undermining the management. Emilie Privas-Lubas, the second wife of the present owner, Valerio Empoli, is attempting together with Valerio's sister Esther, to obtain a majority of the shares and hence ultimate control. Emilie's two children, Philippe Letourneau (by her first marriage), and Nathalie, her stepdaughter, also have their roles to play. Philippe who, for all that he is to inherit the *FETA* organization, has no business sense whatsoever, falls in love with Pierrette and, in order to win her esteem, attempts, in vain, to betray his company's plans; Nathalie, dying of tuberculosis and almost an alcoholic, finally thwarts her stepmother with a Machiavellian maliciousness worthy of her father himself. Caught between these two

59

groups is Beau Masque. An Italian immigrant and Communist sympathizer, Beau Masque has behind him a record of political action. He becomes Pierrette's lover, but always remains an outsider on the fringe of the local political activities, and becomes increasingly jealous of the time Pierrette devotes to them. Ultimately he is a victim of the situation, killed by the *CRS* as he and Vizille, a local former Resistance fighter, attempt to stage their own demonstration. The novel closes with an Epilogue in which, as we shall see, Vailland finally succumbs to the need to point his moral after an action in which, for all their demonstration of solidarity, the workers are brutally suppressed by the forces of authority and accept the new terms offered them by the management.

In spite of Wurmser's enthusiastic comments and of the necessarily foreshortened impression that such a summary gives of the novel, the problem of over-schematization therefore is a real one. Vailland, aware of the danger, attempts in various ways to avoid it. He explores, albeit briefly, the effect of growing industrialization on the local rural areas and population, he analyses in considerable detail the psychological tensions which develop especially between Pierrette, Beau Masque and Philippe. But it is in the stylistic devices he employs that his awareness of the problem becomes most apparent.

In keeping with the principal characteristics of socialist realism Vailland attempts in various ways to convey a sense of authenticity. As in his next novel *325.000 francs* (1955)—and rather like Barbusse in *Le Feu*—Vailland participates in the action of *Beau Masque* as a self-confessed observer. He is confidant to various characters in turn, he has access to a whole correspondence between Philippe and Nathalie (Part III),[7] he reproduces various parts of his own private diary (e.g., pp. 8–19), presents us with a family tree (p. 116) and also with a map (p. 418) to enable us to follow the demonstrators' movements when Johnston arrives. Part V is written like a piece of straightforward day-to-day *reportage*. Certainly, recourse to such devices in no way hides or entirely compensates for the standard use Vailland makes of the omniscient author technique, but they do at least suggest an awareness of its limitations. More typical of his writing is the manner in which Vailland tends to categorize people, often reflecting their moral or political qualities in his descriptions of them. It comes as no surprise therefore that Nathalie for all her nervous energy is consumptive; that Philippe ultimately lacks the fibre to leave his position of security and throw his weight into the workers' struggle for a better deal. Indeed it is typical that what assistance he does give them is based on deceit. On the side of the workers the same device applies. Mignot, secretary of the local section of the *PCF* is serious, unimaginative and ever ready to efface himself; Cuvrot, 'héros de la grande grève de 1924' (p. 39), now leader of the Communist minority on the town council, continues to live in the past; Louise, the delegate of the socialist *Force Ouvrière*, though sympathetic to Pierrette, ultimately accepts a compromise with the management. Against these Pierrette emerges as the lone heroine figure (p. 193). Yet her unquestionable political integrity and standing, reflected in her physical sturdiness and in her independence, is gradually eroded as she becomes involved with Beau Masque. As Mignot suggests to her, 'les camarades responsables se doivent d'avoir une vie privée irréprochable' (p. 339). And even though she does succeed in organizing the demonstration it is, in the short term at least, only partly effective.

It is arguable that in this less than totally optimistic view of the workers' efforts—however bitter his indictment of the repressive measures of the management and of the *CRS* may be—Vailland is already, perhaps unwittingly, hinting at his own reservations and at his later disillusion with the Party. Be that as it may, in 1953 Vailland believed himself to be a fully committed member and it is this which, coupled perhaps with some dissatisfaction with the bulk of the novel and in particular with the portrayal of Pierrette as a vehicle for his ideas, prompted the Epilogue. Here the concern for style goes and Vailland resorts to the kind of sentimental rhetoric that we have already noticed to be characteristic of earlier socialist realism, and in particular of Aragon's *Les Cloches de Bâle*. Returning to Le Clusot a year later he discovers a new energy and enthusiasm among the workers and he allows himself to shift from a factual account of events to pregnant statements of his own convictions. (E.g., 'L'histoire de l'homme était ainsi en train de prendre son "tournant décisif"' p. 443.) Like Aragon, Vailland seems ultimately to have felt himself obliged to spell out his message for his readers, with the result that the novel undoubtedly loses much of its weight and attraction.

By comparison with other novels of this period *Beau Masque* is, at least up to the Epilogue, a much more complex book. At no time is Vailland's presentation one-sided—indeed, even his accounts of the family feud or of Valerio Empoli's business methods are shaded with a degree of admiration. And he is as much concerned in a more abstract way with the position of the 'révolutionnaire professionel' in society, with the problem created by the need for involvement on the one hand

61

and by the inevitable isolation of such a position on the other. It may be true, of course, that in spite of his undoubted political commitment at this time, Vailland had allowed himself too much scope, that he had gone beyond the normal range of the socialist realist novel and that his Epilogue is simply a last-ditch attempt to bring it back into line. Yet Epilogue or not, the real measure of Vailland's success may be seen when *Beau Masque* is compared to novels like André Stil's trilogy *Le Premier choc* (1951–3), a violent attack on Americanism in all its manifestations, the first volume of which was awarded the Prix Staline in 1952 (the Communist's equivalent of the Nobel Prize for Literature), or Pierre Courtade's *La Place rouge* (1961).

Courtade's novel is the account of the political coming of age of Simon Bordes and is written in the form of a metaphorical journey of self-discovery from a starting position of teenage romantic idealism through scepticism to unquestioning (and uncritical) certainty. The novel begins in France in 1935 and ends in Russia in the post-Stalin atmosphere of 1958. It is divided into eight parts of different lengths each relating to a crucial period or incident in Simon's life. It becomes evident early in the book (p. 42)[8] that even if Courtade and his hero are not precisely synonymous they are at least to be closely identified with one another; indeed by the last section of the book Courtade alternates quite regularly between the third and first person singular pronouns to provide him with his narrative voice.

La Place rouge begins quite promisingly. The opening section is an account of a showing of Eisenstein's *The Battleship Potemkin* at which Simon meets a number of friends who are to reappear in the rest of the novel as representatives of different points of view. In the cinema too is Gide who, praised here for his recent support for Communism, will subsequently be violently attacked for what is considered to be a turncoat attitude. Even though he falls well short of Nizan's achievements, Courtade has some success in this section in mixing the political with the personal. Yet as soon as he begins to describe Simon's relationship with Camille (whom he will eventually marry), or Paul Grange's with Paulette for example, sentimentality is never far below the surface. Because, it is implied, of their social position, their love for one another can find an outlet only in a series of nights spent together in various sordid hotel bedrooms; they belong to a depressed class from which escape can only come ultimately in death. Against this, however, Courtade describes Simon's sense of comradeship which Paul and Cazaux (here a member of the *Jeunesse Communiste* but later to become disillusioned with Communism) enjoy. After the performance they all go to the somewhat obviously named café *L'Avenir*. Courtade cannot refrain from pointing the moral: 'Cependant les jeunes gens d'aujourd'hui debout devant le zinc de *l'Avenir* continuaient le voyage du *Potemkine*' (p. 47). Here the sense of comradeship develops as they talk into the night. They are joined by Sacha who is to emigrate to Russia, his papers holding for them an almost religious fascination. Yet it is here that one of the novel's central weaknesses begins to become apparent. Already in the descriptions of Eisenstein's film Courtade's *own* enthusiasm for its political impact has emerged in spite of a token 'pense Simon Bordes' (e.g., p. 42). Now in the café the same hiatus exists between the profundity of the *unvoiced* thoughts of the young men and the way in which when expressed they are full of jargon, repetitive and poorly articulated (pp. 60–70). Indeed it is Camille (the women interestingly taking little or no part in the discussion) who afterwards accuses Simon and his friends of talking 'entre vous'.

As a beginning the first section for all its weaknesses does have some positive qualities. Simon's political and emotional uncertainty are made clear and, even though we are never left in any doubt as to what true values Courtade himself believes in, an illusion of freedom is partly retained. As the novel develops, however, Simon is placed into situations which in true socialist realist fashion are clearly intended to have an instructive effect on him, and much of the internal debate which could have added considerable psychological depth and interest to Courtade's depiction of him is lost. Thus, for example, in Part II he is faced with the view, expressed by Prévôt, that the Nazi–Soviet pact will ultimately be seen to be justified. For Simon who has already visited Russia the choice is between a personal intuitive response and the optimism born of total faith. ('Je te parle de choses que j'ai senties ... enfin ... humainement, et tu me réponds par des abstractions' p. 119.) His romanticism continues; he is unwilling to commit himself to the Party's discipline ('J'aime mieux [. . .] être un bon sympathisant qu'un communiste médiocre' p. 194). Gradually, however, a change occurs neatly corresponding with his meeting Justine, a resistance worker, whom he marries after Camille's death, and by 1954 and now a member of the Party, we find him justifying (in words which could have been those of Vailland) his earlier procrastination by reference to his 'esprit petit bourgeois dont j'avais bien du mal à me défaire à cause de mes origines' (p. 261). From now on Courtade is able to show how Simon has reached full political maturity. Like Prévôt he too has faith

63

and the Stalin trials, while they cause Cazaux to leave the party (again like Vailland 'sur la pointe des pieds', p. 270), are accepted as a necessary link in the chain of historical progress. Finally in the last part of the novel Simon visits Sacha in Moscow. Everywhere he sees evidence of a new prosperity; Sacha's earlier hardships (which he believes he must have exaggerated) are now seen to have been worthwhile. The promise of the Potemkin mutiny has begun to be realized; progress is inevitable. As Sacha remarks in the closing pages: 'Nous construisons le XXIe siècle dans un décor du XIXe siècle . . . Tandis que vous . . ., vous êtes une société du XIXe siècle dans un décor du XXe' (p. 311).

Given his highly selective method, Courtade clearly does not have to rely on the kind of didactic Epilogue which mars *Beau Masque*. His account of Simon's developing political awareness is carefully charted and unlike Aragon in *Les Cloches de Bâle*, for example, he is more than ready to allow a description of working-class conditions to add weight to his political message. Certainly there are some individual scenes, like that of Simon's railway journey and of his subsequent search by the Nazis in Part IV, which are sharply observed, but even these are flawed by his refusal to allow factual description to speak for itself. His reliance on sentimentality, on rhetoric, on authorial intervention, on an increasing confusion between Simon and himself and on pompous theorizing only serve to remind us of some of those weaknesses of socialist-realist writing which we have noted in earlier works and from which there seems ultimately to have been no escape.

Conclusion

As suggested in the Introduction it is possible that an arbitrary selection of this kind will be thought untypical of a period in the history of French literature when ideological concerns have impinged on imaginative writing with ever-increasing force. If we once again recall Orwell's words that this is an age when literature has inevitably to concern itself with the political, then the rather abrupt dismissal of Sartre, Malraux or Camus for example may seem surprising. Indeed such a list might easily be extended: Montherlant, for whom a return to the values of a truly aristocratic society would provide a regenerative force for his ailing nation; Giraudoux, whose work is haunted by the problems invoked by Franco-German relations and whose sympathy for Germany took him to the post of Minister of Information in 1939–40; Saint-Exupéry, whose war-time experiences inspired in him a sense of patriotism and responsibility; even Bernanos, whose concerns might well be thought quite different, carefully charts beneath the surface of his imaginative writing a social and political order that is set in contrast against his Christian-inspired ideal. And so on. But as I have already suggested, politics in the work of these writers is ultimately subordinate to actions and ideas that are essentially *meta*-political in nature. What distinguishes their works from those of Aragon, Drieu or Courtade is an absence—or relative absence—of political tendentiousness and *a priori* assumptions. What political value they do possess is to be found rather in what Gide once defined as '[leur] force d'opposition'[1] or what Sartre in *Qu'est-ce que la littérature?* called 'l'action par dévoilement'.[2]

Once literature moves from this position to one in which it is consciously being subjected to control and used to carry and even impose a political message or to encourage political action, the whole issue assumes a different focus. As we have seen writers' attitudes vary: Drieu, for example, seems to have been much more aware of the potential danger to his art than, say, Aragon (except in his later years). Certainly in the absence of any formal cultural programme or control on the Right in France, works produced by writers politically inclined in this direction do at least tend to offer a wider variety of subject-matter than their counterparts on the Left. Indeed, as we have already noted, they may at first appear less overtly political than much rigidly programmed left-wing writing. Yet when our attention is turned from subject-matter to the more specific question of the ways in which a political message has been imposed on it a remarkably similar and constant range of techniques and methods becomes apparent.

Albeit to varying degrees, Drieu is as 'guilty' as Nizan, Barrès as Courtade: the appearance of or reference to exemplary political figures; the appeal to the reader's emotional sympathy in order all the more easily to convince him of the validity of a certain political stance; parenthetical insertions and direct authorial interventions; naïve symbolism; the use of the third person singular pronoun to voice under the guise of objective and dispassionate observation the personal views of the writer; the change in tone (often denoted by the use of *ils* or *on*) in order to move from an immediate, private action or event to a more general context; the use of final chapters or scenes to point in unambiguous fashion to the true political moral of the work. Considered in this way the kind of distinction implied by Walter Benjamin's remark made in connection with Marinetti that while Communism may be said to politicize art Fascism aestheticizes politics, is less helpful than it might at first seem to be. While in France literature of left-wing inspiration may on the whole be more easily recognizable and definable than its opposite, it is so only because of its subject-matter. Once we concern ourselves with the question of style it is Lukács' notion of a conservative aesthetic that would seem to be more useful in any overall attempt to assess the quality of these works, for what we find in them is an almost total reliance on and often impoverishment of forms and techniques evolved during the nineteenth century. Whatever its political inspiration, writing of the kind we have been discussing depends essentially on what Barthes, modifying Lukács, has termed the convention of the real. Together with its basic re-creation of an external reality there is in these works an assumption on the part of the writer that what he has to say is alone correct. Yet such an assumption, even if it is made only subconsciously and however subtly it may imbue his style, cannot gurantee political effectiveness. In the last resort what matters is the responsiveness of the reader. Whether he belongs to what George Lehmann has referred to as a 'fairly determinate social group',[3] in which case such literature presumably does little more than reaffirm convictions which he already holds, or whether he is a potential convert, in which case his perceptiveness and sensitivity should be of a high order, are considerations with which writers seem only rarely to have concerned themselves. In more recent years in France there can be little doubt that particularly with the vogue for the new novel, political literature has declined both in importance and quality, and where it has survived as we have seen in the case of Courtade's *La Place rouge* it has run dangerously close to caricature. This is not to say that art and politics or even literature and politics have become mutually exclusive, rather that the medium appears to have changed.

It is true that the essay has in many ways continued the tradition of the late twenties and early thirties (orthodox Marxist pieces like Simone de Beauvoir's *La longue marche, essai sur la Chine* (1957) or the more volatile Régis Debray's *Révolution dans la révolution* (1967) for example); but periodicals like *Tel Quel* and *La Nouvelle Critique* have suggested that the notion of 'littérature engagée' is now outmoded, and that political effectiveness must be sought through their more characteristic preoccupations with psychoanalysis, linguistics and structuralism, while a number of individual writers associated with them, like Philippe Sollers, would argue that the very act of writing itself is a politically revolutionary activity: 'L'écriture est la continuation de la politique par d'autres moyens'.[4]

Foreign culture, too, has not been without its influence, especially in the theatre. Brecht's attempts to create objective distance (*Verfremdungseffekte*) between action and audience in order to encourage the latter to think about and hence act in order to correct social or political injustices, 'happenings' and documentary pieces which also aim at involving members of the audience in a direct and emotional way, thereby forcing them to commit themselves have all made considerable impact.[5] Whatever new developments occur, however, it is unlikely that in France at least they will benefit again from the same kind of political climate as that which existed during the first half of the twentieth century. Furthermore in an age that is becoming increasingly reliant on mass media it seems equally unlikely that the writer will ever again be placed in such a responsible and potentially influential position.

Notes

Introduction

1. See for example 'Reflexions on the works of Nikolai Leskov', and 'The work of art in an age of mechanical reproduction' in *Illuminations*, edited by Hannah Arendt (Collins/Fontana, London, 1973).

2. A. Gide, *L'Immoraliste* (1902) Préface: 'Le public ne pardonne plus, aujourd'hui, que l'auteur, après l'action qu'il peint, ne se déclare pas pour ou contre; bien plus, au cours même du drame on voudrait qu'il prît parti [. . .]. Je ne prétends pas, certes que la neutralité [. . .] soit signe sûr d'un grand esprit; mais je crois que maints grands esprits ont beaucoup répugné à . . . conclure—et que bien poser un problème n'est pas le supposer d'avance résolu.'

3. A. Robbe-Grillet, *Pour un nouveau roman* (Minuit/Gallimard, Paris, 1963), p. 46.

4. *Qu'est-ce que la litterature?* (Gallimard, Paris, 1964, Collection Idées), p. 152. First published by Gallimard in 1948. See too Simone de Beauvoir's criticism of the 'new novelists' who, she maintains, have turned their back on political and social issues and have retreated into 'l'antique tour d'ivoire'. *La Force des choses* (Gallimard, Paris, 1963), p. 650.

5. Preface to the 1904 edition of *Un Homme libre* in the 1966 Plon edition of the trilogy.

6. One of the most instructive imaginative accounts of this period is to be found in Martin du Gard's novel *Jean Barois* (1913).

7. Paul Claudel, Francis Jammes, Gabriel Frizeau, *Correspondance, 1897–1938* (Gallimard, Paris, 1952), pp. 274–5.

8. R. N. Stromberg, 'The intellectuals and the coming of war in 1914', *Journal of European Studies*, vol. III, no. 2, p. 115.

9. George Orwell, *Collected Essays, Journalism and Letters*, Sonia Orwell and Ian Angus (eds.) (Penguin Books, Harmondsworth, 1970), vol. IV, p. 464.

10. Mounier quoted in J. Touchard, *Tendances politiques dans la vie française depuis 1789* (Hachette, Paris, 1960); Lefebvre quoted in N. Racine, 'Une revue d'intellectuels communistes dans les années vingt, *Clarté* (1921–1928)', *Revue française de Science politique* (June, 1967)

p. 497. Curtius quoted in H. Massis, *La Guerre de trente ans* (Plon, Paris, 1940), p. 100.

11. *La Guerre de trente ans*, p. 133.

12. For a discussion of the development of these and other groups see J. Plumyène and R. Lasierra, *Les Fascismes français, 1923–1963* (Editions du Seuil, Paris, 1963).

13. Simone de Beavoir, *Mémoires d'une jeune fille rangée* (Gallimard, Paris, 1958), p. 38; see too Sartre's portrayal of the Fleurier family in 'L'Enfance d'un chef' in *Le Mur* (Paris, 1939).

14. For a discussion of some of these, especially of *Ordre nouveau* and *Esprit* see J.-L. Loubet del Bayle, *Les non-conformistes des années 30* (Editions du Seuil, Paris, 1969).

15. See W. M. Johnston, 'The Origin of the Term "Intellectuals" in French Novels and Essays of the 1890s', *Journal of European Studies*, vol. IV, no. 1, pp. 43–56.

16. *Mort de la pensée bourgeoise* (Grasset, Paris, 1929), p. 51.

17. *Les Chiens de garde* (Maspero, Paris, 1971), p. 26. (First published 1932.)

18. The bourgeoisie had enjoyed considerable stimulus from the work of Georges Sorel, notably his *Réflexions sur la violence* (1908).

19. *Les Chiens de garde*, p. 93; 'ces descendants des vieux prêtres donneurs de sacrements'. See too Georges Politzer's essay *La Fin d'une parade philosophique. Le Bergsonisme* (Paris, 1929).

20. *Ibid.*, p. 30. Cf. *Mort de la pensée bourgeoise*, p. 41: 'Tout ce qu'elle [la philosophie française] enseigne, c'est de ne point prendre parti'.

21. 'Une littérature responsable', *Vendredi*, no. 1 (8 November 1935) reproduced in *Paul Nizan, intellectuel communiste*, vol. I, J.-J. Brochier (ed.) (Maspero, Paris, 1970), pp. 138–40.

22. *Les Mots* (Gallimard, Paris, 1964), p. 211: 'Longtemps j'ai pris ma plume pour une épée: à présent je connais notre impuissance'. See too *Politics and Literature*, translated by J. A. Underwood and John Calder (Calder and Boyers, London, 1973).

23. Cf. George Orwell's remark in 'Why I write', vol. I, p. 28: 'When I sit down to write a book [. . .] I write it because there is some lie that I want to expose, some fact to which I want to draw attention'. See too Simone de Beauvoir, *Pour une morale de l'ambiguïté* (Gallimard, Paris, 1947), p. 113. Page references to Sartre's essay are hereafter included in the text.

24. It is worth noting Sartre's words about 'littérature engagée' in

69

'Présentation des Temps Modernes' reprinted in *Situations* (Gallimard, Paris, 1948), vol. II, p. 30: 'Je rappelle que [. . .] l'engagement ne doit, en aucun cas, faire oublier la *littérature* et que notre préoccupation doit être de servir la littérature en lui infusant un sang nouveau, tout autant que de servir la collectivité en essayant de lui donner la littérature qui lui convient'.

25. That is those who judge a book on its political merits while claiming to do so on its aesthetic qualities.

26. Sartre claims it is not possible: *Qu'est-ce que la littérature?* p. 85, note 3, and 'Entretien avec Kenneth Tynan', *Un théâtre de situations* (Gallimard, Paris, Collection Idées, 1973), p. 159. See too Caute's interesting and instructive account of his (and of a white audience's) reactions to D. W. Griffith's film *The Birth of a Nation*, in *The Illusion* (André Deutsch, London, 1971), pp. 49–55.

27. It is also because these writers have already been the subject of a vast amount of critical attention. Given the focus of my approach (not to mention the limited space available) to offer any more than the most cursory of remarks would be to run the risk of total banality. Readers are referred to the following useful recent studies devoted to these authors: E. Parker, *Albert Camus. The Artist in the Arena* (Wisconsin University Press, Madison and London, 1966); G. Brée, *Camus and Sartre: Crisis and Commitment* (Dell, New York, 1972); D. Lazere, *The Unique Creation of Albert Camus* (Yale University Press, New Haven and London, 1973); D. Boak, *André Malraux* (Clarendon Press, Oxford, 1968); D. Wilkinson, *Malraux. An Essay in Political Criticism* (Harvard University Press, Cambridge, Mass., 1967); J. Lacouture, *André Malraux: Une Vie dans le siècle* (Editions du Seuil, Paris, 1973); P. Thody, *Sartre: A Literary and Political Study* (Hamish Hamilton, London, 1960), G. J. Prince, *Métaphysique et technique dans l'œuvre romanesque de Sartre* (Droz, Geneva, 1967); F. Jeanson, *Sartre dans sa vie* (Editions du Seuil, Paris, 1974); S. Julienne-Caffié, *Simone de Beauvoir* (Gallimard, Paris, 1966); F. Jeanson, *Simone de Beauvoir ou l'entreprise de vivre* (Editions du Seuil, Paris, 1966); J. Morand, *Les idées politiques de Louis-Ferdinand Céline* (Pichon, Paris, 1972). It should also be stressed of course that commitment is not necessarily political. It may have become fashionable to see it as such, but books like John Cruickshank (ed.) *The Novelist as Philosopher* (O.U.P., London, 1962) and Rima Drell Reck, *Literature and Responsibility* (Louisiana State University Press, Baton Rouge, Louisiana, 1969), indicate in an important and useful way the full scope of the subject.

28. Cf. Mao Tse-tung, 'Talk at the Yenan Forum on Literature and Art' (May 1942) in *Quotations from Chairman Mao Tse-tung* (Foreign Languages Press, Peking, 1972), p. 302: 'Works of art which lack artistic quality have no force, however progressive they are politically.'

29. Simone de Beauvoir, for example, was aware of this problem as it concerned her own novel based on the Resistance, *Le Sang des autres* (1945): 'le temps passa; les circonstances changèrent et nos cœurs; ensemble nous défîmes l'œuvre que nous avions ensemble imaginée. Reste un livre dont aujourd'hui les défauts sautent aux yeux.' *La Force des choses* (Gallimard, Paris, 1963), p. 50.

30. *Politics and the Novel* (Horizon Press, New York, 1955), p. 20.

Chapter One

1. See for example: R. Rémond, *La Droite en France de la première Restauration à la Ve Republique* (Aubier, Paris, 1954); E. Weber, *Varieties of Fascism* (Van Nostrand, Princeton, 1964) and *Action Française* (Stanford University Press, 1962); J. Plumyène and R. Lasierra, *Les Fascismes français 1923–1963* (Editions du Seuil, Paris, 1963). For the ways in which fascist ideas are projected through literature see in particular P. Sérant, *Le Romantisme fasciste* (Fasquelle, Paris, 1959); P. Vandromme, *La Droite buissonnière* (Les Sept Couleurs, Paris, 1960); T. Kunnas, *Drieu la Rochelle, Céline, Brasillach et la tentation fasciste* (Les Sept Couleurs, Paris, 1972). A. Hamilton, *The Appeal of Fascism* (Blond, London, 1971) (Section Three: 'France').

2. 'The Nature of Fascism in France', *Journal of Contemporary History*, vol. I, no. 1 (1966), p. 28.

3. 'The *Action Française* in French intellectual life', *The Historical Journal*, vol. XII, no. 2 (1969), pp. 328–50.

4. S. Wilson, p. 334. Cf. E. Weber, *Action Française*, pp. 183–4.

5. *La Grande Revue*, March 1934, quoted in Plumyène and Lasierra, p. 93.

6. Drieu la Rochelle, *Socialisme fasciste* (Gallimard, Paris, 1934), p. 111: 'Horrible, de se promener dans les rues et de rencontrer tant de déchéances, de laideurs, ou d'inachèvements. Ces dos voûtés, ces épaules tombantes, ces ventres gonflés, ces petites cuisses, ces faces veules'. Bertrand de Jouvenal, *L'Emancipation nationale* (16 January 1937), quoted in Plumyène and Lasierra, p. 131: 'La France appartient aux pantouflards. Dans la France de demain tout sera aux hommes d'action, rien aux ruminants'. See too P. Sérant, *Le Romantisme fasciste*, chapter I.

7. Brasillach accused the older man of writing about Germany 'avec un respect religieux, devant tout ce que représentent l'Allemagne et l'hitlérisme'. Quoted in B. George, *Brasillach* (Editions Universitaires, Paris, 1968), p. 100.

8. *Introduction à l'histoire de la littérature 'fasciste'* (Paris, 1943), quoted in Sérant, p. 11.

9. 'The Inheritors of Maurice Barrès', *Modern Language Review*, vol. 64, no. 3, July 1969, pp. 529–45. An interesting account of a personal reaction is to be found in Montherlant's three essays on Barrès in *Aux Fontaines du désir* (1927) in which he moves from admiration to scorn. A great deal has been written about Barrès. Studies include J.-M. Domenach, *Barrès par lui-même* (Editions du Seuil, Paris, 1954); J. Madaule, *Le Nationalisme de Maurice Barrès* (Sagittaire, Marseille, 1943); P. Ouston, *The Imagination of Maurice Barrès* (Toronto University Press, 1974); R. Soucy, *Fascism in France: the case of Maurice Barrès* (University of California Press, Berkeley, 1972).

10. See for example *Mes Cahiers*, vols. II, p. 177; VII, p. 275; IX, p. 73.

11. *Ibid.*, vol. XIV, p. 199.

12. *Scènes et doctrines du nationalisme* (Plon, Paris, 1902): 'Nous ne sommes pas des maîtres des pensées qui naissent en nous'.

13. The text is that of the 1909 edition published by the Librairie Félix Juven. Page references are given in the text.

14. P. 74: 'Espacées de cinquante ans sur une même tradition, la grand'mère et la petite fille résonnaient des mêmes chocs'.

15. Barrès writes this section of the novel (pp. 166–76) in the form of a debate.

16. 'Dédicace', p. vi: 'la volonté de ne pas subir, la volonté de n'accepter que ce qui accorde avec leur sentiment intérieur'.

17. The most objective assessments of Drieu to have appeared to date are the books by Frédéric Grover, *Drieu la Rochelle and the Fiction of Testimony* (California University Press, Los Angeles, 1958); *Drieu la Rochelle* (Gallimard, Paris, 1962). A brief but balanced account of his life is to be found in *Pierre Drieu la Rochelle: Secret Journal and other writings*, translated and with an Introduction by Alistair Hamilton (River Press, Cambridge, 1973), pp. vii–xlii.

18. *Socialisme fasciste*, p. 199: 'dès maintenant, la méditation sur un thème nationaliste ne peut plus se faire que dans un cadre européen, même mondial'. Cf. *Mesure de la France* (Grasset, Paris, 1922), p. 92.

19. *Socialisme fasciste*, p. 110.

20. See, for example, *Mesure de la France*, pp. 132–3; *Le Jeune Européen* (Gallimard, Paris, 1967), p. 56; 'Restauration du corps' in *Interrogation* (Gallimard, Paris, 1917).

21. *Chronique politique, 1934–1942* (Gallimard, Paris, 1943), p. 54: 'Doriot, le bon athlète [. . .] qui étreint ce corps débilité [France] et qui lui insuffle la santé dont il est plein'.

22. *Sur les écrivains* (Gallimard, Paris, 1964), p. 79.

23. Preface to *Gilles* written in 1942.

24. *Sur les écrivains*, p. 131.

25. References are to the *livre de poche* edition.

26. References are to the *livre de poche* edition.

27. *Drieu la Rochelle and the Fiction of Testimony*, p. 179.

28. *Ibid.*, p. 364.

29. See Sartre's essay, 'M. François Mauriac et la liberté', *Situations* (Gallimard, Paris, 1947), vol. I, pp. 36–57.

30. Attempts to correct this view have resulted in a number of works that are distinctly apologetic in tone. In addition to the discussion of Brasillach in Kunnas' book the most balanced attempt to date is to be found in B. George, *Brasillach* (Editions Universitaires, Paris, 1968).

31. 'Politics and aesthetics: the Fascism of Robert Brasillach', *The Western Political Quarterly* (February 1965), p. 613.

32. References are to the *livre de poche* edition.

33. Compare these descriptions and reactions with Brasillach's own in *Notre avant-guerre* (Plon, Paris, 1941).

34. E.g. p. 187: 'Tu n'es pas faite pour cette maison. Tu es faite pour la demeure solide de pierres, pour le feu de bûches accolées dans la cheminée, pour le lit large et bas, pour la table et pour la lampe.'

35. Cf. Drieu's assumption that women are naturally attracted to physically strong men. 'Restauration du corps' in *Interrogation*.

36. Cf. p. 253: 'ce blessé qui ressuscitera'.

37. *Œuvres complètes* (Club de l'Honnête Homme, Paris, 1963), vol. v, p. 597.

Chapter Two

1. For an analysis of the history of the French Communist Party see for example J. Fauvet, *Histoire du Parti Communiste Français* (Fayard, Paris, 1964); A. Kriegel, *Les Communistes Français* (Editions du Seuil, Paris, 1968); R. Tiersky, *Le Mouvement communiste en France 1920–1972* (Paris, 1973). The relationship between the *P.C.F.* and writers and intellectuals has been explored by: M. Adereth, *Commitment in*

Modern French Literature (Gollancz, London, 1967); J.-P. Bernard, *Le Parti Communiste Français et la Question littéraire, 1921–1939* (Presses Universitaires de Grenoble, 1972); D. Caute, *Communism and the French Intellectuals* (André Deutsch, London, 1964); J.-M. Domenach, 'Le P.C.F. et les intellectuels', *Esprit* (May 1959); J. Touchard, 'Le Parti Communiste Français et les intellectuels', *Revue française de Science politique* (June 1967). See too P. Loffler, *Chronique de la littérature prolétarienne française de 1930 à 1939* (Editions Subervié, Rodez, 1967); M. Ragon, *Histoire de la littérature ouvrière* (Editions Ouvrières, Paris, 1953); *Histoire de la littérature prolétarienne en France* (Albin Michel, Paris, 1964); J. Rühle, *Literature and Revolution* (Pall Mall, London, 1969) (Chapter 24).

2. Quoted in J. Touchard, 'Le Parti Communiste Français et les intellectuels', p. 476.

3. *Populisme* (Paris, 1931), p. 173, quoted in Bernard, p. 21.

4. *Nouvel Age littéraire* (Paris, 1930), p. 42, quoted in Bernard, p. 24.

5. Touchard, 'Le Parti Communiste Français et les Intellectuels'.

6. For a discussion of this issue see in particular R. S. Short, 'The Politics of Surrealism, 1920–36', *Journal of Contemporary History*, vol. I, no. 2, pp. 3–25; H. S. Gershman, *The Surrealist Revolution in France* (Michigan University Press, Ann Arbor, 1969), pp. 80–116; J. H. Matthews 'Surrealism, Politics and Poetry', *Chaos and Form*, ed. K. McRobbie (Mosaic Essay Series, Winnipeg, 1972), pp. 171–82. See too P. Naville, 'La Révolution et les intellectuels' and 'Mieux et moins bien', reprinted in *La Révolution et les intellectuels* (Gallimard, Paris, 1975).

7. Quoted in Sartre, *Qu'est-ce que la littérature?*, p. 225.

8. Bernard, p. 84.

9. 'Je chante la domination violente du Prolétariat sur la bourgeoisie
   pour l'anéantissement de cette bourgeoisie
   pour l'anéantissement total de cette bourgeoisie,'
The poem is quoted in M. Nadeau, *Histoire du Surréalisme* (Paris, 1964), pp. 333–42.

10. Quoted in Bernard, p. 104.

11. H. Swayze, *Political Control of Literature in the USSR, 1946–1959* (Harvard, 1962), quoted in Caute, p. 322.

12. References are to the text of the first edition published in 1916 by Flammarion. Studies of Barbusse's work include A. Vidal, *Henri Barbusse, soldat de la paix* (E.F.R., Paris, 1953); V. Brett, *Henri Barbusse, sa marche vers la clarté, son mouvement Clarté* (Editions de l'Académie

Tchécoslovaque des Sciences, Prague, 1963). See also *Europe* (January 1969), pp. 3–77 and F. Field, *Three French Writers and the Great War* (Cambridge University Press, 1975), pp. 19–78.

13. After the serialization of *Le Feu* in *L'Œuvre* Barbusse had several hundred copies of the book printed without cuts and allowed it to be presented for the Prix Goncourt. 'Il se trouva que l'Académie Goncourt couronna *Le Feu*. La censure, très embarrassée, craignit le scandale et préféra se taire.' Romain Roland, *Journal, 1914–19* (Albin Michel, Paris, 1952), p. 1127.

14. Letter to Annie de Pene quoted in J. Meyer, '*Le Feu* d'Henri Barbusse', *Europe* (January 1969), p. 31.

15. One of Barbusse's most loyal admirers was Céline whose attempts to convey the total horror of war in *Voyage au bout de la nuit* (1932) is a good example of what he termed 'le "rendu émotif" par les mots'. Letter to M. Hindus, 11 June 1947 in *Les Cahiers de l'Herne*, no. 5 (Paris, 1965), p. 78.

16. It is of course significant that with the exception of Bertrand officers are either ignored altogether or attacked by the soldiers for their incompetence.

17. *Une heure avec Frédéric Lefevre* (N.R.F., Paris, 1925), p. 181. Cf. his aim, stated in his *Manifeste aux intellectuels* (Les Ecrivains réunis, Paris, 1927), to bring about 'l'éclosion d'un art collectif'.

18. *Pour un réalisme socialiste* (Denoël et Steele, Paris, 1935), p. 53.

19. Quoted in B. Lecherbonnier, *Aragon* (Bordas, Paris, 1971), p. 220, note 1. Cf. *Pour un réalisme socialiste*, pp. 56–7: 'Une littérature vraiment sociale [. . .] naît des hommes, de la réalité sociale'.

20. Quoted in R. Garaudy, *L'Itinéraire d'Aragon* (Gallimard, Paris, 1961), p. 320.

21. References are to the *livre de poche* edition of the text.

22. Lecherbonnier, p. 79.

23. Garaudy, p. 371. See too Adereth's view (p. 181) that Clara must be seen as the 'positive' heroine of the novel by contrast with Catherine who has prepared the way for her appearance.

24. *Malraux, Sartre, and Aragon as Political Novelists* (University of Florida Monographs, No. 17, 1964). See too Rima Drell Reck, *Literature and Responsibility* (Louisiana State University Press, Baton Rouge, 1969), pp. 231–2 and p. 246.

25. *Entretiens avec Francis Crémieux* (Gallimard, Paris, 1964), p. 15.

26. Bernard, p. 137; J. Leiner, *Le Destin littéraire de Paul Nizan* (Klincksieck, Paris, 1970). In addition to these and W. D. Redfern's

book mentioned below, studies of Nizan include A. Ginsbourg, *Nizan* (Editions Universitaires, Paris, 1966); J.-J. Brochier, *Paul Nizan: intellectuel communiste* (Maspero, Paris, 1967); J.-P. Sartre, 'Paul Nizan', *Situations* (Paris, 1964), vol. IV; see S. Suleiman, 'Pour une poétique du roman à thèse: l'exemple de Nizan', *Critique*, vol. 30, no. 330, November 1974, pp. 995–1021.

27. Quoted in Leiner, p. 149.

28. References are to the Gallimard edition of the text published in 1968.

29. W. D. Redfern, *Paul Nizan, Committed Literature in a Conspiratorial World* (Princeton University Press, 1972), p. 125.

30. Albert too is passive and believes that he has become the victim of circumstances beyond his control: 'Mais toute la vie d'un homme est un engrenage où il est pris quand il naît' (p. 77).

31. For an account of the attack on Nizan carried out after his death see for example, Brochier, pp. 13–17; Ginsbourg, pp. 84–106; Redfern, Chapter Six. The character Brunet in Sartre's *Les Chemins de la liberté* is modelled on Nizan.

Chapter Three

1. Caute, *Communism and the French Intellectuals*, p. 327.

2. L. Casanova, *Le Parti communiste, les intellectuels et la nation* (Editions de la Nouvelle Critique, Paris, 1949), p. 119. Cf. p. 141. 'Sa foi dans l'avenir, dans la justice de notre cause, continuera d'animer les millions de communistes qui luttent partout dans le monde pour le bien de leurs peuples et la paix des hommes libres'. Zdhanov's works were first translated into French in 1948.

3. *Ibid.*, p. 59.

4. *Ecrits intimes* (Gallimard, Paris, 1968), p. 304. Studies of Vailland include F. Bott, *Les Saisons de Roger Vailland* (Grasset, Paris, 1969); J. E. Flower, *Roger Vailland. The Man and his Masks* (Hodder and Stoughton, London, 1975); M. Picard, *Libertinage et tragique dans l'œuvre de Roger Vailland* (Hachette, Paris, 1972); J. Recanati, *Esquisse pour la psychanalyse d'un libertin. Roger Vailland* (Buchet-Chastel, Paris, 1971). See too a special number of *Entretiens*, (ed. M. Chaleil) (June 1970).

5. *Le Colonel Foster plaidera coupable*, *Œuvres complètes* (Editions Rencontre, Paris, 1967), vol. IV, Act I, Scene II, p. 194.

6. *Op. cit.*, *Œuvres complètes*, vol. V, p. 190.

7. References are to the *livre de poche* edition.

8. References are to the 10/18 edition.

Conclusion

1. *Retour de l'URSS* (Gallimard, Paris, 1936), p. 79.

2. *Op. cit.*, p. 30.

3. 'The Writer as Canary', *Journal of Contemporary History*, Vol. 2, No. 2, April 1967, p. 22.

4. Quoted in S. Heath, *The Nouveau Roman: A Study in the Practice of Writing* (Elek Books, London, 1972), p. 242.

5. See for example Sartre's lecture 'Mythe et Réalité du théâtre' given at Bonn, 4 December 1966, and reproduced in *Un théâtre de situations* (Gallimard, Paris, 1973).

Acknowledgments

Thanks are due to the following publishers for permission to reproduce copyright material:

Editions Gallimard: Simone de Beauvoir (*Mémoires d'une jeune fille rangée*); Paul Nizan (*Le Cheval de Troie*); Pierre Drieu la Rochelle (*Gilles, Interrogation, Fond de Cantine*).
Librairie Ernest Flammarion: Henri Barbusse (*Le Feu*).

WRITERS AND POLITICS
IN MODERN GERMANY

Foreword

The term 'political literature' like 'committed literature' with which it is frequently associated has become an accepted part of the language of literary history. Yet however convenient, it is, on examination, surprisingly imprecise and misleading. The whole area of the interaction between politics and literature is a vast and complex one which has yet, especially on a European scale, to be fully and comprehensively charted. Certainly invaluable contributions do already exist: Jean-Paul Sartre's *Qu'est-ce que la littérature?* (1947), George Woodcock's *The Writer and Politics* (1948), Jürgen Rühle's *Literatur und Revolution* (1960), Irving Howe's *Politics and the Novel* (1961), John Mander's *The Writer and Commitment* (1961) for example. There are, too, as the bibliographical information contained in the individual essays in this series will reveal, a number of equally important books which deal with the issue in purely national terms. With few exceptions, however, these, like many of the more general studies, suffer from the same defects resulting in the main from a failure to distinguish adequately between 'political literature' and what might be termed 'social literature', and from an incomplete assessment of changes both in political climates and in the writer's relationship to society as a whole. Yet, even when the area of investigation and terminology has been more carefully ascertained, we often find that these books are principally concerned either with an examination of the political ideas *per se* contained in various works of literature, or with an assessment of the ways in which parties and movements have controlled and used to best advantage writers and intellectuals who claim political allegiance. More recently Roland Barthes in *Le Degré Zéro de l'écriture* (1967), George Steiner in *Language and Silence* (1967) and David Caute in *Illusion* (1971) have suggested a wider perspective, outlining some of the problems of style and form which an imaginative writer has to face when he offers his pen to a political (or social) cause. On the whole, however, it is fair to say that the majority of critics have concentrated more on *what* ideas are expressed than on *how* they have been. In addition therefore to attempting to define the concept of political literature more precisely and to exploring such issues as the suitability of imaginative literature as a vehicle for political ideas or the effect such literature

can have on the public for example, one of the principal concerns of these essays is to attempt to examine ways in which an author's political sympathy or affiliation can be seen to affect or even dictate the way in which he writes. In some countries—in Russia, France or Spain, for example—direct influence of this kind is more apparent than in others. Elsewhere, notably in Britain, where political directives concerning art and literature have not been the rule, the problem is in some ways more difficult to assess. Indeed national variation of this kind is one of the principal contributory factors to the complex nature of the whole question. Thus while the subject is best illustrated and examined in the literature of France and Germany during the interwar years, it is after the Second World War that it fully emerges in the works of Italian and Scandinavian writers. Furthermore literary experiment seen and approved in some countries as an expression of a progressive, even revolutionary, political position is considered in others to be characteristic of subversion and decadence.

Given such problems as these and given too the amount of space available, these seven small volumes can do little more than hope to encourage a new approach to political literature. While free to explore the subject in the way they believe to be most useful within the context of the literary history of their particular countries, contributors have been encouraged to balance general comment with examination of specific examples. Inevitably therefore the essays appear arbitrarily selective. But like the literature which they choose to examine it is hoped that they will be judged not only for what they contain but also for the ways in which they deal with it.

John Flower

General Bibliography

The following are a selection of those books which discuss some of the general problems associated with this subject. Suggestions for further reading are contained in the notes to individual essays.

BARTHES, Roland, *Le Degré Zéro de l'écriture*, Editions du Seuil, Paris, 1953 (Translated: *Writing Degree Zero*, Cape, London, 1967).

CAUTE, David, *Illusion: An Essay on Politics, Theatre and the Novel*, Deutsch, London, 1971.

CROSSMAN, Richard, *The God that Failed: Six Studies in Communism*, Hamish Hamilton, London, 1950.

HOWE, Irving, *Politics and the Novel*, Horizon Press, New York, 1955.

MANDER, John, *The Writer and Commitment*, Secker & Warburg, London, 1961.

MUIR, Edwin, *Essays on Literature and Society*, Hogarth Press, London, 1965.

PANICHAS, George A. (ed.), *The Politics of Twentieth-Century Novelists*, Crowell, New York, 1974.

RÜHLE ,Jürgen, *Literatur und Revolution*, Kiepenheuer & Witsch, 1960 (Translated: *Literature and Revolution*, Pall Mall, London, 1969).

SARTRE, Jean-Paul, *Qu'est-ce que la littérature?* Gallimard, Paris, 1948 (Translated: *What is Literature?* Methuen, London, 1951).

STEINER, George, *Language and Silence: Essays and Notes, 1958–66*, Faber, London, 1967.

TROTSKY, Leon, *Literature and Revolution*, University of Michigan Press, Ann Arbor, 1960.

WINEGARTEN, Renee, *Writers and Revolution: the fatal lure of action*, Franklin Watts, New York, 1974.

WOODCOCK, George, *The Writer and Politics*, The Porcupine Press, London, 1948.

Contents

'. . . a human situation is characterizable only when one has also taken into account those conceptions which the participants have of it, how they experience their tensions in this situation and how they react to the tensions so conceived.'

Karl Mannheim

Preface

The history of political literature in Germany has yet to be written. What follows is a contribution to the story of literary commitment in our century. But I have restricted the scope of my enquiry still further, to the years 1918 to 1945. This decision was only in part dictated by lack of space. It is my belief that the development of political writing in Germany since the Second World War has not fundamentally altered the issues in debate or the lines along which the aesthetic battle has been fought. Of course certain techniques have been refined. But others such as socialist realism or *Heimatdichtung* stubbornly survive in their respective halves of Germany. Something akin to the 'internal emigration' of the Nazi era has emerged in the lyrical poetry and allegorical prose of the GDR, while in the Federal Republic the debate about 'proletarian literature' has progressed little since the last years of Weimar, except that the tables have been turned on the Zhdanovites and the disciples of Tolstoy. If overt fascists no longer enjoy a hearing among the intellectuals, the argument between conservatism and radicalism, between *l'art pour l'art* and commitment, continues unabated, with all the sterility of reiterated ideological prejudices. And the homeless centre-left still finds itself in no-man's land, a third force of perpetual opposition, preserving its integrity but apparently condemned to impotence or to being modishly patronized.

Yet some things clearly have changed, above all the writer's relationship with his public. In the Weimar period intellectuals on all sides enjoyed a rare *rapport* with their audience and a firm sense of their own 'representative' position, of their allegiance to a particular social group or class whose values and interests they were pledged to articulate. The growing awareness that a decisive ideological and political battle was impending helped to simplify the issues and to justify commitment. The prestige of the intelligentsia inspired them with confidence in their ability to have a direct and immediate impact upon the course of events. Since then Hitler, Stalin and the development of Western society have between them reduced this confidence to a mere shadow of its former self. The issues have grown labyrinthine in their complexity. Ambiguity and irony seem more reliable lode-stars than faith. Pessimism is our

3

birthright. We can no longer delude ourselves into believing that ideology can cure our ills. In many respects the post-war debate about commitment in literature came to an end with the Cold War. The political function of the writer is now seen as something far more modest and more fundamental than was once the case—the liberating of language itself from corruption and manipulation, not for the sake of aesthetic purity, but in the interests of social man. Thus I return to my starting point: the Weimar Republic and the Third Reich offer a paradigm of German political writing in our century, intensified, concentrated, exaggerated even, but exemplary in its range of possibilities. Where the nature of post-war commitment diverges from it, we find a systematic narrowing-down rather than an amplification of its erstwhile hopes and methods.

Within the period 1918–45 I have again had to be selective for purely practical reasons. In an attempt to combine a sense of context and perspective with the particular detail of the individual work, I have provided in each section a general impression of the literature associated with my various themes, followed by a closer look at representative examples. The choice of examples is based on their significance in the intellectual or political climate of their time, as attested by debate or controversy; or on their sales figures, a criterion which may be debatable as an indication of literary value but at least suggests a documentary interest and a potential political importance. Occasionally I have relied on my own subjective judgement in selecting works to complement the alternatives suggested by the first two criteria. I have kept biographical information down to a minimum and have dealt very selectively with Bertolt Brecht and Thomas Mann whose careers and achievements are familiar far beyond the purview of German literary historians. Moreover I have deliberately omitted Austrian writers from the present study, since I have already dealt with them in an earlier book, *The Broken Eagle* (London, 1974). There the reader will find discussions of Hugo von Hofmannsthal, Karl Kraus and Joseph Roth, among others, which are also relevant to the current theme.

A major part of my task I saw as the attempt to piece together a coherent pattern of development, and to make available the conclusions of more detailed studies of particular authors and situations. There is thus a strong synoptic bias in my account. I have tried to balance the discussion of theme and subject with a commentary on formal techniques and language, whenever the latter seemed to warrant attention. But since it is in the nature of committed literature to stress content at the expense of aesthetics, the reader will inevitably discover a predominance of interpretation over formal analysis. A 'close reading' of the conventional is a sure recipe for boredom. I have borne in mind the needs of fellow Germanists whose interests have not yet extended to this field of enquiry; and the needs of those students of the subject whose knowledge is based on the literature of other nations. May the former forgive me for often stating the obvious, and the latter for sometimes not being explicit enough. But may they both find here something of interest.

Acknowledgments

In a study as wide-ranging as this it would be invidious to record every single debt. The works listed in the footnotes to my general sections will give some idea of the intellectual sources on which I have drawn. I am also grateful for the often unwitting co-operation of colleagues and students who participated in discussions on these topics. My original interest in the subject dates back to a seminar on twentieth-century German literature given by Professor J. P. Stern at Cambridge in the early sixties. No mere acknowledgment can convey the measure of my indebtedness to him.

Introduction

The Apolitical Tradition

The problematic relationship between spirit and power, right and might is a thread which runs through German intellectual history from the eighteenth century onwards. What has come to be known as the peculiarly 'non-political' quality of the German tradition implies not so much apathy or lack of insight—though these often accompany it— as a fundamental scepticism with regard to the meaning and value of political activity.[1] To be non-political in this sense is to believe that politics has no bearing on the essential areas of human experience, that it is a peripheral affair of concern only to the politicians. This attitude initially produces indifference or contempt towards the political sphere. But under the pressure of events it produces an allied pheno- menon: the justification of political power by reference to spiritual, metaphysical or moral principles—what Alfred Döblin once called 'den Kurzschluss in die Mystik'.[2] A tradition which begins by devaluing political activity ends by participating in it on wholly false assumptions. Instead of seeing politics as the art of acquiring and exercising power, or as an area of practical arrangements in an imperfect world, the non- political mind ignores the mundane criteria of political realism and insists upon transforming the political struggle into a conflict of spiritual principle. From being viewed as the sordid squabbling and manoeuvring of inferior men, politics becomes the arena of world-historical individ- uals, the preserve of the national leader or of a ruling elite. Politics is now seen as a matter of statesmanship and foreign policy, while internal party politicking continues to be treated with contempt. Though the hypostasization of political issues is a familiar feature of other nations at certain points in their history, what is characteristic of Germany is the way in which this process becomes a substitute for the political emancipation of the bourgeoisie.

The non-political tradition was rooted in philosophical Idealism and the social and political conditions of the eighteenth century.[3] The individualism of Kant, Goethe, Humboldt or Schiller had encouraged

7

withdrawal, indifference, contempt and withal acquiescence in the *status quo*. The collectivism of the Romantics, however, produced a witches' brew of mysticism and economics, *Realpolitik* and ethical imperatives, nationalism and spirituality. The individualist strand of Idealism predominated while the class which espoused it was not yet confident enough of its ability to win political power. The collectivist strand predominated when the bourgeoisie grew more conscious of its political importance but chose to ally itself with the old ruling class in the face of pressures from a foreign enemy or from 'the enemy within', the organized working class. Admittedly the period between 1830 and 1848 saw determined attempts to establish another alternative.[4] Liberal and socialist writers applied the methods of rational analysis to their society; they acknowledged the necessary link between the individual and society but argued the case for a critical, dissenting intelligentsia or even ideologically committed literature. The *Jung-Deutschland* Liberals, however, if not Idealists, were still victims of the non-political tradition. In their inexperience and intellectualism, their subjectivism and naïve rationalism, they showed themselves far less interested in social problems than in literary freedom and personal emancipation. Their 'aestheticism' was rejected by the ideological socialists of the 1840s, who renounced creativity in favour of rhetorical didacticism. Heine was the only major imaginative writer who straddled both these literary generations and whose unashamed subjectivism went hand in hand with a perceptive, undogmatic concern for social and political realities. But there was no place for such a voice in Germany either then or later.

The *débâcle* of 1848, when even the Liberals showed themselves attached to class interests and national ambitions, ensured the survival of the authoritarian state. In the years between the abortive revolution and the unification of Germany, many former Liberals escaped into the Idealist tradition; they repudiated *Realpolitik* but allowed Bismarck to pursue it unhindered, provided the state did not interfere with their ability to cultivate the inner life of culture, learning, pure philosophy, the arts and other creations of the spirit.[5] But some intellectuals, like Treitschke, justified Bismarck's policies in spiritual or ethical terms, as the Romantics had glorified feudal absolutism before them, while the National Liberals followed suit on a more mundane level. The crowning success of 1871, the foundation of the German Empire, reinforced these tendencies. The result was not merely an unpalatable idealization of the existing state and its imperial ambitions (following Hegel), but the distraction of educated opinion away from the concrete problems of

8

industrialization and urbanization to hazy notions of the German 'mission' or the vindication of the German 'spirit'. A bourgeoisie dominated by the military and the bureaucracy, uncertain of its own values and deprived of an effective public voice, sought in national aggrandizement a substitute for the rational modernization of its own society.

As Sombart pointed out, the intellectual, confronted by the alternatives of conformism or futile opposition, often turned his back on politics altogether.[6] Wilhelmine Germany can display few commentators with the lucid scepticism and critical irony of the later Fontane, or with the satirical wit of Heinrich Mann. Naturalist descriptions of working-class misery were characterized by a doctrinaire determinism, as contemporary socialist critics were quick to complain. The George circle provided a focal point for the cult of aestheticism and an elitist indifference to politics. When Stefan George proceeded in the early years of the century to formulate an ideal of social hierarchy and charismatic leadership, of heroism and brotherhood, his poetry was remote from concrete realities, yet coincided with the general aura of Wilhelmine authoritarianism.[7] He provides a classic example of the wrong sort of fusion between *Geist* and *Macht*, of power sanctioned by dedication and service to values that derive from a transcendent authority. He was devoted to spiritual and cultural renewal, but by 1914 he was calling for a holy war to purge the sins of liberal materialism and individualism, like the *völkisch* writers before him. In his own rarified idiom George echoed the 'unspoken assumptions' of the age and helped to obscure the real political issues behind a smokescreen of indefinable abstractions.

The wave of national fervour which surged through German society as through much of Europe in August 1914 bore the vast majority of intellectuals along with it. Their impassioned discovery of patriotic feeling stemmed paradoxically from their widespread alienation from politics in the preceding years.[8] Welcomed in from the cold, they rejoined the community of the nation with the fervour of the proselyte. But the war experience, which directly affected so many areas of individual existence hitherto kept apart from the public sphere, served only to increase political awareness without providing the opportunity for political responsibility.[9] Censorship and a form of military dictatorship prevented proper political debate. If the cult of totally detached inwardness became virtually impossible, the nature of political involvement was still governed by the Idealist legacy, now mobilized in an assault on liberal-democratic, 'Western' values. Perhaps the most

9

radical—and certainly the most tortuous—disavowal came from the pen of Thomas Mann in his *Betrachtungen eines Unpolitischen*. Somewhat late in the day Mann tried to reaffirm the individualist cult of inwardness, the need for an inviolate private sphere, within the framework of political authoritarianism.

Under Weimar the tragic consequences of political inexperience became clear; a failure to appreciate the true nature of the difficulties besetting the Republic, and an inability to assess the actual possibilities of the situation or to envisage the political forms that idealism was bound to take in practice. This dangerous lack of insight was compounded by an equally perilous moral intransigence which scorned the compromises and manoeuvring of workaday politics and attempted to realize its dreams and visions in all their pristine strength and purity. This intransigence, as Max Weber foresaw during the winter of the Revolution, and as Heine had prophesied many decades earlier, could all too easily topple over into chiliastic zeal which brooked no obstacle or delay.[10]

There can rarely have been an era so productive of political writing and ideological conflict, or so receptive to committed literature as the Weimar years. But the period also demonstrates the limitations of literary commitment. A generation of German writers which plunged into the political arena as no other had done before it, came to realize how helpless they were to control or influence events through their art. The lesson of Weimar and the Third Reich was not only the need for an intellectual attitude that encompassed socio-political issues in a critical fashion, not only the acknowledgement that the claims of commitment and aesthetic freedom are not easily reconciled: it was also the realization that political literature could at best hope only for oblique and indirect results. The ultimate measure of political writing lay less in the extent to which it inspired political action than in the extent to which it shaped human consciousness. That insight, however, implying as it did that *all* literature has a latent political function, sounded the knell of a tradition which for so long had thrived on a particularly insidious form of false consciousness.

Chapter One
The Literature of War

In the first post-war decade, books about the War were neither numerous nor—with one or two notable exceptions—widely read. It was not until after the publication of Remarque's *Im Westen nichts Neues* in 1928 that a spate of war novels, diaries and memoirs poured on to the market. The majority were influenced by the increasingly violent political conflicts of the final years of the Republic and played a role in preparing the public emotionally and intellectually for the appeal of fascism.[1] Books such as Franz Schauwecker's *Aufbruch der Nation*, Werner Beumelburg's *Sperrfeuer um Deutschland* or his *Gruppe Bosemüller*, Hans Zöberlein's *Der Glaube an Deutschland*, Josef Magnus Wehner's *Sieben vor Verdun* and fresh editions of Walter Flex's wartime work *Der Wanderer zwischen beiden Welten* all helped to shape an image of the war experience which had its parallel and extension in the right-wing ideologies of the Weimar period. Though some of these war books were more explicitly political than others, together they created a myth of the *Kriegserlebnis* which estranged a substantial and militant section of the population from the political realities of the Republic. Their point of departure was the banality and lack of authenticity of Wilhelmine Germany, a world of careerism, material greed, irrelevant examinations and deep social divisions. Most of the heroes of these books are sons of well-to-do bourgeois families, educated and idealistic, sickened by the petty cares of the parental world. Through the War they achieve a spiritual liberation, a breakthrough to a more meaningful and mysterious existence. The touchstone of their moral worth is their reaction to the *Materialschlacht*, the battle of attrition. The books avoid reasoned analysis of the causes or consequences of the War; instead they seek to reproduce the experience which the authors have undergone. Thereby, however, they remain in thrall to the experience, completely subject to its emotional impact and incapable of rising above it to view it with critical detachment. At best they transcend it only through nebulous metaphysical speculation. The War often appears as an inevitable decree of Fate. A naïve religiosity informs many of these accounts, absolving the individual from traditional ethical responsibility and transferring the conflict on to a cosmic plane. Yet the Spirit, Law or Idea which the heroes obey cannot be named, nor can the nature of the new world which they anticipate be described. What is fundamentally at stake is the value of self-sacrifice as such, irrespective of the cause in whose name it occurs. When the vague idealistic gloss on that sacrifice became politicized after the War, it took the form of a Messianic nationalism remote from the concrete possibilities of the time. Paradoxically the war writers condemned the ideological abstractions of contemporary politics and felt that their generation could forge a new reality out of the living experience of the War. One of their prominent themes was that of the comradeship of the trenches which afforded the hope of a better society. The 'community' at the front was classless and united. It judged a man not by material possessions or artificial prestige or an accident of birth but by a supreme test of his moral worth. The unique experience of the front line divided it from the civilian world so that it was able to preserve the values of sacrifice and solidarity at a time when the *Volksgemeinschaft* at home was being betrayed by defeatist politicians. And since the Weimar state was a creature of that cowardly treason, the nationalist ex-servicemen pitted themselves determinedly against what they felt to be its gross utilitarianism, its anarchic party divisions, its moral flabbiness or decadence, and its cult of self-interest. There was a conviction that the war generation had shed its blood for the sake of a new future—the regeneration of the *Volk* which was increasingly identified with the rebirth of a strong, united German state. Such was the context in which the nationalist war writers selected and interpreted their material. They wrote not merely to record or to exorcize their experiences but as part of an ideological campaign. After 1933, even if particular authors fell out of favour with the National Socialist regime, their war books often retained the seal of Party approval because it was felt that they stiffened the moral fibre of the nation. (Ernst Jünger's *In Stahlgewittern* was a case in point.) An older book, Edgar Spiegel's *Kriegstagebuch U202* (1916), was reissued during the Third Reich to become a best-seller, while politically acceptable writers such as Ettighofer produced new war books which found an avid market. Together with the novel of peasant life the literature of war was the most frequently mined seam in the literary life of the Third Reich.

1. Ernst Jünger: *In Stahlgewittern* (1920); *Der Kampf als inneres Erlebnis* (1922)

Jünger was one of the earliest and most influential of the German war writers. He speaks not for a generation but for an elite, a select few who were able to face up to the horror of war and seek in it a validation of their existence quite independent of the political goals for which the War was fought. The value of a cause or an idea is measured in Nietzschean terms by the intensity with which its champions defend it, not by any objective criteria, thus rendering on the political level the theme of the 'dear purchase' which one critic deems to be a dominant motif of the greatest literary achievements and the ruling ideology of the age: a salvation whose value is relative to the degree of difficulty, arduousness and hardness that attends it.[2] What Jünger tries to articulate is the impact of war upon his sensibility and the implications of the war experience for post-war society and for the contemporary image of man. He does not attempt to minimize or glorify the carnage; part of his task is to depict it as dispassionately but as graphically as possible, for the horror is a measure of the test which he has to endure.

The elite Jünger describes are superbly trained beasts of prey, embodiments of the will of the nation, a new unique race of death-defying *Landsknechte*, intoxicated by danger and exhibiting a heightened vitality. Jünger invariably speaks of them in phrases redolent of Nietzsche, for they possess the characteristic combination of the Superman—ruthless courage and intelligence, animality and intellectual alertness. The theme of regression to primeval instinct with its echo of the *furor teutonicus* sounds repeatedly in Jünger's description of the psychology of the battlefield. Characteristic of this state is the complete suspension of the rational mind and the conscious will, the transcendence of individuality and a sense of being at one with the chthonic forces of existence. It is a state more akin to the Dionysian world of *The Birth of Tragedy* than to military text-books. The animal aggression, Jünger reminds us, establishes a link with the primitive phase of human culture when man moved in bands through the wilderness, constantly threatened by his environment and driven to defend himself tooth and nail. It is an orgy of the instincts recalling Freud's interpretation of the War as an inevitable deliverance from the repressive taboos of civilization. Jünger's depiction of his elite conjures up a timeless mythic image of the Warrior of whom his storm troops are but the modern embodiments. It follows that warfare is treated not as the outcome of political events but as a law of nature, as basic to human existence as the sexual drive. Jünger, heir to an egregious Social Darwinism, confuses a putative aggressive instinct with its political manipulation, war.

However, Jünger is too immersed in the German intellectual tradition to forgo an Idealist transfiguration of the activities of his predatory beasts. Again and again he reminds us that their victory over self, their manly courage and determination, constitute a *spiritual* triumph. In an apotheosis of violence he describes battle as a sacred ritual, a divine judgment on two opposing ideas (put more crudely, might is right). Courage is an expression of the profound awareness that man embodies eternal, indestructible values, while a brave death demonstrates his inner nobility. The *Landsknechte* are unconscious tools of the *Weltgeist*, men at the front (we are told) are the material which the Hegelian Idea consumes for its own purpose. Invisibly connected with the great streams of vital energy, the soldiers are driven on by a higher will as the potential force of the Idea becomes actual within them. Jünger's metaphors culminate inevitably in the death wish: self-sacrifice for a conviction is man's supreme ethical accomplishment.

Clearly there is a contradiction between Jünger's primitivism, his celebration of animal instinct, and this idealistic gloss. It is difficult to reconcile obedience to a primeval blood lust with fulfilment of a spiritual imperative. Similarly there is a contradiction between the image of the elite as beasts of prey and his anachronistic references to chivalrous values. The sense of an ageless pattern of conflict is at odds with his desire to depict the horrors (and therefore the moral victories) of *this* war as unique and unprecedented. There is an unresolved tension between the reality of the war of attrition and Jünger's emphasis on the decisive importance of human qualities. And there is an uneasy marriage between Jünger's natural elitism and his wish to stress the collective unity of the *Frontgemeinschaft*, the comradeship of the front line. Behind all these, however, a more fundamental paradox can be glimpsed. Jünger's glorification of hardness, courage, and blood-lust, his search for existential validation in the jaws of death, is a desperate attempt to overcome his incipient awareness of futility and meaningless destruction. The last metaphysical activity within the framework of European nihilism is not aestheticism, as Nietzsche maintained, but Jünger's apotheosis of violence—though it might be argued that barbarity arises precisely out of the aestheticization of horror. The mythic image of the Warrior and the hypostasization of his struggle barely shroud that chilling vision of the void which Jünger was vouchsafed in the mud of

Flanders. The fear of chaos and nihilism stalks these early pages despite the defensive barriers of Idealist philosophy. The inner serenity of Idealism has become a rictus of hopelessness on the face of the living dead. To Jünger, as to his great mentor Nietzsche, history appears as a bleak vista of endless power struggles, a *perpetuum mobile*, whose futility and brutality can only be kept at bay through aesthetic trans-figuration and defiant self-affirmation.

Although this is not the place to examine Jünger's career as an influential publicist or to assess his contribution to the ideology of German fascism,[3] his war books clearly raise the question of how the war experience was to inspire a restructuring of society. He felt that the war generation, an elite with a strong group consciousness moulded by common experience, had it in their power to fashion a new social order. The worship of technological production, the presumptuous belief in the power of reason and in the inevitability of progress, the cult of positivism and materialism, the notion that the scientific spirit held the key to true wisdom—these and similar nineteenth-century heresies had been belied and discredited by the War and the unleash-ing of atavistic passions. The War was not the end but the beginning of an age of violence. In the face of such a vision the republican world of the twenties appeared cowardly, vulgar and escapist. The pronounced fatalism with which Jünger had greeted the War as a historical event, his consistent refusal to question or even discuss the political issues at stake, lasted only as long as the authoritarian, hierarchical structure for which he had fought. During the republican years he threw himself into the political fray on the side of the extra-parliamentary opposi-tion.[4]

When one looks at a later ideological statement such as *Die totale Mobilmachung* (1930), one sees that Jünger is still endeavouring to apply the lessons of the War to the contemporary social and political situation. His notion of total mobilization, of the harnessing of every citizen, every area of activity, to the national effort, was the corollary of the age of the masses and of advanced industrial technology, and therefore part of the ineluctable process of history. Jünger has clearly resolved some of the contradictions inherent in his earlier war books in favour of an enthusiastic affirmation of what he deems to be the dominant tendencies of the age. There remains a painful acknowledg-ment that the traditional heroism of the warrior-caste is redundant in an era of democratic rationalization, that the wars of knights, kings and even citizens have ceded to those of the Worker (not the economic class of Marxist definition but the anonymous, socially undifferentiated drone who exists for the purpose of maximum achievement in a totally mobilized society).

Jünger argued that socialism and nationalism were the two great millstones between which the vestiges of the old world were being crushed. They stood for the forces of mass organization, anonymity and conformity, the total eclipse of individualism, and a fetishism of the machine. They would end by destroying even Progress itself—and, with a strong echo of Spengler's *Kulturpessimismus*, Jünger again betrayed that nihilism which had confronted him in the vortex of war. The future, he predicted, would be a 'glacier world' of pain and death: it behove us to prepare for it. His attempt to conceal that icy vista in a fog of high-mindedness fails. The helpless disaffection of the new Caesars cannot identify with any existing social blueprint and their vaunted 'superfluity' of life culminates only in death.

Yet in its very febrile aimlessness this attitude was helping to forge a new reality which would be far removed from its idealistic abstractions. Jünger's concept of total mobilization is fundamentally an attempt to devise a new solution to the problems of modern industrial society as an alternative to Marxism. What in fact emerges is an ideological equivalent of economic rationalization, stamped with the hallmark of fascism. In practice it became the world of Goebbels, Himmler and Speer. When the future finally materialized, Jünger withdrew in disgust from the political scene.

2. Arnold Zweig: *Der Streit um den Sergeanten Grischa* (1927)

Of course, the overtly militarist books did not have the field to themselves. Erich Maria Remarque's *Im Westen nichts Neues* sold far better than any single nationalist war novel. With its insistent theme of a whole generation uprooted, disillusioned and alienated by the War, it touched a profound chord in the hearts of contemporary readers. The hero Paul and his friends repudiate the Wilhelmine world and will remain as alienated from post-war civilian society as Jünger or his fellow radicals. They share with right-wing war literature the sense of regression to a more primitive state of being. But Remarque avoids any ideological extrapolation. The scene in a crater, where Paul, face to face with the Frenchman he has just killed, delivers a rhetorical set-piece on the brotherhood of man, has no practical consequences for him, and even in its formulation of the problem avoids the crux of the matter:

the social conditioning of human behaviour. The curiously illogical, conciliatory manner of Paul's timely death; the emphasis on the discomfiture of authoritarian bullies or on erotic escapades; the banality and sentimentality of the language; the absurd narrative technique involving a first-person narrator who tells his story in the historic present tense yet is dead by the end of the book; the lack of coherence and substance in the character of Paul; the contradiction between his self-conscious crudity or primitivism and his occasional non-committal ripple of humanitarian feeling—all this adds up to a true 'best seller' that confirms and affirms, but does not challenge or elucidate the readers' experience.

Another well-known war book, Ludwig Renn's *Krieg* (1928), consistently excluded any sense of self-pity. It is a laconic and detached account of the infantry war in the West, an example of unpretentious but authentic reportage. Here too the political dimension is absent, except in the rudimentary sense that Renn rejects patriotic clichés or indicates the antipathy of the fighting troops towards the revolutionaries and mutineers in the rear.[5] Hans Carossa's *Rumänisches Tagebuch* (1924) was a far more 'literary' work, full of impressionistic descriptions of sky and landscape, accounts of the author's dreams, and ethical or philosophical reflections. Its interest lies in the manner in which it shows a latter-day Idealist trying to come to terms with the War through a devalued metaphysic of nature. The inherent aestheticism springs from his inability to respond with compassion to the impact of pain, anguish and death. The narrator's sense of inner freedom is bought at the cost of empathy and involvement. It represents an avoidance, rather than a transcendence of experience. A surrogate religiosity bereft of any true object leads not to God, but back into the self. The corruption of the most important ethical precept of Idealism—the Kantian admonition that no man should serve as means to an end—manifests itself in the narrator's readiness to abstract lofty spiritual edification from the suffering of others.[6]

Zweig's novel *Der Streit um den Sergeanten Grischa* differs from the majority of German war books in being set wholly behind the lines. The author is concerned not simply with the impact of the 'storm of steel' on the individual sensibility but with the historical context in which the War was fought. Through the story of an escaped Russian prisoner who is recaptured and sentenced to death, and the people with whom he comes into contact, Zweig sets out to reveal the true social and political motives behind the War and their consequences for ordinary men. His

novel is a document of analysis and protest, bodied forth in the individual characters and their fate.

Though Grischa's death is morally and legally unjustified, the
German High Command is determined to prevent revolutionary and
pacifist ideas from infecting the Army (the year is 1917) and to this end
insists on ruthless disciplinary measures. Grischa's death is a warning
to defeatists, potential deserters or mutineers that the military authorities will deal implacably with any attempted defiance. Furthermore the
machinery of military justice must neither admit a mistake nor exhibit
leniency, for to do so would impair the respect and fear it commands.
However, Grischa is also a pawn in a secondary conflict, the personal
relationship between two German generals—which in turn represents
a power struggle within German society. Schieffenzahn, Commander-
in-Chief and a bourgeois meritocrat, has had throughout his life to
pit his wits against the stupidity and arrogance of higher-born comrades. Confronted with von Lychow, the local divisional commander
who protests against the death-sentence, he sees himself once again face
to face with the old feudal traditions, the narrow-minded *Junkertum*
that is inimical to the new, technologically rationalized society of
Wilhelmine Germany. A class score is settled—and Grischa dies.

The political ambitions of this new Germany are made clear enough.
They involve the acquisition of vast territorial gains in the East. The
German people are predestined to play a role of conquest and world
domination that is only just beginning. But who are the German 'people'?
It is equally clear that these expansionist dreams belong to the ruling
class of militarists and industrialists, and to the bourgeois managers
and civil servants who live comfortably off the misfortunes of others.
There is a parallel between their pursuit of territorial gains and their
social dominance in pre-war Germany; they will rule the new subject
peoples with the ruthless determination which they showed towards the
German working class up to 1914 and especially from that fateful
summer onwards. Thus the machinery of German militarism in which
Grischa is enmeshed is linked to the social structure of a Germany
divided into exploiters and exploited. Instead of the division between
the two nations, the front line and the civilian population at home,
which figures frequently in nationalist war books, Zweig presents us
with a different tension—the social gulf between officers and men, a
leitmotif of German anti-war literature.

Lest the picture appear too simplified, however, Zweig supplies
differentiated portraits of individual members of the officer class in

18

such a way that those who still preserve some vestiges of decency and compassion are seen to be no less imprisoned by the system than Grischa or any other common soldier. Conversely, the theme of working-class solidarity, central to Communist writing, is treated in a realistic fashion. Fellow-feeling cannot break the compulsive hold of discipline and overcome the fear of retaliation. Only in the closing pages of the novel does the theme of comradeship sound a triumphantly sentimental note. The political corollary is then suggested: the working class whose cooperation is essential to the prosecution of modern warfare also have it in their power to bring the War to an end.

The tendentious nature of Zweig's book is not in dispute. What is remarkable, however, is the extensive historical analysis which he manages to integrate into the story of a relatively obscure character, and the objectivity with which he presents a wide spectrum of social allegiance and political opinion. Nowhere is this objectivity more evident than in the portrait of von Lychow, who grows in stature as the novel proceeds, without being able to transcend the limitations of his background.

If the strength of Zweig's novel lies in its depiction of various reactions to Grischa's dilemma with their intermingling of private, social and political factors, its main weakness lies in the portrait of Grischa himself. He is too much the amiable, sympathetic, unwitting victim, too literary a creation altogether for the Russian peasant he is supposed to be. This is well attested in the dream which he has on the eve of his execution and through which he achieves a measure of acquiescence in his death. He sees it as an atonement for the blood he himself has shed earlier in the War as an ordinary soldier. Leaving aside the sophisticated sequence of images and the highly articulate consciousness revealed here, one cannot help querying the propriety of this religious insight in a novel predominantly concerned with political realities. The logic of Grischa's dream is that he deserves to die. But this is at odds with the message of the novel as a whole. Zweig does not distinguish carefully enough between Grischa's subjective religious acceptance of his impending execution and the need to indict the social evil which it epitomizes.

Der Streit um den Sergeanten Grischa remains one of the most sober and wide-ranging of German war novels. It eschews the abstract idealism of the pacifist writing of the Expressionists. It is alive to the suffering of individuals but sets this in a historical context. It succeeds in conveying a poignant sense of the diminishment which Grischa's death inflicts upon his fellows, and intimates the richness and abundant sweetness which life might have held for him. Here at least the realism of the novel does not falter. (Compare the contemptuous abstractions of Jünger, his disparagement and repudiation of compassion and love.)[7] Above all it manages to convey the corruption and inhumanity of a social system which inhibits a man's best instincts and treats individuals as means not ends.

From his combination of social analysis and humanitarian protest Zweig was eventually to move into the Marxist camp. He continued to write in a social-realist mode and slowly completed a whole cycle of novels depicting the First World War as the cataclysm of bourgeois civilization.[8]

Chapter Two

The Literature of Revolution

A. Expressionism

Like the political revolution to which it ran parallel, the literary revolution of Expressionism had its roots in the pre-war period.[1] And like the political upheavals of 1918–19 it was given a decisive impetus by the War. The Russian Revolution of 1917 had little immediate impact on German writers opposed to the Imperial regime but the November Revolution in Germany itself inspired an upsurge of literary commitment. Early Expressionism had, it is true, sometimes produced a poetry of social protest but the commitment of a man like Franz Pfemfert, editor of one of the leading Expressionist periodicals *Die Aktion*, was shared by few members of the younger literary generation before the War. *Die Aktion* kept up its political criticisms during the War within the narrow limits allowed by censorship. The political comment was often implicit and indirect, achieved for instance by the publication of the war poems of serving soldiers or by the reprinting of texts by French and Russian writers that intimated a common experience. From April 1915 Pfemfert regularly published extracts from the press and current publications, demonstrating without comment the inhumanity of the pro-war faction. (No gloss was needed in the context of *Die Aktion* whose editorial values were already familiar.) *Die Aktion* also supplied reports on the course of the Russian Revolution. Another widely circulated Expressionist periodical *Die weissen Blätter* remained mainly literary even after its move to neutral Switzerland in 1916, but it did print occasional anti-war pieces by Leonhard Frank, Becher, Barbusse, Rolland and others. Whereas Pfemfert saw the War as a political event, *Die weissen Blätter* inclined towards a historical fatalism, regarding the War as the inevitable crisis of technological civilization out of which some new world would dawn.

By the end of the War the political activism of the 'rhetorical' Expressionists was gathering momentum. This second phase was relatively homogeneous in its ambitions and techniques. The Expressionists repudiated the bourgeois world of their parents with its ruthless economic doctrine, its obsessive materialism and its aggressive individualism. They threw off the shackles of nineteenth-century determinism, whether sociological or biological, and condemned the shallow rationalism of the old world. They sought to penetrate to the essence of reality and to articulate an intuitive vision of the Idea. They cultivated emotion, intoxication, ecstasy as the means of experiencing noumenal truths and of establishing a link with cosmic forces. Imbued with religious, even Messianic zeal, they created universal patterns of experience and archetypal figures, abandoning psychology for mythic abstractions, the better to release the Spirit from the vessel of the phenomenal world. In all this the Expressionists reveal a curious affinity with the conservative or conservative-revolutionary response to the War such as can be seen in Carossa or Jünger. Where 'rhetorical' Expressionism differs from conservative idealism is in its activist impulse to change the world. Where it contrasts with the national revolutionaries is in its humanist compassion and faith in universal brotherhood, though its religious emotionalism is not without a certain moral ambivalence. Expressionism posits the transformation of the individual soul as a prerequisite of the transformation of human society and accordingly preaches a Tolstoyan gospel of love and peace. Here for the first time German Idealism found itself actively involved in a revolutionary situation.[2] The story of that involvement is also the story of the limitations of the tradition itself when faced with the challenge of social change.

The Expressionist endeavour to unleash a spiritual and moral revolution was accompanied by the exploding of conventional literary forms and techniques. A dynamic vocabulary, a convulsive paratactic syntax in which ideas followed one upon the other without logical connections; rhetorical inversions; repetition and accumulation; the isolation of key words for emphasis; the omission of articles and inflexions; ellipsis and condensation—these were some of the linguistic features manipulated by the Expressionists to sustain a mood of rhapsodic intensity and to assault the emotions of the reader or audience. In the theatre, light and sound effects were exploited to reinforce dream-like (or nightmarish) visions and to impart a breath of infinity; geometric and abstract designs universalized the settings and heightened the emotional impact; and a deliberately 'theatrical', declamatory style of acting aimed at sweeping the audience off its feet, overwhelmed by the power of a spiritual experience. The dramatic structure abandoned along with psychology and dialogue the notion of a plot and a carefully integrated development: the characteristic pattern was a series of almost autonomous scenes, each marking a significant 'station' on the hero's road to sacrifice and fulfilment. Expressionist drama depicted not reality but the image of reality in the mind of the subject.[3] Consequently there was no room for dramatic irony, merely for a series of revelations. In fact the stage was invaded by fundamentally undramatic qualities,[4] conducive not of character portrayal but of typological abstractions, not of dialogue but of declamation, not of action and conflict but of a predetermined irresistible attraction towards the magnetic pole of spirit.

When the Expressionist generation threw itself into political activism, it opted for emotional impact and immediacy both in the genres it favoured and in its relationship with its public. The novel was neglected in favour of poetry, the drama of prophecy and revelation flourished, and public readings vied with little magazines, pamphlets and brochures as the most popular outlet for Messianic fervour. The aesthetic experience was seen as a ritual of conversion and dedication, prior to a direct attack on reality. Expressionist writers did not attempt to argue, define or convince: they launched key words and slogans at their audiences in a bid to suspend rational thought and impart a religious enthusiasm. It has been rightly observed that the core of Expressionist writing, even when it attempted to grapple with social and political issues, remained 'a personal religious transformation'.[5]

In all this the Expressionists anticipated the emotional impulses which would be exploited and manipulated by National Socialism. Their intense willingness for self-sacrifice, their ecstasy in suffering, their powerful sense of community, and their experience of mystical inspiration sprang from a belief in sublime radicalism as an end in itself. Though the circumstances of the religious experience might be questionable and the consequences of these emotions catastrophic, the Messianic drive was self-justifying. There was a danger of the symbolic dramatic action ceding to an appeal for a more literal imitation of the sacrificial mode: Hanns Johst's *Schlageter* (1933), a play commemorating one of the early Nazi 'martyrs', bears the hallmark of its author's Expressionist origins, with its quasi-religious vocabulary of the Passion, a faith unto death, a service which is its own reward, a love which atones for all errors—and its final ecstatic summons to Germany to erupt into a cleansing conflagration. Heyricke's *Neurode* or Richard Euringer's *Deutsche Passion 1933*, featuring the Unknown Soldier as a Christ figure, likewise demonstrate the transition from ethical abstractions to fanatical commitment. The true precedents for this fatal confusion of

23

ethical imperatives, social radicalism and apocalyptic criminality are the millenarian movements of the Middle Ages; its heirs are the myrmidons of the new millennium proclaimed in 1933.[6]

Inevitably the febrile atmosphere of the Expressionist era, the opportunities for self-exposure, the unfocused abstractions and the primacy of feeling encouraged a degeneration into mannerism and emotional cliché. Subjectivism declined all too easily into exhibitionism and self-deification, and this crisis itself became an excuse for endless self-analysis. The conflict between the generations released too much uncontrolled adolescent vitality, while the liberation of poetic form rapidly turned into anarchic licence. As the social world proved intractable to the voice of the Spirit and the emotional intensity was dissipated, Expressionist idealism rallied briefly in an inverted form to bury its old hopes beneath a layer of sadistic cruelty and animal vitalism, and a welter of scatological imagery. But by about 1924 even this satanic impulse was spent, and the murky metaphysics was assimilated to more timely radicalisms.

The 'rhetorical' Expressionists spurned conventional political routine and the existing parties. Their sympathies were with the Left but their idealism tempted them into trying to vault over the area of political organization altogether. Their image of man deliberately erased the influence of social forces to which the individual is subject in the modern world and their utopianism thus amounted to little more than a whistling in the dark. One of the rare instances of an attempt to grapple with particular social problems can be seen in the *Aktivismus* group led by Kurt Hiller whose quixotic blend of social reforms, private obsessions and unabashed elitism met with short shrift from the revolutionary workers of Berlin.[7]

The pattern of enthusiasm and bitter disenchantment that marks Hiller's Activism likewise informs the contemporary trilogy by Georg Kaiser, one of the best known dramatists of his generation. The plays bear the titles *Die Koralle*, *Gas I* and *Gas II*. The action is characteristically remote from the concrete revolutionary situation, while yet presenting symbolic parallels to the crisis of capitalism and the war of attrition, and offering a challenge to create a new Heaven and a new Earth. What is interesting here is not merely the indictment of an inhumane civilization or the acknowledgment that the New Man has been repudiated like the first Messiah; we witness too the helplessness of a reformer who perceives the evils of economic rationalization and alienation without being able to offer any alternative other than 'three acres and a cow' or a withdrawal into inwardness. The dilemma is not Kaiser's alone but that of Expressionist idealism in general. Equally significant is the chiliastic zeal with which the hero of *Gas II* destroys his fellow workers for the good of their souls, casting aside all immediate moral responsibility in his thirst to achieve an untrammelled victory for the principle he represents.

Ernst Toller: *Die Wandlung* (1917–18) and *Masse-Mensch* (1919)

Of all the Expressionist writers Ernst Toller was the one most deeply enmeshed in practical politics.[8] While his early work manifests many of the characteristic features of 'rhetorical' Expressionism, it has the advantage of being moulded by first-hand experience of a revolutionary situation. In November 1918 Toller was one of the intellectuals who played a leading part in the short-lived socialist revolution in Munich (where Gustav Landauer and Erich Mühsam were among his colleagues). Subsequently Toller spent five years in prison for high treason.

His play *Die Wandlung* (written 1917–18), subtitled 'Das Ringen eines Menschen', belongs to the optimistic, enthusiastic phase of Expressionism. It depicts the development of the hero from a confused, alienated outsider to the status of a redeeming prophet. The emphasis lies on his individual purification and spiritual fulfilment—the extension of this into the social world takes place not in a historical situation but in a solipsistic wish-dream. Ushered in by a surrealist attack on the German war machine, the play articulates the vibrant hope of the 'rhetorical' Expressionists that out of the feast of death and horror a regenerated humanity would emerge. A febrile intensity and a breathless sequence of images, nightmarish or transfigured, sustain the drama, which is divided into 'stations' alternating between relatively realistic scenes played front-stage, and shadowy, dream-like inserts enacted at the rear of the stage. The spectral scenes counterpoint Friedrich's experience in the social world, showing the reality beneath the clichés and deceptions of bourgeois civilization.

In the final scene Friedrich delivers a long exhortation, urging that spiritual renewal must precede social upheaval; any change in the social world must be effected in a spirit of love and forgiveness. And he concludes on a note of millennial optimism, with a direct appeal to his audience in the spirit of 'rhetorical' Expressionism. (So too Walter

Hasenclever's *Antigone* (1917) had ended with the heroine's voice calling from the grave to urge prayer, atonement and forgiveness instead of violent retribution.)[9] When (to adapt Friedrich's peroration) the powers that be proved deaf to the 'organ voluntaries' of the masses, when the soldiers turned their swords on the revolution instead of turning them into ploughshares, when the citadels were found to be made of stone not of brittle slack, the Expressionist fervour collapsed. Its influence survived only as an aesthetic and emotional legacy. As Brecht sardonically commented, it freed itself only from grammatical rules, not from the toils of capitalism.[10]

After the defeat of the revolution Toller became a critical socialist whose ethical idealism was tempered by a realistic awareness of the problems and limitations of political activity. His play *Masse-Mensch* records an early stage in this process, when he faces up to the problem of violence and the relationship between means and ends. With memories behind him of the conflict between moderate and extremist revolutionaries in Munich, and having experienced himself the savage retaliation of the reactionary regime, Toller tries to articulate the dilemma and the tragic alternatives facing those who would destroy a corrupt but still powerful social order. The form, the style and the intensity of the play are still characteristic of 'rhetorical' Expressionism. The insight which the play affords, however, goes far beyond the attitudes of most of Toller's Expressionist contemporaries and his own earlier position. Here the conflict is not so much between the old world and the new as between two opposing ideas of change, as embodied in the Woman who clings to her humanist principles, and the anonymous agitator who believes in the necessity for ruthless revolutionary violence. Do the ends justify the means? Is the agitator any better than the system he attempts to destroy? Can the idealist impetus of revolution survive a recourse to violence? Can the established order be defeated in any other way? Can might and right be reconciled? Can future gain be purchased at the price of present loss? The Woman remains true to an idealism which refuses to reduce individuals to means and will not countenance bloodshed for the sake of the cause she believes in. The agitator remains relentlessly pragmatic. There is no compromise, no resolution. The Woman fails to persuade the world to accept her values and can only be effective as a martyr of the revolution she deplored, with the blood of innocent victims on her hands. In order to alleviate the impact of this tragic dilemma, the ending diverts our attention from the issue of political morality to the tentative hope of personal contrition and regeneration, a shift from the political to the religious plane which betokens the failure of Idealism to come to terms with revolutionary activism.

B. Proletarian Literature

One of the major tasks confronting left-wing writers during the Weimar years was the need to develop their own distinctive art forms in the struggle against capitalism and fascism.[11] When in 1925, after a period of fragmentation and disarray among left-wing factions, the German Communist Party emerged as the sole revolutionary alternative to the Social Democrats, it had no official aesthetic doctrine, except in so far as the reviews in the Party newspaper *Die Rote Fahne* had shown a high regard for the bourgeois classics of the eighteenth and nineteenth centuries and a negative attitude towards aesthetic modernism. Indeed the KPD was suspicious of literary activity altogether on the grounds that it was ineffective and superfluous. Writers were welcomed purely as agents of propaganda of the crudest kind, pending the successful revolution which would lay the foundation of a truly proletarian culture. But the translation in 1924 of Lenin's *Party Organisation and Party Literature* and the 'Bolshevization' of the German Party in the mid-twenties did set in train a theoretical discussion of the tasks facing the Communist writer.

The general aims of Communist writing were to create a literature which satisfied the reading needs of the proletariat, revealed to it the truth about capitalist society and reinforced its class consciousness. Such a literature had a paramount didactic purpose: to mobilize the masses for the class struggle, but it also had a cultural aim, the combatting of the conservative, even philistine artistic tastes of the working class as mirrored in its preference for the sentimental trash which poured from the bourgeois presses of Ullstein and Scherl in cheap editions. There remained, however, the basic problem of defining the nature of 'proletarian' literature. Was it something written by or for the working class—or both? Should it employ new forms or merely new subjects—or both? Should it confine itself to the conditions and experience of the proletariat? Or should it take a wider view, retaining a revolutionary perspective on society? What is clear is that by the late twenties 'proletarian' literature was generally thought to be determined not so much by the class origins of the writer as by his philosophical and political commitment. On the other hand, there was still a strong tendency to favour working-class authors. Proletarian writers were seen as the main reservoir of socialist art. Workers were encouraged to try their hand at writing, first through short reports or personal accounts for the Party organs, then progressing to short fictional forms (the 'worker-correspondents' movement sanctioned by Lenin and Sinovjev). Working-class theatre groups were also active, devising their own agitatory material. In 1930 the 'Roter Eine-Mark-Roman' was launched, a series of novels written by working-class authors for the masses and depicting the life of the proletariat in factories, mines, tenements or on the barricades. The first titles included Hans Marchwitza's *Sturm auf Essen*, Klaus Neukrantz's *Barrikaden am Wedding* and Willi Bredel's *Maschinenfabrik N. und K.* Like the fully fledged 'socialist realism' of which these books were harbingers, the ostensible endeavour was 'to gain and make meaningful for literature the area of workaday life which bourgeois realism' had neglected. But the attempt was frustrated from the start by the stereotyped ideological patterns, the predictable, over-simplified evaluations and impoverished clichéd language.[12]

In 1928 a major organizational development occurred with the founding of the *Bund proletarisch-revolutionärer Schriftsteller* to co-ordinate the literary offensive of the KPD. Its programme was based on the Soviet WAPP programme of 1924 and its activities were funded direct from Moscow. Initially it considered the value of progressive bourgeois allies—that is, middle-class intellectuals who had joined the Party or who supported the Communist cause—to lie in their ability to play midwife to the nascent creative talents of the proletariat.

These early attempts to reconcile the demands of agitation, diversion and literary ambition proved disappointing. Johannes R. Becher, as editor of the *Linkskurve*, the official journal of the BPRS, urged writers to turn to pamphleteering as a more useful application of their talents. Other voices indicated the need to evolve a revolutionary aesthetic form corresponding to the revolutionary political message that it was intended to convey. The dramatist Berta Lask argued the case for moving away from the individualism of bourgeois literature towards a sense of the collective; such a change might involve mass dramas, revues and choral recitation. The individual character should be presented not as an autonomous personality but as an exponent of the historical role of his class. (Her own plays, e.g., *Thomas Münzer* [1925] and *Leuna 1921* [1927], depicted events in the history of the working-class movement, using huge casts and epic spectacles under the influence of the *proletkult* and Meyerhold.)[13] In 1930 the 'proletarian novel' was the theme of a radio discussion between the German-speaking Czech Communist F. C. Weiskopf and Kurt Hirschfeld. Weiskopf could do no more than aver that the genre was still in a formative stage. The features it would display included an emphasis on collective action and collective feeling, and the extension of the boundaries of fictional form to include reportage and the chronicle style. The language of the 'proletarian novel' would need to encompass the vocabulary of the political and trade union movement, the vernacular of the cities and the shop-floor. If such suggestions were still little more than crudely tentative, more cogent and forceful ideas were being advanced by Brecht whose 'epic' theatre envisaged a form that broke with nineteenth-century bourgeois drama in order to meet the changing needs of an age of revolution.

By the beginning of the thirties a rift was evident between the 'modernist' writers who were seeking new forms, and the conservatives who were beginning to follow the increasingly intolerant and traditionalist Moscow line. Their dissension illustrated the wider political problem of a German Communist Party which had come to be dominated by Soviet-inspired policies often at odds with conditions in Germany. On the one hand Becher, Andor Gábor, Alfred Kurella and Georg Lukács, the controlling voices in the BPRS and the *Linkskurve*, moved in the direction of socialist realism. On the other hand Brecht, Walter Benjamin, Hanns Eisler and Ernst Bloch advocated more progressive forms. Lukács argued that modernist experiment was the expression of a decadent bourgeoisie. The burden of the radical position was that form was determined by the technical possibilities of communication and reproduction, and by the changing structure and needs of the audience. But Lukács insistently advocated the combination of a Tolstoyan totality and breadth with a Marxist analysis of society. His conservative aesthetic paradoxically abandoned immediate political impact for the sake of a higher task, the creation of the great proletarian work of art. Although Lukács attacked the avant-garde deviationists, he never quite became a proponent of socialist realism as taught by Zhdanov, with its deliberate mixture of description and prescription and its singular lack of objectivity. The critical debate was to continue even after 1933, notably in the public exchange of letters between Lukács and Anna Seghers over the problem of realism, and in the arguments about Expressionism.[14]

Within the KPD it was the conservative line that triumphed. In 1935 the KPD declared the need to mobilize the 'classical' bourgeois heritage

29

in the struggle against fascism. One of the curious results of the conservative victory was that the highly 'bourgeois' and self-consciously modernist novels of Thomas Mann were hailed as prototypes of the new realism, while the aims of Brecht and his associates were denounced as decadent and formalistic. The BPRS ended by advocating a novel of milieu concerned with all the groups and tendencies within the working class and the lower middle class. Such a literature would extend the nineteenth-century realist tradition and was (in theory) to be committed without being crudely didactic. It would reject the idea of a collective literature where the masses themselves became the protagonist, preferring the use of representative individuals. It would avoid the overt intervention of the author or narrator. The conservative line similarly attacked the documentary principle, the use of reportage and all 'naturalism', advocating instead character portrayal and psychological interest. Mimesis triumphed over demonstration, illusion and empathy over cool appraisal, a would-be total view over the instructive singular example.

When one surveys the products of left-wing writing in Germany between the wars, it seems that the only successful importation from the Soviet Union was the idea of agitprop theatre. Here it was a case not of literary achievement but of public rituals designed to confirm and strengthen political resolve. The merits of agitprop lay not in any text, for it aimed at the obliteration of art forms other than the cartoon, the sketch and the poster, but in the collective experience and revolutionary fervour it inspired. It preached to the converted, and bored or infuriated the rest. A significant feature of the Socialist theatre of the twenties was the *Sprechchor* movement. Ernst Toller was among the first dramatists to write choral works for amateur performance—'semi-dramatic compositions with spoken parts for individual voices, groups and full chorus, recited to musical accompaniment'.[15] Toller also wrote for trade-union festivals so-called *Massenfestspiele*, scenarios or pageants that were performed outdoors by enormous casts. Brecht's own *Lehrstücke*, the didactic plays of the late twenties and early thirties, are rooted in this workers' theatre.[16]

The commercial pendant to the workers' pageants, parables, choral works, revues and Marxist morality plays was to be found in the theatre of Erwin Piscator.[17] Piscator too was anxious to find alternatives to the individualist literature of the bourgeoisie. But he was not content merely to depict man in the mass in order to show that an individual fate was shared by thousands. Rather, he set out to reveal the social and economic causes which turned individual conflict into class conflict. Drama, he believed, should reach out beyond the confines of the stage and establish direct links with social reality by documentary methods. Piscator had already presented early agitprop pieces in Berlin with amateur casts. In the mid-twenties he put together two revues, *Revue Roter Rummel* (1924) and *Trotz Alledem!* (1925), which became models for many subsequent agitprop productions. Indeed the revue form replaced the mass spectacles and choral works as the favourite vehicle of workers' theatre groups. This tendency was reinforced by a visit to Germany in 1927 of a Moscow troupe specializing in the 'Living Newspaper' technique. Through music, mime and dance they enacted and interpreted items of current news. In 1929 there were 180 agitprop groups in Germany with a potential audience of three and a half million. The limitations of the agitprop tradition were, of course, its built-in obsolescence.[18]

From 1927 Piscator relinquished agitprop in favour of an attempt to revolutionize the conventional theatre—an attempt in which the technical resources of the stage were to be of supreme importance as befitted the age of technology. Piscator emphasized the economic and social background of the action at the expense of character. He emphasized visual impact over the spoken word. He emphasized mechanics over acting and dialogue, frequently overreaching his resources in the process. He used captions, exposed the stage machinery, utilized narrator figures who commented on events and addressed the audience, introduced film and documentary material. There was no attempt at creating any illusion of reality on stage: events were self-consciously enacted. Props were used to supply information, not to reinforce illusion. Yet Piscator still endeavoured to involve his audience totally in the theatrical experience, therein marking a crucial distinction between his ideas and those of Brecht's 'epic' theatre.

1. Friedrich Wolf: *Die Matrosen von Cattaro* (1930)

Discontent and rebellion in the Imperial Navy had been an important factor in the revolutionary upheavals of 1918. As the War entered its fourth year, sporadic outbursts of unrest heralded the coming storm. During the later Weimar period the sailors who had been savagely punished for their part in the initial unsuccessful mutinies figured in several works by left-wing writers, where they were accorded a martyr's status similar to that given to the *communards* of 1871 or the Russian revolutionaries of 1905. Theodor Plivier's reportage-novel *Des Kaisers Kulis* and Toller's documentary drama *Feuer aus den Kesseln* both dealt with a mutiny in the German fleet in 1917 after which the ringleaders had been shot. Piscator dramatized Plivier's story. And Friedrich Wolf, after a number of social plays, turned for his next subject to the mutiny in the Austro-Hungarian navy at Cattaro early in 1918. Whereas Plivier and Toller were both concerned to attack the system against which the mutineers had rebelled (a system whose spirit survived in nationalist circles) and to commemorate their sacrifice, Wolf went a stage further. His drama sought to teach a lesson by exposing the fatal errors of the naval mutineers and drawing explicit consequences from their defeat. As a writer firmly committed to the KPD line and to the agitatory function of art, Wolf treated his subject in an openly didactic fashion. Plivier, who was not a Party member and was in fact considered an anarchist by the Marxist–Leninists, attempted to reproduce the total wartime experience of the German sailor in the objectivist mode. Toller for his part tried to explain how and why the mutiny occurred and to attack the real offenders. Wolf compressed the underlying causes of the Cattaro revolt into a documentary preface listing the men's grievances as confirmed by an official enquiry of the time. His play opens on the very eve of the mutiny. Not the causes but the results are at the centre of his intention: *Die Matrosen von Cattaro* is an object lesson in Leninist tactics.

2. Anna Seghers: *Die Gefährten* (1932)

It was not easy for the KPD to find writers who could combine a correct ideological attitude with a degree of creative ability. Many of the writers sympathetic to the socialist cause avoided presenting the Party's policies or its activities in a direct fashion. Plivier's account of the German Fleet dealt with figures who were not politically organized. Renn's *Krieg* spurned political discussion altogether. Anna Segher's prize-winning *Aufstand der Fischer von St Barbara* depicted (before she joined the Party) a forlorn rebellion and an almost existentialist hero in a manner far removed from the notion of art as a 'searchlight' or 'weapon'. Brecht, it is true, set out to draw a revolutionary moral from a picture of the Party at work in *Die Massnahme* but thereby failed to satisfy the orthodox Party critics. The majority of his didactic plays are moral parables abstracted from a concrete political situation. Only in one play —his adaptation of Gorki's *The Mother*—did he show the development of a revolutionary consciousness culminating in commitment to the Party (and there he chose a context at several removes from the ideological or tactical debates of the Weimar years). Among the targets of orthodox critics were books in which the workers appeared as a sullen mass, crippled by exploitation and erupting in futile rebellion (e.g., Wolf's novel *Kreatur* of 1926); works which showed the proletariat dependent upon bourgeois leaders for positive direction (e.g., Wolf's play *Kolonne Hund* of 1927); and writers such as Plivier who supported the theory of spontaneous rebellion and misconstrued the role of the Party in its relationship to the workers.[19] Anna Segher's novel *Die Gefährten* which was intended to depict the anti-fascist struggle of a hydra-headed Party in many European countries represented something of an exception in its immediate depiction of the current situation and its stress on Communist organization and agitation. Yet the novel contains significant omissions. There are no discussions of ideology, merely the portrayal of attitudes towards it. There is no critical attempt to get to the bottom of the contemporary position of the Party, but only a series of tributes to the courage and tenacity of those who fight for the cause. And although many of the characters visit the Soviet Union, although several of them live in Germany, there is no analysis of the problems and difficulties facing the Soviet Party or the KPD: in other words the Party in power or the Party in legal opposition within a parliamentary framework. Segher's attention focuses on those countries such as Hungary or Bulgaria where the Party must work clandestinely and where the mere problem of survival obviates the need to consider present tactics or ultimate purposes.

In *Die Gefährten* the novelist attempted to write a fictional work that departed from conventional realism, above all a work which reproduced that sense of collective experience often mentioned as characteristic of the proletarian work of art. The novel is anti-individualist in both its theme and its form. It traces the story of numerous Communist agitators and organizers from the collapse of the Hungarian revolution in 1919 to a point later in the twenties. The scene shifts between Hungary, Poland, Italy, Russia, Germany, Bulgaria, France and China. The novel rarely devotes more than a few pages at a time to any one character before cross-cutting to another. This episodic structure is designed to preserve a sense of the myriad ramifications of Party activity and to inhibit emotional involvement on the part of the reader. In short, it is an attempt to evolve a fictional equivalent to Brecht's 'epic' theatre, albeit perhaps too mechanically conceived. Our attention is

33

firmly fixed on the political attitudes and activities of the characters: personal relationships and emotions impinge upon the novel only in so far as they issue from or affect political behaviour. The theme of forsaking one's family (Matthew x.37) is only one of several religious motifs and images in the story. There is little psychological discrimination between the various characters, while the episodic structure often omits narrative links and explanations of cause and effect. This ellipsis extends even to the style itself, lending it greater tension and imaginative interest than will be the case in Segher's later novels which revert to more conventional techniques of realism.

3. Bertolt Brecht: *Die Massnahme* (1930)

The anti-individualism of Segher's novel, together with the revolutionary didacticism of Wolf's play, are both to the fore in Brecht's drama *Die Massnahme*. It tells of a group of Communist agitators who have just returned from a mission to China and who now explain through a series of re-enactments how they were forced to eliminate a young comrade in order to safeguard the success of their mission. As in Toller's *Masse-Mensch*, the conflict is between the emotional humanitarianism of the individualist and the unremitting logic of the faceless revolutionaries who know no loyalty except to the Party.

The structure of the play is neatly symmetrical. In each episode a preliminary narration introduces the scene and this is rounded off by a brief discussion between the agitators and the tribunal on the moral to be drawn from the preceding incident. The young comrade is criticized for separating *Gefühl* and *Verstand*, for surrendering to righteous indignation, for seeking to preserve his moral integrity and for placing his own emotional fulfilment before the long-term success of the movement. He tries to alleviate present misery or to effect superficial amelioration instead of working determinedly, clandestinely and detachedly for the transformation of the whole system. He cannot—ultimately—bring himself to sacrifice the present for the sake of the future. His reluctance to compromise himself morally, to dissimulate, to lie, to suppress his instinctive compassion will prevent him from ever helping to destroy a system which is itself completely ruthless and unscrupulous.

Commentators on *Die Massnahme* are inclined to reduce the point at issue to the conflict between emotion and reason, and the repugnant political conclusions of the piece. But surely the play indicates that intellect and feeling must be effectively combined if there is to be any real chance of changing a violent and corrupt world. The final lines do not condemn emotion as such: they accord certain productive feelings a proper place in the revolutionary attitude—but also stress the need for adequate understanding of social mechanisms and for infinite patience. Moreover the decision to eliminate the young comrade is neither unfeeling nor taken lightly. '*Furchtbar ist es, zu töten*' are the only words in the text which Brecht italicizes. There is even a gesture of *Freundlichkeit*, that supreme Brechtian virtue, in the comfort they give the young comrade at the end when they cradle his head in their arms. Yet the glib acquiescence arouses suspicion: perhaps the case is too neatly presented, the structure too symmetrical, the language too carefully constructed. By anticipating the audience's reservations and seeking to meet them in advance, by systematically dismissing all logical alternatives to the measures taken, the play impels the critical observer to resent this preemption of his judgment and to take stubborn issue with the arguments put forward, even to the point of defending the ostensibly illogical solution which would be no less credible as a political response to the dilemma. Not until a decade or more later would Brecht's imaginative writing betray the poignant sense of moral diminution occasioned by his assent to violence. Even now he does not seek to glorify violence or to transfer the responsibility to some indefinable metaphysical instance, after the manner of the right-wing radicals. His acceptance of the logic of revolution involved a strenuous effort to face up to the world as it was.

The anti-individualist theme of the play determines its techniques, such as the symbolic use of masks or the collective voice of the control-chorus representing a tribunal of the movement. The agitators (one of them a woman) take it in turns to play the role of the young comrade and to act the parts of all the other characters in the reconstructed scenes, a highly theatrical way of demonstrating that they have no fixed private personalities any more and are completely *disponible*, at the behest of the Party. But this role-playing is also an important element in the technique of 'alienation', the critical distancing of the audience from the dramatic events. Not the characters themselves as individuals but their story (and what we should learn from it) occupy our attention. The task of the 'epic' theatre is not to involve but to demonstrate. Hence the play-within-a-play which presents events at several removes. Hence the analytical discussions at the end of each episode, hence the narration which sets the scene, hence too the use of songs to interrupt the action and comment on the issues involved. Such

35

a structure, together with the impersonal, reflective, stylized language, is designed to encourage cool appraisal and lucid thinking on the part of the audience.

Yet the play does not always maintain this atmosphere of detachment and intellectuality. The almost religious praise of the Party, for example, smacks more of the over-zealous convert than of analytical reason. It is here that the truly 'Stalinist' aspects of the play lie, in the stress on the infallibility of the Party, in the idea of being re-united with the Party by accepting guilt and expiation, in the self-indictment of the sinner, and in the determined avoidance of tragedy through the resolution of all conflicts within the Party—the Party being somehow free from the contradictions and antagonisms that otherwise dominate historical development. Brecht, of course, was not alone in his obeisance. From Ernst Fischer's retrospective account of his own experiences in Moscow in the late thirties, we gain a pertinent insight into the stratagems devised by the intellectual who, for the sake of the cause he passionately believes in, deliberately renounces scepticism, individualism and critical reason in favour of conformity and discipline. Fischer's words are equally applicable to the Brecht of the *Lehrstücke*:

> . . . he is forever calling himself to heel in the name of the collective to which he belongs and yet, in his critical self-assertion, does not belong to fully. His consciousness tells him that he is imperfectly aligned and his conscience reproaches him for it, a conscience that has not been forced upon him but was born of his own free decision, and the more refractory the rebellion of the primary, anarchic self, this irrepressible *no* of the consenting intellectual, the more vehement, out of his self-imposed conformity, will be his defence of discipline—that to him so antipathetic discipline—against insubordination, against the heretic that is himself.[20]

The notion of heresy, like the religious imagery of *Die Massnahme*, hints that the *sacrificium intellectus* was due to more than mere self-discipline. The surrogate creed which Brecht professes in his *Lehrstück* has its parallels with the debased religious longings voiced by Expressionism and later exploited by National Socialism. It is ultimately a question of what Nietzsche had called the 'instinct of weakness', the desperate need for faith, certitude and authoritative guidance, whereby the only kind of self-assertion still felt to be possible is fanatical dedication to a self-proclaimed ideal. (In Brecht's first play *Baal* metaphysical rebellion still had the courage of its anarchic, vitalist convictions.)[21]

After 1933 Brecht's ideas about the relationship between politics and literature grew more complex. His view of human character and its role in drama likewise became less simplified. The technique of *Verfremdung* was further developed and refined. Other things, however, remained constant. Brecht continued to attack bourgeois morality as a weapon in the class war. He never doubted the argument that violence could only be defeated by violence, or that the end justified the means. Even through the worst excesses of Stalinism, both in the Soviet Union and in Ulbricht's Germany—despite the Moscow trials, the Nazi-Soviet pact and the events of 1953 and 1956—he never acknowledged publicly the possibility that the means might corrupt the ends to the extent of rendering them unattainable.

C. Towards the National Revolution

1. Hans Grimm: *Volk ohne Raum* (1926)

The popularity of war literature and *Heimatromane* in the closing years of the Weimar Republic and in the Third Reich has already been mentioned. Perhaps it was because Grimm's novel managed to combine elements of both that it made such a mark on the German reading public. By 1940, despite its enormous bulk, it had sold almost half a million copies.[22] Its interest for us lies in the fact that it provides an illuminating index of the confusions besetting German conservatism in the twenties, of the degeneration of provincial literature into *völkisch* obsessions, and of the relationship between imperialist expansion and petit bourgeois resentment.

Volk ohne Raum is the major novel of German colonialism. It traces the fortunes of Cornelius Friebott from his village in Lower Saxony to the farm lands of German South-West Africa in the years between 1887 and the Weimar Republic. And it attempts to explain all the social and political problems of those years as the product of the lack of *Raum*, or 'living space' as the notion later became familiar.

The novel's criticisms of industrial Germany run parallel to many a socialist analysis and for a time the hero is drawn to the Social Democrats. Yet when it comes to national destiny and a remedy for Germany's ills, it is not socialism that provides Cornelius with his answer. His ideology is based on a belief in the mystic relationship between man and his soil, on the conviction that like the giant of mythology men can be restored to health and vigour through contact with the earth. The economic equivalent is a race of independent farmers tilling their hereditary land. The neglect of the small land-owner and the industrial explosion in the last three decades of the nineteenth century destroyed this relationship in Germany and accounts for the malaise of modern society. The nation is overpopulated and overcrowded. Its young men are forced to emigrate to alien lands and foreign colonies in search of fresh air and opportunity. Adventurous souls, we are told, become criminals because there is no proper outlet for their energies. One out of every three girls remains unmarried, her life blighted. These haphazard and contradictory reflections fall into place when Cornelius comes across a book on the colonial question written by a socialist, Hildebrand. It postulates the primacy of the productive agricultural class over the proletariat and industrial production. It advocates that private ownership of land be upheld and defended. No country, it argues, can afford a population greater than it can feed from its own resources. Since Germany is patently incapable of sustaining its population, it must expand into colonial territories. This simple argument is hammered home repeatedly by Cornelius and other characters and finally by Hans Grimm *in propria persona*.

What the novel therefore propagates is in effect a non-Marxist alternative to the problems of late capitalism, an alternative far more concrete and particular (but also more regressive) than Jünger's typological *Arbeiter* and his concept of total mobilization. Grimm seeks to deliver his compatriots from *Lohnknechtschaft*, from being enslaved by the wage-packet, from alienation, overcrowded slums and wasted lives. His solution is not class conflict and violent revolution but a national expansion which will bring reconciliation of conflicts and freedom from aggression within, while at the same time revolutionizing the quality of national life. (It was an argument rooted in the *völkisch* writings of Lagarde and Langbehn.) Where Jünger took the logic of economic rationalization and technological determinism to its ultimate conclusion, Grimm offers nothing more original than a recourse to *petit bourgeois* values. For all his indictment of capitalist evils, what he urges is a return to an earlier stage of economic history, to the age of the small-scale entrepreneur or peasant farmer with his alleged individualism, his independence, his readiness to seize opportunities and his cult of *Leistung* or achievement. In sociological terms the theory envisages not the restoration of the traditional *Bürgertum* but the enthronement of the lower middle class. Here surely is one of the reasons for the novel's enormous popularity under a regime which was carried to power on the fears and grievances of the *petite bourgeoisie*. Indeed the book contains various echoes of the original Nazi programme for social and economic reform.[23]

Grimm's perverse reasoning whereby an economic phenomenon is interpreted in geo-political terms is merely a symptom of the disease it ostensibly sets out to cure. Moreover, it is accompanied by indications of a biological racialism. Clearly these are endemic in the literature of European imperialism. The point is that Grimm's novel appeared not on the flood-tide of colonial expansion before 1914—during the author's formative period—but eight years *after* the War. In the light of the practical impossibility of then regaining a foothold in Africa, the book must inevitably have been read in relation to Nazi ideas of winning 'living space' in the eastern lands of Europe. Indeed it is now clear that Alfred Rosenberg in his *Mythus des Zwanzigsten Jahrhunderts* drew on Grimm's novel in arguing his case.[24] Rosenberg, the nearest to an ideologue that the NSDAP produced, demanded living space in much the same terms as Grimm. He too quoted declining population statistics in Germany. He too made the automatic connection between inner freedom and *Lebensraum*. The treatment of the plight of the peasants and of the industrial wilderness, the image of the Germanic character and achievements, the colonialist racialism are common to both. Rosenberg, like Grimm, distinguished between the trading English and the Germanic English; like Grimm too he condemned the *Entente* for leading native levies against their fellow white settlers. But Rosenberg in an attempt to win British support looked quite openly to Eastern Europe as providing the opportunity for fresh expansion and colonization.

Although nationalist resentment at the terms of the Versailles Treaty manifestly stimulated the popularity of Grimm's novel, it possessed other qualities calculated to appeal to a lower middle-class readership. Its enormous length stems from an endless accumulation of incident which combines a primitive desire for story-telling with a complete dearth of emotional or intellectual demands. Much of it is, in the words of one critic, 'an adventure story in the style of Karl May'[25] on whom several generations of German adolescents have fed their heroic fantasies. Grimm's hero remains static, an honest, diligent, fair-minded and ingenuous German Michel, who neither changes nor develops his personality but merely finds confirmation of his existing ideas. He embodies all those qualities such as simplicity, earnestness and fidelity which have traditionally been associated with the word *deutsch* since the eighteenth century. It is of course a prerequisite of crudely didactic writing of this kind, whatever the ideology behind it, that the dimension of critical distance be abolished and with it all intentional irony. The novel is written in an archaicizing, semi-literate style where the accumulation of emotive adjectives and a pseudo-Biblical syntax lend a spurious authority to the statements. *Volk ohne Raum* is generically a debased *Bildungsroman*, a novel of 'education and initiation', in which the vitality and moral insight of the original tradition have been swamped by sentimentality and pontification.

In the case of Grimm, as with so many contemporary intellectuals, we are reminded of Hegel's aphorism:

> An diesem, woran dem Geiste genügt, ist die Grösse seines Verlustes zu ermessen.
>
> (*The poverty of what now serves to satisfy the spirit is a measure of how much it has lost.*)

2. Ernst von Salomon: *Die Geächteten* (1931)

Grimm's bourgeois nature, his attachment to property, his uncomprehending attitude towards technology, his sentimentality, and his hostility towards the Soviet Union marked him off from the more radical and violent national revolutionaries. This younger generation of nationalists found a spokesman in Ernst von Salomon, as their French contemporaries turned to Drieu la Rochelle. His best-known work *Die Geächteten* is part autobiography, part reportage, part (though not overtly) fiction. It is a personal account of the *Freikorps* campaigns in the period immediately after the First World War and of the political conspiracies which led to the assassination of Walther Rathenau. Its interest lies less in the military or political facts of these campaigns than in Von Salomon's interpretation of events. The ideological framework of the book is familiar from studies of the 'conservative revolution'. What is unique is the experience of a lived ethos which no abstract analysis can produce. In its own perverse way it is a far more impressive achievement than Johst's *Schlageter* which deals with a similar theme. In the narrator's opening account of the chaotic days of November 1918 two features emerge which prove characteristic of the rest of the book: the primacy of idealistic values over material factors and the insidious use of highly charged emotional language which anticipates (or mirrors) the concepts of an ideology. The narrator displays a now familiar unwillingness or inability to entertain a rational political debate or analysis. He is not prepared to acknowledge the political will of the masses or any objective justification for their rebellion. Instead of a working population driven to desperation by four years of war, virtual famine and repression, he sees only a mob epitomizing the red peril of Bismarckian days.

In the men who enlist for frontier defence in the East, the desire for self-liberation and fulfilment is ultimately more significant than patriotic pride. The campaigns in the East offer a chance to compensate for the unacknowledged defeat in the West. These volunteers live for the intensity of combat and are dedicated to the cult of action. They feel a constantly repeated need to prove themselves in the face of danger and hardship, to demand of themselves the utmost in courage, strength and endurance. The narrator vividly describes the intoxication of battle, the delirious excitement, the mindless impetus, the blood lust which demands consummation, the almost erotic elation that he experiences in the fusion of man, weapon and victim. The mystique of violence is invoked no less powerfully than the mystique of *Blut und Boden*, of the rich soil which was once fertilized by the blood of earlier German conquerors and which the *Freikorps* are now pledged to defend. The narrator's ambivalence towards the Bolsheviks, the mixture of hatred and respect that he displays, anticipates the National Bolshevism of Ernst Niekisch.[26] The common enemy of both the Bolsheviks and the German patriots is the capitalist West. The narrator comes to feel that in the Baltic he and his comrades have allowed themselves to be used as the instruments of sordid political scheming. If the *Freikorps* had already made one fatal blunder in helping to restore law and order in Germany in 1918–19, they have now committed a second error in permitting themselves to be used as mercenaries of the *Entente* against the Red Army and against a nation which, like the Germans themselves, is struggling to achieve its freedom.

In *Die Geächteten* political discussions are dominated by the powerful clichés of unreason. Politics for their opponents is a matter of self-interest, a means of satisfying material needs. For the narrator and his comrades, however, it is a question of obeying a metaphysical law and partaking of a deeper reality. The notion of Fate or Destiny is frequently invoked as the ultimate arbiter of human events or as the justification for political action. The *Freikorps* feel they have a mission to mould the as yet inchoate Reich (a millennial fiction not to be confused with actual political boundaries) according to their will, their vision. For this they are prepared to sacrifice not only their lives but even their conscience and their integrity. Ultimately the conflict in which they are involved is hypostasized into a struggle between God and the Devil, with themselves as a doomed elect, a generation of provisionals. Thus their position is unassailable by reason. Convinced that they are the chosen, they interpet even practical failure as temporary, for History is on their side. And the strength of their faith itself betokens its validity. The value of a belief is measured not in any objective terms but by the degree of personal commitment it commands. For the time being they are content with intuitive apprehension or the instinctive response of the blood. The reward for perseverance and steadfastness will be full revelation and knowledge. The ends are so absolute as to justify the most squalid political means: murder, robbery, sabotage, torture. Various aspects of the Idealist tradition are brought together here in their ultimate, catastrophically travestied form. The inwardness and other-worldliness, now so terribly at odds with political realities, issue inevitably in death. In the glorification of death as a return to the womb of Nature this political romanticism achieves its appropriate culmination.

The assassination of Rathenau in 1922 marks the climax of the terrorist campaigns of the *Freikorps* men after they have been driven underground. Rathenau, Foreign Minister and living symbol of the Weimar Republic, must die because he threatens to restore Germany's self-confidence and to persuade the people to live according to his values which to the radicals are those of a fossilized corrupt world, in other words lukewarm patriotism, bourgeois materialism, servility and a sentimental cosmopolitanism. The narrator is subsequently sickened by the failure of Rathenau's death to bring about any change in the seamy, cliché-ridden world of German politics.

Von Salomon's book may not be always a strictly accurate record. There are certain minor inconsistencies between *Die Geächteten* and the autobiography and apologia he published in 1951 entitled *Der Fragebogen*. Moreover the account of his own exploits in the Baltic campaigns begins to strain our credulity somewhat when we realize that he was still a boy of seventeen with no wartime experience behind him. He casts himself in a mould that strongly suggests adolescent wish-fulfilment. Yet this matters little if one considers the undoubted fidelity with which he articulates the feelings and aspirations of his social group, the young intellectuals who flocked to the conservative anti-democratic movements of the Weimar Republic. These student idealists who together with uprooted and disinherited war veterans made up the majority of *Freikorps* recruits, helped to encourage hostility towards the Republic and to foster the cult of violence.[27] But in 1933 the hour of reckoning came for Von Salomon no less than for Ernst Jünger and Gottfried Benn. The archival material entrusted to him by his old *Freikorps* comrades was hastily presented to the national archives lest it should be confiscated by the Gestapo or the Party, and he himself eked out a comfortable if inglorious existence until the end of the War as a film-script writer with Ufa, the state-controlled film studio.

The Literature of Constatation

Neue Sachlichkeit

If the Expressionist mode corresponded to the turbulence of the War and its immediate aftermath, the kind of writing known as *Neue Sachlichkeit* belonged properly to the years when the Weimar Republic achieved a brief and illusory stability. The term itself was coined in 1925 when G. F. Hartlaub used it in the title of an exhibition of neo-realistic painting at Mannheim. After the pathos and emphatic rhetoric, the utopianism or the bizarre nightmares of the Expressionist years came a period of disenchantment and reassessment. The 'objectivism'[1] of writers such as Erich Kästner, Hermann Kesten or Joseph Roth sprang from a determined acceptance of contemporary social conditions. It involved a laconic attempt to reflect the reality of the day. Inevitably, however, in the context of the time, this was tantamount to committing oneself to 'Western' values. With their ironic scepticism, their fascination with urban and industrial life, their journalistic idiom and their terse functionality, the objectivists appeared profoundly un-German to the right wing and to those 'apolitical' intellectuals who were already plunging into mythopoeic irrationalism. Under the pressures of Weimar the very choice of subject and its treatment involved—perhaps unwittingly—an ideological decision, no matter how non-committal the overt position of the writer. As the economic and political crisis came to a head at the turn of the decade, most objectivist writers found themselves left of centre. Some became Marxists and joined the KPD. The majority formed a nucleus of what was called a 'white socialism', an attitude that was increasingly critical of capitalism and impatient with the failure of liberal democracy. They even adopted a Marxist terminology, although without necessarily accepting its basis in dialectical materialism. Up to the end of the decade *Neue Sachlichkeit* was the literary home of an ideologically homeless left.

As Lukács pointed out in his attack on Ernst Ottwalt,[2] the initial one-sided stress on content had nevertheless led to a degree of formal experiment. For in order to be true to modern experience, to reproduce it in an adequate manner, the objectivist writers had to seek new techniques. Their most characteristic literary innovation was the documentary form. The documentary in this sense sprang from the desire to authenticate a literary statement about contemporary life or the recent past by overt reference to verifiable historical data. It differed from the traditional use of historical documents in literature in several ways. First, it was concerned to make a relevant statement about current issues, not about a remote historical situation. Secondly, it was not interested in setting off individual characters against a recognizable background but rather in conveying the texture and flavour of a contemporary social milieu. The emphasis lay on circumstances rather than on personalities. Thirdly, the use of documents or authentic sources was built into the work itself, either in the form of a preface and appendices or as an integral part of the text. Documentary literature moves away from traditional realist *Gestaltung* towards montage and reportage. The writer sees himself as an editor rather than an inventor or creator, though there can be wide and crucial divergences in the extent to which his material is selected, shaped, structured, refined and adapted.

An early German example of the genre, anticipating the objectivist use of the documentary by several years, is Karl Kraus' anti-war drama *Die letzten Tage der Menschheit*, the earliest scenes of which date from 1917. In his preface Kraus claimed that he had done little more than body forth speeches, dialogues and printed documents. In fact, however, Kraus had not merely edited his material or amassed a series of quotations. He had also stylized and recreated it in dramatic form. Though the dialogue is brilliantly realistic in its use of slang, colloquialisms and professional jargon, and though many situations are authenticated, the particular speeches and characters are for the most part invented. Though there is no conventional dramatic plot or protagonist, the play is given a dramatic unity and a structured development through the use of recurring motifs, repetition, contrast and balance. In the last act Kraus' imagination reaches mythic proportions. Cinematic sequences are combined with grotesque Expressionist fantasies, ending in the Apocalypse. His successors a decade later imitated the documentary approach but self-consciously kept their imagination in check. Thus Ernst Ottwalt notes at the beginning of a novel exposing the prejudices, chicanery and corruption of the German judiciary, that he is prepared to answer any queries from his readers as to the factual basis of his accusations. Theodor Plivier's 'novel of the German Fleet',[3] which records a group experience and abounds in technical descriptions

45

of running and maintaining a ship, introduces in its final section a first-person narrator to assure the reader, somewhat lamely, of its authenticity. Ernst Toller tackled his documentary drama *Feuer aus den Kesseln* (1930) more methodically, reproducing in a lengthy appendix the sources upon which he had drawn. But he also changed locations and chronology in the interests of dramatic concentration or effectiveness and felt free to invent new characters.[4] He reserved his right to distinguish between creative art and mere reportage, while agreeing that on matters of substance artistic statements must be congruent with historical truth. In fact it is clear that Toller adapted his material just as much in the interests of a political message as in those of artistic form. Toller's play reveals a move away from his earlier, more dialectic drama towards direct agitatory impact. His play was not only a tribute to revolutionary action but also an indictment of the political justice of 1930. The prosecutors and judges of 1917 were still members of the judiciary and Toller publicly challenged them to answer his charges. For a final example of the documentary genre one might look at Erik Reger's novel *Union der festen Hand* where he drew on his first-hand experience of working for Krupp and barely disguised the historical models for his exposure of German industry (Krupp, Stinnes, Thyssen, Hugenberg and others). They are given fictitious names only to raise them to a representative level.[5]

Documentary writing had an obvious appeal in the age of the film camera and the radio microphone. Nowadays much of it has only a documentary interest. Its only aesthetic (as distinct from didactic) justification is surely the means it offers of articulating a reality whose horrendous perversity seems to surpass and paralyse the literary imagination. There are a small number of examples (Kraus' play is one, Weiss' *Die Ermittlung* another) which, in the very act of confessing their inability to devise an adequate aesthetic equivalent for a reality that defies the imagination, reassert their creative power and transcend their dilemma. Only through a documentary approach can they avoid 'aestheticizing'—in other words, betraying and attenuating—the experiences which furnish their terrible subject matter. Yet that kind of 'documentary' is no mere accumulation of *faits divers* where bareness threatens to become barrenness. It is still informed by meaningful patterns or by a search for the overall meaning of events.[6] The discreet artistic shaping is synonymous with an existential interpretation—socio-economic in the one case, apocalyptic in the other. The documentary writing of objectivism, however, is not of that order.

The World of Weimar

In a world in which the laws of the market place dominated even literary life, two best-sellers conveyed a sense of the alienation and despairing passivity that were so widespread among the non-aligned Weimar intellectuals. Erich Kästner's novel *Fabian* (1931) is probably the closest German equivalent to the Berlin stories of Christopher Isherwood. It traces the adventures of the ingenuous hero through the Berlin of the Depression, when republican democracy had already ceded to authoritarianism and the extremists on either side were vying with one another for the final victory. Fabian stands in the centre of the ideological storm. His only defence against society is a rather flippant wit and a battered but still basically sound sense of personal integrity. Clad in this inadequate armour he drifts through the frenzied, chaotic life of the city, unable to discern any purpose or meaning in existence, helpless to influence or challenge his milieu. Nightmare visions embody his experience of social alienation and the vicious, predatory nature of advanced capitalism. And whenever Fabian considers the political scene his wry *aperçus* convey his pessimism and resignation. Beneath his ironic, self-deprecating charm Fabian suffers not only from his personal inadequacies but also from the pestilence of the age in which he lives. His scruples, his mistrust of power and his sceptical insight into his contemporaries' motives prevent him from seeking a remedy in any given political cause. But his resignation is painful and his isolation hard to endure.

Hans Fallada confined his novel *Kleiner Mann—was nun?* (1932) to a worm's eye view of the lower middle-class victims of the Depression. The protagonist, Pinneberg, struggles to defend his private happiness against the encroachments of the economic crisis. His intermediate position between the established middle class on the one hand, and a proletariat he despises on the other, proves in the long run untenable. In his gnawing insecurity, his ever present fear of redundancy, Pinneberg realizes that the grey masses of the proletariat are the only conceivable comrades for him. Yet he dreads being reduced to their social level and having to abandon his hard-won status, however little it avails him. The historical consequences of his predicament are not drawn: instead of voting for fascism like his contemporaries, he finds solace in a sentimental domestic idyll. Likewise Fallada offers no objective analysis of the economic crisis. His hero appears to be at the mercy of anonymous, threatening forces, the plaything of a malevolent fate. He is thus effectively absolved of personal responsibility, while his helpless passivity amounts to an affirmation of events. The novel faithfully mirrors the plight of the *petite bourgeoisie* instead of providing a critique of it.

Ernst Toller's play *Hoppla, wir leben!* (1927), a work which takes us into the heart of Weimar political life, was the product of close co-operation with Erwin Piscator and shows his influence on the technical side of its production with its use of film, loudspeakers and a 'construc- tivist' set.[7] Using a traditional device of *Verfremdung* Toller examines his own society through the eyes of a stranger, a former revolutionary recently released from a mental hospital to which his traumatic experi- ences in 1919 had condemned him. Karl Thomas is a *revenant* who reminds his former comrades of the ideals for which they once fought and faced death. And his naïve bemusement at their new-found prag- matism is a measure of the debasement of those ideals at the 'dirty hands' of politics.[8] The hero realizes that the one great event of his life, the only thing that gives meaning to his existence and sustains him against the threat of despair, has become a mere episode in the eyes of others, to be glossed over in silence or forgotten under the pressure of new events and fresh challenges. His final speech transcends the political scene and opens up a vista of metaphysical absurdity. Yet that vision is Karl's and his alone: it is not the final statement of the play. At the very moment of Karl's suicide the dramatist provides a pointed reminder of the social evils which remain to be combated, and the value of comradeship is affirmed anew by the reactions of Karl's friends in the adjoining cells. We are left with a feeling of chagrin that a man of impassioned humane idealism should find no place in this society. But we are also left with the assurance that his comrades will persevere in the fight to make the world a more tolerable place to live in.

1. Erik Reger: *Union der festen Hand* (1931)

Hitherto I have briefly mentioned works which reproduce the texture of Weimar life. A more probing, analytical treatment is to be found in Reger's *Union der festen Hand*. The subtitle of the novel reads 'Roman einer Entwicklung' (the story of an evolution). The allusion to the *Bildungsroman* tradition seems deliberate. It arouses expectations of a tale of moral, intellectual and emotional development from youth to maturity. Just as deliberately the book soon explodes those expectations, for the novel belongs unmistakably to the twentieth century. Its foreground deals not with the development of a single individual but with the economic and social history of Weimar Germany, with a period when personality is defined in terms of social function and occupation rather than in terms of intrinsic human qualities. By implicitly drawing our attention in this way to the reinterpretation of the fictional task, Reger arouses our critical alertness. It is a minor example of a technique applied throughout the book: the distancing of the reader from the personal histories narrated and the maintaining of a critical detachment vis-à-vis social and economic developments. Reger's novel is an attempt to 'alienate' the reader from his environment in the Brechtian sense of making the familiar appear unfamiliar. And where Brecht drew on various technical resources of the theatre or modified the structure of his dramas to achieve *Verfremdung*, Reger evolves methods more appropriate to the narrative mode. The results are not perhaps as rich or as diverse as in the case of the 'epic' theatre. Yet they prove highly effective in the context of this unjustly neglected novel.

Reger divides the book into five sections whose titles chart the successive stages in the history of industrial power from the end of the War. And at the close of each section he introduces a newspaper report which sums up the main developments in the preceding period or complements these by reference to events elsewhere in Germany. These reports also serve to set the scene for the next section. The contrasting reportage style interrupts the flow of the narrative and encourages a pause for reflection not only on the events themselves but also on the way they are reported in the press. The reader is urged to study the functioning of the mechanisms exposed here, so that after the fifth section he will be able to write his own newspaper summary. This appeal to critical reflection is reinforced by another device. At intervals political slogans and clichés are printed in upper case, without comment, in a context which reveals only too clearly the disparity between what they ostensibly denote and the reality in which they are glibly invoked. Reger also recognized the importance of the narrator as a foil to the flow of events. His narrative voice, unlike Fallada's, is not content merely to record the surface of events from a private perspective: it explains, analyses, demonstrates, makes significant connections and retains a rational insight into the milieu it describes even when the milieu is raised to an irrational power. On the other hand, faced with the outcome, the narrator cannot offer any simple remedy.

The major achievement of Reger's novel is to have exposed the process of economic rationalization in Germany after the War and to have traced the manner in which heavy industry preserved, entrenched and expanded its power under the Republic. When we meet a representative group of industrialists at the end of the War, it soon becomes clear that Reger intends to go far beyond the caricatures of party propaganda. His concern is to differentiate between the various generations of industrial chiefs to show the development of the capitalist system itself, from the self-made entrepreneurs of the *Gründerjahre* (the first phase of industrial expansion after the unification of Germany), to the commercial adventurers of a later phase, the industrial bureaucrats, and finally the *Händler*, the faceless financiers of the 1920s.[9]

In this final stage we hear of massive exchanges of shares, complex deals, intricate partnership arrangements, numerous take-overs and instances of asset-stripping, manoeuvres so involved and obscure that the public cannot keep track of events. In the name of rationalization Hillgruber, the archetypal *Händler*, instigates the formation of a trust, a monolithic monster that devours all competitors. Only a few meaningless balance sheets reach the outside world. Shareholders are powerless to control the company directors. Workers no longer know who really employs them and lose interest in the destination of the things they produce. Hillgruber in short introduces a totalitarian phase in industrial history. Moreover, it is equally clear that these cartels, syndicates and trusts dominate and threaten to devour even their creators. The human mind can no longer keep pace with its own monstrous progeny.

The emergence of this ultimate stage in the development of capitalism cannot be separated from the history of relations between industry and government. The relationship is governed by weakness and miscalculation on the one hand and by unscrupulous self-aggrandizement on the other. The government looks on helplessly as the process of rationalization gathers momentum, for it is now evident that industry and finance rule the state, not the politicians and least of all the electorate. Intimidated by the spectre of unemployment, cabinets hasten to equate the profits of heavy industry with the national good. When rationalization fails in the long run to produce the expected economic miracle, when the consequences of colossal mismanagement make themselves felt, the industrialists turn the Weimar Republic into a scapegoat for their own blunders. They make its social policies responsible for the sickness of the economy. With seductive logic, with a masterly balance of lucid exposition and rhetorical appeal, a combination of emotional, idealistic and materialistic formulations, the industrialists argue that the German workers are pricing themselves out of the world markets. They claim that the true enemies and exploiters of the working class are not the employers but the politicians and bureaucrats who put their self-interest and careers above all else. With this assault on the republican hands that have fed them, the industrialists begin to campaign for the removal of all the safeguards and agreements won by the trade unions since the War. Lay-offs, redundancies and lock-outs further wear down the resistance of the workers. Meanwhile, behind the scenes the industrialists have established contacts with the Nazis, as part of their plan to smash the residual power of the unions. They regard the Nazi ideology as insane but concede that the Party has a useful function to perform in bringing pressure to bear on other social groups and on foreign opinion. The 'Union der festen Hand', as the industrialists' alliance is known, considers the Nazis to be completely under its control. The Nazis for their part are eager to be all things to all men, an opportunism facilitated by the vagueness and confusion of their slogans.

Reger's novel is not only a highly perspicacious account of the growth of industrial power during the Weimar Republic. It is also a relentless exposure of the *débâcle* of working class militancy during these same years. Here we find no heroicization, no myth of the collective, no dogged determination, no tragic pathos. Reger's sometimes sardonic analysis of the self-seeking quietism of the average German worker goes a long way towards explaining why socialism failed and fascism triumphed during the lifetime of the Republic. The workers believe they have far more to lose than their chains: there is the discount store, the doctor, the maternity home, the social club and the company pension. The political implications of *embourgeoisement* become clear. The workers would exchange all their hard-won rights and concessions for a few extra pfennigs an hour. One of the employers reflects on the desperate desire of many workers to see themselves or their children graduate into the ranks of the bourgeoisie. Their models, their goals, their mental attitudes are governed by bourgeois precedents. The fourth estate, he concludes, is no more than a degraded middle class bent on rehabilitating itself. Even when, as in 1918–19, the workers have a measure of power, they fritter it away for want of effective leadership and a clear political purpose. During the Weimar years they grow successively more demoralized and indifferent. Radical gestures give way to bureaucratic protest. The legacy of political authoritarianism has left them steeped in a quasi-military discipline: if their songs have socialist texts, the melodies are old army tunes. And as times become harder the workers prove susceptible to the appeals of the *Stahlhelm* (the militant, right-wing ex-servicemen's organization), and the Nazis. Finally, a free newspaper, expensively and skilfully edited, is launched to overcome the workers' sense of alienation, to instil management values and reconcile them to their lot.

The character through whose experience we witness much of this demoralization and decline is Adam Griguszies, who begins as an arrogantly stupid Communist agitator but ends by uttering the last hopeless lines of the novel:

Was bedeuten sie?	(*What do they represent?*
Veteranen der Arbeit?	*Horny-handed sons of toil?*
Opfer des Kapitals?	*Victims of capitalism?*
Erwachendes Deutschland?	*Germany awakening?*
Soldaten der Roten Armee?	*Soldiers of the Red Army?*
Du lieber Gott. Du lieber Gott.—	*Dear God in Heaven . . . Dear God in Heaven . . .*)

The present-day reader is well placed to supply that final newspaper report which Reger withheld so as not to anticipate the course of events.

2. Thomas Mann: *Mario und der Zauberer* (1930)

In his epic novel *Der Zauberberg* Thomas Mann escorted his young hero through a series of ideological and existential temptations to an epiphany of love and hope. Hans Castorp was the symbol of a Germany faced with a choice between Western values and its own Romantic heritage, between a dark irrationalism pregnant with disaster and new, life-enhancing patterns of thought and feeling. In the novel the hero glimpses where the choice should lie—in mediating between and transcending the opposites—without having the strength of conviction and moral will to commit himself to it. And the depiction of his tempters and mentors is likewise hedged about with ironic ambiguity. But if this aesthetic statement is complex and qualified, with a conclusion which posits no solution within the novel but appeals to the historical responsibility of the reader to shape his own answers in the social world outside the book, Mann's publicistic support for the Republic after 1922 grew increasingly forthright. He was one of several leading German intellectuals (among them Ernst Troeltsch, Friedrich Meinecke and Walther Rathenau) who moved from a conservative, authoritarian position to one of realistic acceptance of the post-war state, thereby earning for themselves the title of *Vernunftrepublikaner*.[10] Though intellectually convinced of the need for a Republic, they weakened their standing and their cause by being less than passionately committed to its support, particularly in the early years. Mann's own initial statements contained a good deal of shameless casuistry. However, his special contribution was to elucidate the perils of the non-political tradition of which he had once been such a determined advocate, and to emphasize the dangers of a misguided idealism.[11] He defined the greatest temptation of the modern intelligentsia as the desire to slough off the principle of individuation, to regress to mythic, unconscious depths, to return to the instinctive springs of being. It thus became susceptible to political totalitarianism. Mann was under no illusion as to the facile optimism and shallow positivism of so much 'democratic' thinking. But he felt that under the circumstances the Republic offered the best—indeed, the only—chance of defending the moral and cultural values which he subsumed under the notion of *Humanität*. Shortly after the crucial elections of 1930 he appealed to the German bourgeoisie to support the Social Democrats in future polls in order to check the rise of fascism.

If that same public had read his latest story *Mario und der Zauberer*, it might understandably have questioned the connection between his political rhetoric and this tale of an Italian hypnotist. The point is that Mann's *novella* transposes into the setting of a seaside entertainment the author's ideas on the nature of political leadership in a fascist dictatorship.[12] Furthermore it hints at private doubts and reservations which election speeches could only mask, never suppress. Not once is it stated that this apparently simple tale of a hypnotist shot dead by one of his subjects is a political parable. However, a series of internal references and allusions suggest parallels with the fascist Italy in which the story takes place. From the outset the narrator establishes the chauvinism of the Italian bourgeoisie, its servility, authoritarian injustice and self-conscious puritanism. Cipolla's own asides to the audience express a self-assertive nationalism. His commentary repeatedly points to the problem of political power and leadership and at one stage he even gives Mario the fascist salute in honour of the heroic tradition of the Fatherland.

Cipolla is physically repugnant, an asthmatic hunchback with bad or broken teeth. His bitter malice towards the strong, the healthy and the virile hints at the compensatory function which his highly developed will-power fulfils. He is full of contempt for his victims and relishes their humiliation. His voice proves stronger than reason, virtue, duty, pride or love—cynically belying, in fact, all the qualities which as a patriot he is pledged to uphold. It seems that his victims succumb to the negativity of their position. They simply try to resist Cipolla's will without being very clear or convinced about what it is they champion. Their liberty has become an abstraction, an end in itself, rather than a truly positive value linked to the achievement of definable goals. The story thus suggests that the audience's susceptibility is due, at least in part, to a disjunction between the ethos it wishes to uphold and the social or political forms in which those values ought to be cast—an inconsequentiality rooted in a loss of faith which Cipolla knows full well how to exploit.[13] Cipolla's will to power is by contrast concerted and dynamic. Yet to sustain it calls for a constant, unflagging effort, with frequent recourse to stimulants to revive his stamina. Thus he presents himself as the suffering, self-sacrificing leader and even appeals to his audience's compassion, assuring them that to command is synonymous with obeying.

But Cipolla is not only a clever hypnotist, he is also a master of rhetoric. And the welter of paradox and mystification with which he surrounds his act is only too familiar from justifications of the *Volksdiktatur*, whereby the leader's will to power is sanctioned as the voice of the people. There can be little doubt as to who is the master in that sultry seaside hall. Yet Cipolla's words suggest a dependence which is not entirely fictitious. Though not in the way he describes, there is indeed a mutual bond between him and his audience, for he needs them as the objects of his will. In fact he is even emotionally dependent upon them. This is no detached, superior master-mind but a lonely, deformed, all-too-human figure who can only make contact with his fellow men by dominating them. The will to power in Cipolla represents a perversion of the desire to be loved, as can be seen from the transvestite substitution in which his act culminates. And it is precisely at this point that Cipolla's concentration falters. By allowing his dependence to come to the fore, Cipolla weakens the willpower into which it has been channelled. His hold over the young waiter Mario slackens and allows the hapless victim to awaken to a dazed realization of the humiliation inflicted upon him. Mario is the only victim who remembers what has happened in the hypnotic trance—because Cipolla's will was not strong enough to erase the memory. Cipolla is not destroyed by any external agency or force triumphantly pitted against him—paradoxically, Mario is a far more ineffectual figure than many of the previous victims —but by his own weakness, his own loss of self-control.

Whom did Mann have in mind, if anybody? The obvious example of physical deficiency in the Nazi hierarchy was Goebbels, with his club foot and hypertrophic intellect. It was Brecht who, in *Der aufhaltsame Aufstieg des Arturo Ui*, obliquely suggested this connection by calling his own caricature of Goebbels 'Givolla'. Goebbels, the intellectual apostate, may well have been more interesting to Mann than Hitler's semi-literate banality. But then Cipolla's whip also recalls Streicher, while the perversity of his sexual constitution contains an echo of Röhm's notorious homosexuality.

What of Mann's narrator who witnesses and recalls these events, who provides us with a critical view of the performance and seems to possess a more lucid insight into Cipolla's behaviour than anyone else present? The narrator is in fact a distinct personality, not merely an anonymous voice. And before long he gives us the impression of being on the defensive, as though he were anticipating objections which he is anxious to discount. It emerges that despite his moral misgivings the narrator is clearly fascinated by Cipolla's act and is prevented from leaving or interrupting the performance by his desire for further revelations and instructive experiences, however pernicious or uncanny they may prove (a mark of the 'true' moralist, according to Mann's *Betrachtungen eines Unpolitischen*). The real source of his uneasiness and guilt is not the neglect of his parental duty. It is the tacit recognition that he has become Cipolla's accomplice. His sin of omission has helped to bring about a catastrophe which his intelligence and moral insight might have prevented. The narrator may present himself as a detached, objective observer but in reality he is as much in thrall to Cipolla as anyone else present. The degradation suffered by the individual victims dishonours the whole audience, as the narrator himself tells us. But whereas the others are unsuspecting and gullible, oblivious to the full implications of what is going on, the narrator by virtue of his insight and acquiescence is *guilty*. We may perhaps conclude that his fascination is aesthetic in origin: he recognizes and admires in Cipolla a masterly performer, an artist in language, a 'brother in the spirit'.[14]

It would be egregious to identify Mann with the narrator. The latter gives himself away precisely because of the ironic distance between the novelist and his character. Yet irony is itself an aesthetic, not a moral quality. We do well to bear in mind Mann's admission when he justified his abandonment of the conservative position:

Ich habe vielleicht meine Gedanken geändert—nicht meinen Sinn.[15]
(*I may have changed my opinions—but not my drift.*)

55

Chapter Four
The Literature of the Third Reich

A. Nazi Writing[1]

When Hitler came to power the racial and political purge of national institutions proceeded apace. Every aspect of cultural activity was rapidly integrated into a tightly organized system of direction and control. The majority of democratic or socialist writers went into exile. Those who stayed, either by design or because they failed to escape in time, ended in prison or in the camps. The reconstituted Prussian Academy of Arts included among its new members Hans Carossa, Hans Grimm, Gustav Frenssen and Guido Kolbenheyer. The *Sektion für Dichtkunst* wanted to elect Stefan George as president in place of Heinrich Mann but since George had emigrated to Switzerland in spite of Goebbels' inducements, they had to settle for the erstwhile Expressionist playwright Hanns Johst. Three separate censorship authorities controlled literary production. Overnight the sole criterion of literary merit became ideological correctness, while literary criticism was reduced to a matter of eulogy or defamation. By 1936 analytical criticism and evaluation were formally abolished by Goebbels in favour of a purely interpretative *Kunstbericht* which would simply pay tribute to and describe a work of art.[2] Goebbels' directive to the German theatre on 9 May 1933, laying down the guidelines for the official aesthetic, contained a typical self-contradiction, but also an unambiguous threat:

> Die deutsche Kunst der nächsten Jahrzehnte wird heroisch, wird stählern, romantisch, wird sentimentalitätslos sachlich, wird national mit grossem Pathos, sie wird gemeinsam, verpflichtend und bindend sein oder sie wird nicht sein.[3]
>
> (*German art in the coming decades will be heroic, steely, romantic, it will be unsentimental and down to earth, patriotic with great fervour, it will be communal, committed and binding or else it will cease to exist.*)

The aims of such a literature were to preserve the *Volk* and the State from dangerous influences, to be an instrument of political education and to bear witness to National Socialist achievements.

One of the main characteristics of Nazi literature, then, was its anti-intellectualism. For reason and critical analysis, it substituted instinct, intuition, unquestioning faith and the bonds of racial unity. It condemned the Enlightenment spirit as un-German, shallow, decadent and destructive, and instead glorified the German 'heart' or 'soul' with its associations of inwardness and metaphysical profundity. But it also repudiated the complexities and ambiguities of aesthetic modernism in favour of a much-vaunted clarity, simplicity and directness. Nazi writers set out to invent a new mythology based primarily on a free interpretation of the heroic Nordic past. They identified *deutsch* with *germanisch* and cultivated a barbaric paganism to which even Christianity was subordinated. Together with the party ideologues they provided the political take-over with a pseudo-philosophical superstructure. A Darwinistic view of society and history, notions of biological selection and mutation, helped to justify the regime's right to rule. The will to power was affirmed as the driving spring of human creativity. At the same time the blood of the race was propounded as the mythic ground of being, providing both internal cohesion and an exclusive homogeneity in the face of influences or assaults from outside. The *Volksgemeinschaft*, the racial community, harmonious and united, was contrasted with an atomistic, mechanistic *Gesellschaft*, riven by strife and constantly threatened by anarchy.

The literature of National Socialism invoked a historical fatalism in its ideological struggle against doubt and scruple. Fate was the ultimate controlling power in human affairs, mysterious, unfathomable, absolute in its compulsion—and the test of heroism was the instinctive commitment to Fate's decrees, the 'decision' which produced action and deed with no thought for personal suffering or loss. The cult of heroism in this sense of pursuing one's destiny to the bitter end figured prominently in Nazi writing. The Führer was presented as the tool of history or Fate or some other transcendental force. His charismatic leadership was invested with a religious or mythic awe and personal fulfilment could be sought only in the execution of his will. As far as the outside world was concerned, however, the relationship between *Führer* and *Gefolge*, overlord and vassals, was transformed into the basis of a new imperialism, a justification of the natural right of the German people or the Aryan race to rule over subordinate or inferior nations. The virtues which were said to have laid the foundation of Germany's greatness were

57

simplicity, honesty, obedience, loyalty and discipline. The life of the individual was dedicated to the service and glory of the *Volk*. The concept of a 'Prussian socialism' sought to fuse the patriotic militarist heritage with the anti-liberalism and anti-Marxism of the conservative middle class. These German values had to be preserved through racial hygiene and physical purity, through the cult of health and beauty. The *Volk* had to be constantly on its guard against possible polluters of the nation and other unwholesome influences.

Nowhere was the stress on racial purity and strength more prominent than in the *Heimatdichtung* and the formula of 'blood and soil'. The bond of blood, of heredity and heritage, was reinforced by a pseudo-mystic communion with the soil which had the property to purify and regenerate human nature. The formula was associated with a cult of elemental passions and fertility, of full-blooded manhood and the earth-mother. An anti-urban polemic which had once praised the qualities of health, uprightness, simplicity, *Gemüt* and a rough-hewn authenticity, now degenerated into primitivism, brutality and fanaticism. The German peasant farmer was mythologized no less than the front-line soldier: he became a timeless figure, strong, defiant, grave and brooding, his own ploughman, sower and reaper, master of his land and fate, more interested in ritual than artificial fertilizer.[4] Idealization and deliberate archaisms combined to produce an anti-historical genre which eschewed concrete economic or social problems in favour of ideological wish-fulfilment. Significantly, what we here find projected on to a rural setting are the dreams and fears of an *urban* lower middle class seeking to escape the consequences of its absorption into a modern, pluralist industrial society. Such 'novels of the soil' soon accounted for more than half the fiction titles recommended each year by the Party.

The motifs of the war experience and of the '*Volk ohne Raum*' complemented the mythic presentation of peasant life in the repertoire of Nazi literature. Other standard themes involved the glorification of the 'brown battalions', the Party militant, and the plight of the *Auslandsdeutschen* who dwelt amid hostile, jealous nations and yearned to be reunited with the fatherland. Yet the regime failed in two important aspects of its literary policy. It was unsuccessful in its efforts to manipulate for its own ends the vogue of historical fiction; and similarly, it failed to encourage the writing of novels devoted to contemporary social and political realities, the *Zeitroman*.

There was nothing revolutionary about the language of Nazi literature. Whether in prose or poetry, it was markedly epigonal.[5] Stefan George was hailed as the father of the new lyric on the basis of *Das Neue Reich* (1928) and a handful of other poems such as 'Krieg'. He seemed to preach a new racial consciousness and the need for a strong *völkisch* state and leader (though in fact his was a millennial vision vouchsafed only to a spiritual and aesthetic elite). His heroic pathos was readily imitated, as were his metaphors of flame and blood. But the primitive eclecticism of the Nazi ideology was matched by the indiscriminate exploitation of a variety of literary and linguistic sources. The forms and rhythms owed much to the nationalist poetry of the Napoleonic era and the 1840s. Wagner's alliterative Nibelung style also left its traces. The vocabulary of '*Blut und Boden*' mingled with a Germanic or medieval idiom. Religious terminology reinforced and sanctified the Party's claim to power. The eulogizing of Hitler again deliberately invoked religious, especially Messianic associations or reiterated hackneyed historical images. Nazi poetry was a public affair, the profession of a creed, recited at social gatherings, festivals, or celebrations. Choral songs of the collective alternated with liturgical *Fahnen-* or *Weihesprüche* in which the individual pledged himself to serve the Party and the *Volk* and appealed to others to follow his example. The high-minded idealism of sacrifice and dedication accorded ill with outbursts of brutal aggression against the enemies of the people. Attempts at dramatic innovations—*Chorspiele*, cantatas, *Thingspiele*—looked suspiciously like the mass theatre favoured by the Socialists in the days of the Republic; at all events they failed to capture the imagination of even a well-disposed audience.

In retrospect it seems as though the most important fascist literature was written before 1933. Thereafter, for one reason and another, not least because of the profound disparity between ideology and reality, it appears to lose its impetus and inspiration. Many of the successful works of the Nazi period were new editions or impressions of older books. Authors of repute to whom the Nazis looked for support (above all George, Jünger and Benn) refused to harness their imaginative energies to the Party. By the late thirties only the ageing Gerhart Hauptmann allowed the regime to benefit from his international prestige. Consequently these years saw the flowering of a literary mediocrity so banal and incompetent that even the Party leaders themselves became concerned about the lack of creative talent. In short, Nazi literature remained versified ideology produced by inferior poetasters who, in the words of one critic, tried to stimulate their readers with a meaningless torrent of emotive clichés designed to have an indeterminate irritant effect.[6]

Modernism was linked in the Nazi mind with biological decadence, Jewish perfidy and the Weimar Republic. Nazi writing thus remained sealed off from contemporary literary developments abroad. Conversely Nazi authors had no influence outside the German-speaking lands. An example of the Nazi attitude towards aesthetic modernism can be seen in their campaign of vilification against Expressionism. Goebbels was in favour of certain artists on the grounds of their primitivism, their rebellion against materialism and their links with Germanic mysticism (not least, perhaps, because it was in Expressionism that his own literary roots lay). Rosenberg, on the other hand, condemned Expressionism outright and urged the adoption of neo-romantic or monumental neo-realist forms. Hitler himself always detested the Expressionists. Though some visual artists survived the first purge of decadent art in 1933, none escaped a second assault which began in 1936 and culminated in the notorious Exhibition of the following year. Many literary Expressionists had, of course, been associated with humanist or socialist values and were therefore condemned from the outset.[7] In the course of this campaign the Nazis turned their wrath on one of the foremost German poets of the twentieth century, Gottfried Benn, finally compelling him to 'emigrate'—as he called it—into that 'aristocratic' form of exile, the German army.

B. Gottfried Benn

The case of Gottfried Benn illustrates the susceptibility of certain intellectual circles to the appeal of fascism, and their subsequent disillusionment when it proved impossible to maintain any kind of intellectual independence or to pursue any literary development which did not accord with the tenets of the Nazi ideology and aesthetic.[8]

In the early twenties Benn had withdrawn into a nihilistic aestheticism. By the end of the decade his regressive irrationalism translated itself into an anti-Marxist polemic. Finally his aestheticism toppled over into a glorification of barbarity. In the first months of the Third Reich he proclaimed his commitment to the regime and attacked its opponents. Yet he was ignorant of much of the party programme, had never attended a political meeting or rally, and had not read *Mein Kampf*. In fact it was not political considerations in the narrower sense that determined his attitude but his fears of cultural disaster. He believed that rationalism had destroyed human values and the totality of nature. Western man was undergoing a process of progressive cerebration which threatened to culminate in his own extinction, with the rapidly multiplying peoples of Eastern Europe spilling over to take his place. The only power capable of transcending nihilism was artistic form: here was the affirmation that could bridge the abyss of violence, chaos, and contingency. How Benn came to identify this Nietzschean affirmation with the 'national revolution', to make the transition from a purely private response to a collective ideological solution which he had always spurned, can perhaps only be explained by the degree to which he had hitherto felt alienated and isolated in the society of his day. It was a precarious enough alliance but, while it lasted, fervently and zealously proclaimed.

Various speeches and addresses supported the regime against its liberal or socialist critics, and saluted its dynamism, its rediscovery of the mythic ground of Being.[9] But Benn still had to live down his suspect past: his aesthetic modernism. The only way to convince the regime of his reliability would have been to produce an appropriate literary work in full accordance with the new cultural policy, as Johst and Bronnen did. But this contribution Benn could not make. He had nothing but contempt for Nazi literature. His reputation therefore continued to bear the stigma of *'entartete Kunst'*, though in a defence of Expressionism he did try to present it as an Aryan phenomenon fully compatible with National Socialism. At one point he was accused of being a Jew and forced to establish his racial credentials in public. But his cosmic pessimism was hardly attuned to the millennium which had just dawned. And his idea that creative genius went hand in hand with physiological decadence was closer to turn-of-the-century aestheticism than to the heroism of the new era. Many of his theories were too esoteric or recondite for comfort. By August 1934 Benn was admitting in private his thorough disenchantment with the Third Reich. The *putsch* against Röhm and the S.A. had been the last straw. Early in 1935 he rejoined the Army. It was only his good relations with his military superiors (and their distaste for the Party) which enabled him to survive the attacks on him in the S.S. journal and the *Völkischer Beobachter* in 1936. The campaign was renewed the following year in a book bearing the eloquent title *Säuberung des Kunsttempels* and finally in March 1938 he was expelled from the *Reichsschrifttumskammer* and forbidden to publish.

Benn's reaction to the disappointment of his political hopes had been once again to endeavour to separate entirely the spheres of spirit and power, a distinction for which he had argued in his polemic against left-wing committed writing in the last years of the Republic. This apparently so modern poet fell back on a familiar tradition once his brief outburst of political radicalism had spent itself.

C. The *'innere Emigration'*

Not all the literature written in Hitler's Germany was Nazi-inspired or crypto-fascist. Between 1933 and 1935 some one hundred contributions by members of the *Bund proletarisch-revolutionärer Schriftsteller* were smuggled out of Germany to appear in the *Neue Deutsche Blätter* in Prague. One of the Berlin leaders of the *Bund* was Jan Petersen. His chronicle *Unsere Strasse* was sent to Czechoslovakia and published in Berne, Moscow and London. It was the only work written inside the Third Reich which directly depicted the resistance struggle. There was, too, a literature of the camps and prisons ranging from anonymous verses to sonnet cycles, from Werner Krauss' novel *PLN* to private letters.[10] But the phenomenon known as the *'innere Emigration'* implies a different kind of writer and a different kind of experience.[11]

There were many conservative writers such as Hans Carossa or Ernst Wiechert who chose to remain in Nazi Germany, not necessarily because they were impressed by the Führer personally or by his policies, but because they saw the impetus behind the national movement as a token of moral renewal. National Socialism was able to tap a vast reserve of idealistic passion among the bourgeois intelligentsia who heard only the high-minded clichés and ignored the sordid, brutal political realities. There was an initial identity of interest between conservative writers and the Nazis in that the conservatives shared their dislike of aesthetic modernism, their hostility towards the alleged materialism of modern civilization, their contempt for liberalism and a vulgar hedonism, their fear of social anarchy and nihilism. Moreover some conservatives were prone to glorify Prussianism and patriotic sentiment. Where the conservative writers differed from the Nazis was in the matter of basic values and the solutions they proposed. Instead of the abolition of class conflict in a total mobilization of society, they postulated the return of social harmony through a hierarchic structure based on estates. Instead of totalitarian subordination to the will of one man and one ideology, they advocated a semi-feudal authoritarianism. Instead of a message of hatred and violence, they preached a return to traditional moral values and brotherly love. Instead of the will to power, they urged detachment from the things of this world and a cultivation of inwardness. Instead of biological racialism, they endorsed a spiritual elitism.

Clearly the differences between the conservative intellectuals and men like Jünger or Benn, to say nothing of Rosenberg or Goebbels, were enormous. What is remarkable is the degree to which these differences were obscured or ignored in the common struggle against rationalism, Marxism, decadence and liberal society. The conservatives were so imbued with the Idealist tradition, so unaccustomed to political analysis and ignorant of the possibilities and limitations of political systems, that they were easily deceived by a semantic confidence trick. They believed in the rhetoric and silently acquiesced in the tactics. They recognized the signals of a common heritage and purpose, and dismissed any contrary indications as unfortunate excesses or deviations. Only after the Nazis came to power and the full implications of totalitarian rule made themselves felt did German conservatives begin to feel uneasy. It took a lost war finally to impel them into abortive action or clandestine commitment.

The notion of an '*innere Emigration*' became an issue immediately after the Second World War, particularly as a result of the public correspondence between Frank Thiess and Thomas Mann.[12] The often vituperative debate revolved around such questions as whether everything written within Nazi Germany represented a token of acquiescence in the regime; or was it possible to have published without compromising one's integrity? Was everything that did not oppose Nazism necessarily its ally? Or had an intellectual resistance existed? There is little point in reopening the argument on the level of personalities or of sweeping moral judgments. But it is worthwhile looking back to the situation which gave rise to the controversy.

The term '*innere Emigration*' has always been somewhat elastic; it has been applied to a variety of attitudes ranging from courageous resistance to gross opportunism, from total silence to veiled criticism. As a term of literary history the concept is most usefully reserved for those writers who overtly and expressly distanced themselves from the regime and who propounded their opposing values in full awareness of their political implications. The possibilities for expressing dissent were of course extremely limited. The disciples of inwardness had no con-

63

ception of the extent to which the totalitarian state would control the hearts and minds of its citizens. Writers whose whole philosophy was based on the separation of politics and literature, of Life and Spirit, of Caesar and God, awoke to the realization that all intellectual activity was now politicized. Nothing was passed for publication which did not seem useful to the regime, however indirectly. Naturally the censors made mistakes, and conflict between rival organs of the State and the Party undermined the system's efficiency in this as in other spheres, but a writer who wished to communicate his dissent could not count on the fallibility of the functionaries responsible for reading his manuscript. In practice he was left with three choices. He could adopt a highly oblique method of criticism such as allegory, parable, fable or historical analogy; or he could circulate his work clandestinely, which for practical reasons meant poems or pamphlets; or he could publish abroad under a pseudonym. If the last two methods were fraught with personal danger (to his credit, Werner Bergengruen used both), the first ran the risk of being ignored or misinterpreted by virtue of its very indirectness. It has been claimed that people became adept at reading between the lines and attuned to the accents of the 'language of slavery',[13] through which critics of the regime communicated with each other without betraying themselves to the dictators. But if the *Sklavensprache* had to be camou-flaged beneath the language of the masters, was it always so easy to distinguish between the true and the false? Could the dissenters dis-guise their purpose in this way without radically modifying their aims? Was the price they paid in order to appear at all—too great? For all the veiled criticism in Bergengruen's *Der Grosstyrann und das Gericht* the novel won Party approval as a glorification of the 'leadership principle', while the fervent Prussian ethos of Jochen Klepper's novel about Frederick William I, *Der Vater* (1937), ensured its official promotion despite its equally intransigent Protestantism. One commentator concludes that with the best will in the world the writers of the '*innere Emigration*' 'involuntarily helped the regime to build up a facade of spiritual freedom and cultural continuity in spite of the concentration camps . . . In this way they were integrated into the collective organiza-tion and, in effect, strengthened it'.[14] What is certain is that even when the '*innere Emigration*' spoke with an unequivocal voice, it never transcended the fateful errors which had led to its predicament in the first place.

The literary forms favoured by these writers were the novel and the lyric. The drama, which required a public forum, was virtually closed to them. Above all they cultivated historical fiction, for in the past they could rediscover a clear design and a human autonomy which the present denied. Or, to view it more negatively, one could say that they fled from a confused, unyielding present reality that seemed to shatter their image of man and his world to historical material which they could mould according to a preconceived and comforting pattern. Nazi writers sometimes resorted to the historical novel in order to glorify a heroic model and to seek historical sanctions for Germany's current destiny. Non-political authors turned to 'antiquarian' *pointillisme* and romanticized biography for light relief. But the conservative religious writers of the '*innere Emigration*' sought out the past in order to find parallels that demonstrated man's weakness, guilt and presumption, his need of divine mercy, and his ability to find redemption. (Hence, for instance, Gertrud von Le Fort's *Die Magdeburgische Hochzeit* or Stefan Andres' *El Greco malt den Grossinquisitor* or Reinhold Schneider's *Las Casas vor Karl V.*) But since they lacked political or historical insight into their own times, they found it difficult to discover an adequate equivalent in the past, and much of their writing seems curiously beside the point. By viewing events *sub specie aeternitatis* they attributed them solely to moral decisions and posited remedies for social evils in the spiritual conversion of individuals, especially those in positions of power. In this respect they repeated the historical error of the 'rhetorical' Expressionists, as exemplified in Kaiser's *Die Bürger von Calais* or Hasenclever's *Antigoné*. Later, particularly during the War, when the intractable corruption of Germany's leaders had become only too clear, history was transformed into apocalypse and the sole remaining hope was seen to reside in God's mercy. What is missing from this writing is any impulse to social revolution: its attitude to rebellion is determined by Luther's interpretation of Romans XIII (the powers that be are ordained of God . . .).[15]

Not surprisingly the search for design and meaning is reflected in the poetic forms favoured by the conservative writers, above all the sonnet.[16] The sonnet was 'untimely' in more senses than one in Nazi Germany. It was a strenuously classical form far removed from hymns to the Führer or S.A. marching songs; and it was an alien, non-Germanic form equally remote from the romantic *Lied* and the Wagnerian *Stabreim*. The choice of poetic medium was thus itself an implicit gesture of dissent, at least against the official aesthetic. The sonnet was used in a firmly traditional manner, with no attempt at either structural or linguistic experiment. Its strictness, discipline and clarity convey, like the recourse to historical fiction, the desire to affirm an absolute law that controls and shapes a chaotic material world. Behind this formalism lies a strange paradox. Emigré writers were beginning to despair of the power of art to achieve any impact in the real world: but the writers of the '*innere Emigration*' who were compelled to witness the daily repudiation of all their most cherished values clung to their belief in the moral influence of artistic form and to a Johannine interpretation of the Word. It was not simply the desire for didactic clarity that accounted for the absence of innovation, but rather their unquestioning faith in an older heritage, an older language even—in short, in an Idealist equivalence of world and word. Through language and art they tried to counteract the process of brutalization and distortion. Yet all too often they remained imprisoned within a highly stylized convention, suffused with archaic or idyllic elements and pseudo-Biblical pathos.

What function did such writing fulfil? It was produced for an educated middle-class readership, a group of like-minded people who found themselves involved in a political process of which they disapproved but which they were helpless to change. This conservative literature sought to reassure and console by invoking the ultimate victory of the spiritual principle. Although the explicitly critical writing circulated privately, often in verse form, among small groups and in a local area, the more indirect expressions of dissent which appeared in print attracted a large following. The appeal was partly escapist, partly compensatory, and in human terms it is easily understood. In political terms, however, it was little short of disastrous. While it reinforced the prejudices that had originally led to Hitler's electoral successes, it obscured the question of specific responsibility by hypostasizing the theme of guilt into the myth of original sin. Instead of trying to understand how evil had taken on the particular form of National Socialism or how the Nazis had come to dominate German society, the '*innere Emigration*' contented itself with proclaiming the sinfulness of the whole of mankind. By demonizing Hitler into an embodiment of Satanic power, it neglected to study the all-too-human social and economic process that had brought him to the fore. In short, it was informed by a fatalism no less insidious than that of a Jünger or a Benn. And in a world which demanded that they rethink their faith, their philosophy, above all their attitude towards evil, these conservative writers proved incapable of learning from their experience.

An early example of this failure can be found in Werner Bergengruen's novel *Der Grosstyrann und das Gericht* (1935). Set in Renaissance Italy, it relates the search for the murderer of a high official amid an atmosphere of corrosive fear, greed, suspicion and betrayal. Yet after confusion and violence appear to have shattered the divine order and beauty of the world, the reality of God's mercy is reasserted. In its reflections upon the relationship between justice and power, the novel evinces an idealism which sanctions political activity only in the execution of a higher spiritual purpose and which disparages a more pragmatic view of politics as mechanical and bureaucratic. By dint of ignoring the implications of the inevitable disparity between might and right, Bergengruen lapses into a pious optimism which flies in the face of all the evidence of his own age. Logically he faces a choice between the tragedy of moral compromise or the martyrdom of the intransigent idealist. The unreal alternative which in fact he offers, a vision of earthly and divine power reconciled through the conversion of the hubristic despot, was irrelevant to the situation of 1935 and could only have encouraged a retreat into inwardness on the part of those who contemplated the desolate political vista of their age.

Much of the Christian writing of the '*innere Emigration*' is armoured against experience in a highly questionable manner. The victory of the Cross is hollow indeed unless it encompasses and transcends the full measure of anguish, suffering and despair. It is not the religious optimism in itself that is suspect but the ease with which it is invoked. Like others of their generation with very different moral values, these writers betray a terrifying failure of imagination in the face of the unprecedented disaster all around them. All too often their vocabulary and imagery convey not so much a living experience as a defence against it.

Another instructive example of the limits of the '*innere Emigration*' is provided by Ernst Wiechert who enjoyed a considerable literary following during the Third Reich. He also earned the unenviable distinction of being one of the few writers to survive a period of correction in a concentration camp.[17] His experiences in Buchenwald were recorded in *Der Totenwald*, written in 1939 and buried in his garden until after the War. For all its sententiousness and rhetorical pathos, the book remains a sombre record of his shame at having compromised with the regime, and of the barbaric circumstances of his imprisonment, a dark night of the soul illuminated only by the humanity of fellow prisoners who helped him to survive, many of them Communists.

In 1939, however, Wiechert's overt literary activity took the form of

67

a novel called *Das einfache Leben* which offered a seductive escapist alternative. It was eagerly seized on by his readers, for over a quarter of a million copies were sold in two years.[18] The book is a mixture of utopianism and mawkishness with a strong undercurrent of depressing nature philosophy. It issues in an uncritical fatalism, all-affirming, anti-individualist and regressive. Again one cannot but wonder at its sheer irrelevance to the problems that it is ostensibly meant to resolve: the final decline of a military and feudal society, the advent of a modern industrial culture and, by implication, the development of totalitarianism. There is an inherent falseness in the advice of landowners and *rentiers* that one should resort to honest toil as the solution to all ills. There is a despairing helplessness in their propounding of duty and diligence when the ultimate meaning of their existence has been called into question. Instead of grappling with the uncertainties, conflicts and complexities of modern life the hero can only retreat into a simplicity and 'authenticity' the desire for which had already played a fateful part in the calamity of 1933. The religious affirmation in which his story culminates turns out to be an atheism that lacks the courage of its convictions: for the law which he acknowledges is nothing less than 'the final absurdity of existence', glossed over by sentimental remnants of traditional piety. Small wonder if in the face of these confusions, this incipient nihilism, Orla's favourite image is that of the 'stone on the river bed', the pre-conscious mineral stillness at the heart of the natural world. It is the last escape of all.

Ernst Jünger represents a third possibility of the '*innere Emigration*': aristocratic detachment. When the reality of the Third Reich became clear to him, his natural elitism reasserted itself and he remained aloof from the vulgarity and crudeness of those whom he had helped to achieve power. Only once did he indicate in public his attitude to the regime, in the novel *Auf den Marmorklippen* (1939). The implications of the book were eagerly discussed at the time in the circles of the '*innere Emigration*' (though advertisements for the book were forbidden, it sold well over 10,000 copies by 1940).[19] After the War apologists spoke of a bold gesture of resistance. This allegory of the rise of fascist terror in a decadent world shows the narrator's sanctuary threatened by the encroaching powers of a sinister *Oberförster*. The marble cliffs have eventually to be abandoned and a new life sought in exile. But the central message of the book lies in the experience of inner victory, the triumph of the spirit over instinct, adversity, pain and fear. This was the strength of the Mauretanian elite when the narrator belonged to their number: the stillness in their souls as in the heart of a cyclone. This too is what validates the death of a young prince—the quiet smile of serenity that betokens the casting aside of weakness and the revelation of the 'great order' of Being. Inspired by this sight (on a severed head) the narrator declares that it is better to die with the free than to march in triumph with the slaves. The book envisages no possibility of defeating the *Oberförster* by political or military means and indeed suggests that this is irrelevant, provided the struggle gives one the chance to attain the necessary sublimity. Moreover, the novel is ethically flawed, in that the victory over fear appears to be synonymous with a victory over all feeling. The stillness at the heart of the cyclone denotes not only indifference to one's own suffering but an aesthetic detachment from the anguish of others. The narrator's principal response to the rule of the *Oberförster* is one of repugnance. At best he experiences a fleeting moment of sadness as when he glimpses the prince's mutilated features. But in general the book gives the impression of feeling rigidly controlled or suppressed. A cool, impersonal style fails to capture any sense of the moment. At one point there occurs a revealing statement that like the cosmos the human world must necessarily be engulfed in flames from time to time in order to purge and renew itself. The *Oberförster* and his rule of terror are symptoms of just such a periodic holocaust which the narrator observes with acquiescent, clinical interest.

Chapter Five

The Literature of Exile

The event which precipitated the flight of so many intellectuals from Germany was the Reichstag fire of 27 February 1933.[1] The Nazis used the fire as a pretext to round up their opponents, who included not only the Communists but anyone known for his anti-nationalist or pro-democratic views. Ossietzky, Mühsam, Renn, Bredel, Seghers, Kisch and Hiller were among those arrested. By the autumn of 1933 all the significant emigré writers were out of Germany. Scarcely any had taken care to transfer funds while they still had the opportunity or made mental preparation for going into exile. And to begin with, few believed that the extraordinary situation would last.

The exiled writers were a motley band.[2] Some had left because of their political views, others for racial reasons, many for both. A few were non-political modernists who left in pursuit of aesthetic freedom. Ideologically they included Communists, Social Democrats, non-party left-wing radicals, liberals, monarchists, even national revolutionaries. These divisions in turn produced a variety of interpretations of the Third Reich. The conflicts of the republican era continued in exile, exacerbated by the consciousness of defeat and the search for scapegoats. The financial resources of the exiles varied enormously, a factor which was important in determining the different treatment meted out to them by their 'host' countries. As the emigrés spread out all over Europe and beyond, they shared only a common predicament: that of writers who overnight had been deprived of their natural readers or audiences and cut off from the living community whose language they wrote. The need to produce work that would sell in translation combined with their sense of having to preserve a national heritage and encouraged a conservatism of form and language. A writer like Musil who resolutely pursued his modernist experimental fiction was dependent on private charity.

The popularity of historical fiction inside the Third Reich was paralleled among exiled writers such as the Mann brothers, Lion Feuchtwanger and Stefan Zweig—and for similar reasons, sometimes escapist, sometimes didactic. Likewise the sonnet form was cultivated not only inside Germany but also—improbably—in Moscow by Johannes R. Becher, who turned his hand to this and other classical forms.

One can distinguish between three broad categories of response to the challenge of exile. The first was fatalistic and escapist (the flight of Döblin or Werfel into Catholicism, mysticism and inwardness). The second response came from those writers who concentrated on preserving a humanist and liberal heritage, the ideals of the two Weimars, and who, although opposed to Hitler, resisted the calls for a committed art in an agitatory sense. Unlike the Communists, for example, they did not participate in everyday political activity, nor did they support any particular party or organization. The third kind of writer was actively anti-fascist, continuing the struggle from other European countries and later from the Americas. (Among this category one might include Toller, Joseph Roth, Heinrich Mann and the KPD authors.) In the early years many exiled German authors sought to enlighten the world as to what was happening inside Germany and to warn of the threat to the rest of Europe: hence Feuchtwanger's exposure of anti-semitism and *Gleichschaltung* in his novel *Die Geschwister Oppenheim* (1933).[3] The Communist activists even tried to keep up contact with the socialist underground, such as it was, and to smuggle writing both in and out of the Reich. A series of left-wing novels described the struggle of the resistance groups in an optimistic spirit, in the deluded belief that the regime would itself soon bring about a decisive swing to the left among the proletariat. As late as 1935 Communist exiles in particular still expected the imminent collapse of National Socialism either through violent uprising or through its own inherent weaknesses. There is, however, a noticeable difference in Anna Segher's *Das siebte Kreuz* (1939) which no longer maintains the fiction that any organized opposition survives within the Reich and which holds up the moral commitment of individuals as the only hope for the future. In the late thirties, as the regime consolidated its hold and the international community accepted fascism as a *fait accompli* or even welcomed it, the emigrés experienced disillusionment and a growing sense of futility. With the outbreak of the War and the early German successes, a second wave of emigration spilled out of Europe and a series of suicides charted the fear and despair that dogged the footsteps of so many exiled intellectuals. Even committed writers saw their activism apparently rendered irrelevant.

The year 1933, however, marked a far less decisive point in the *literary* development of many writers[4] than the hiatus in their private lives suggests. For in the second half of the twenties a reaction against the laconic matter-of-factness and exclusively social themes of objectivism, or against left-wing demands for commitment, had already made itself felt in various ways among bourgeois writers. There was a rediscovery of the natural world and a nostalgic return to the past or the private self. Some explored the realms of myth, legend and mysticism. These tendencies were reinforced in exile, so that writers like Thomas Mann or Roth could reconcile their anti-fascist publicistic activity with the exploration of artistic worlds far removed from the sphere of 'telegrams and anger'.

1. Bertolt Brecht: *Mutter Courage und ihre Kinder* (1941)

Cut off after 1933 from a readily available theatrical context, from a rapport with a familiar audience, Brecht found it difficult to discover an appropriate form for the directly activist pieces which he continued to write in exile and which remain relative failures. A measure of detachment from the immediate struggle was necessary before he could begin to strike the right note, whether in the reflective ironies of the *Flüchtlingsgespräche*, the lyricism of the Svendborg poems, or the dramatic achievement of the major plays. In these latter works the immediate political conflict receded into the background and Brecht emerged as a Marxist *moraliste*, articulating problems of human behaviour and exploring the possibilities of human freedom within the framework of a materialist interpretation of consciousness and society.

The opening scene of Brecht's play *Mutter Courage und ihre Kinder* which is set in the Thirty Years War contains in essence the theme of the action as a whole: Mother Courage's attempt to live off war without giving it anything in return. The purpose of Mother Courage's career as a canteen owner and camp-follower is to sustain and preserve her family. Yet by the end of the play that career has destroyed the very thing it is meant to protect. Again and again her commercial instinct causes her to neglect her children and to hasten their death. Mother Courage is as much a victim of war as a parasite on it. This hard, experienced, worldly-wise woman fails to see the one simple truth about her position: that the means of life have become the ends, and that life itself is the sufferer. And all the time it is her mute daughter Kattrin who witnesses and experiences this truth.

Inarticulate and timid, cut off from ordinary social relationships, Kattrin has not developed a protective skin between herself and the world. The vein of feeling throbs only just beneath the surface. She responds directly and instinctively to the spectacle of suffering and anguish, amid a society conditioned to ignore them in the interests of survival. She is the most important single instrument of *Verfremdung* in the play, for by observing her reaction to events we ourselves are made to see afresh the consequences of her mother's indifference to pain and deprivation. When a Catholic army prepares to attack Halle, Kattrin achieves a moral freedom and a chance to act which have hitherto been denied her. What begins as another impulsive reaction becomes a conscious decision. As the intimidated peasants pray and throw themselves (and those about to be slaughtered) on God's mercy, Kattrin climbs on to a stable roof from where, in defiance of all threats and entreaties, she drums out a warning to the unsuspecting town. Although she is shot, the sleeping garrison is roused to the danger and Halle repulses the attackers. The virtues of her two brothers (honesty and boldness) were heavily qualified in our eyes by their deaths: her quality of compassion and self-sacrifice is validated by the saving of the town.

If ever proof were needed that Brecht's 'epic' theatre did not aim at excluding emotion or that the emotion did not creep in inadvertently, the final scene of the play provides it. The poignancy of Mother Courage's loss is not diminished by the reminders of her incorrigible shortsightedness. Conversely the sight of her grief and her resilience does not weaken our conviction of her personal responsibility. Sympathy and critical detachment merge in the indictment of a system which reduces everything to a price and perverts even the best in man. For whenever men behave in a harsh, stupid or cowardly fashion in the play, it is invariably in defence of their material welfare. Only Kattrin overcomes this material compulsion.

It was not important that Mother Courage should learn her lesson, commented Brecht, provided that the audience learnt theirs.[5] What the play tells us is that wars are instigated by the ruling class for the sake of their personal power and gain. That ideological crusades are a smokescreen for political ambitions. That bourgeois 'virtues' are a luxury which no poor man can afford in a society built on acquisition and exploitation. That in such a society love is a dangerous folly which only makes one easier to exploit. That the ordinary people upon whom the mighty depend for their subjects, soldiers or congregations are always the losers. But the mighty do not live for ever. True, it is pointless to rebel unless your wrath is strong enough (and cunning enough) to sustain you. Yet you cannot escape the consequences of the system by hoping to find a safe and comfortable niche. What then is to be done?

Mother Courage and Kattrin embody two possible responses to the world as they find it. The mother consistently points out that the individual must submit to social pressures. Kattrin in her own small way does something to change society. Both options demand their penalties. But whereas Mother Courage thrives on suffering and destruction, Kattrin prevents it. What is equally instructive is the manner in which her sacrifice is presented. The conventional Idealist associations— nobility, dignity, sublimity—are absent. In their place we see an example of suffering humanity driven to desperation, a half-demented, frightened, sobbing girl who knows only that if *she* submits to coercion, the children in the town will die. The literature of inwardness cannot muster a single instance of sacrifice that speaks to us so vividly and so directly. Brecht does not suggest that Kattrin's actions are the sole means of changing the world. But hers is a symbolic gesture which emphasizes the moral commitment that is essential if anything is to be changed. (Hence too Brecht's modified conception of Galileo in another play of these years: from approval of his pliability to a dialectical critique of his cowardice and compromise.) In the long run, the play implies, change can only come from those who have taken the measure of society like Mother Courage but do not share her greed and capitulation. It can come only from those who have it in them to emulate Kattrin's commitment at critical moments but who also possess the insight into social mechanisms which she lacks.

2. Thomas Mann: *Doktor Faustus* (1947)

Thomas Mann's initial reaction to the 'seizure of power' was an attitude of wait-and-see. On his children's insistence he did not return to Germany from a lecture tour abroad. But in the autumn of 1933 he went so far as to try and rid himself of the suspicion of anti-fascist activity by dissociating himself from the journal *Die Sammlung* edited by his son Klaus. Silence seemed to Mann the best way of maintaining contact with his public inside Germany. Gradually he realised that he had no choice but to commit himself openly, and from early in 1936 he became an unrelenting opponent of the Hitler regime. This activism was clearly a condition of his being able to remain (in Hölderlin's words) a *Dichter in dürft'ger Zeit*. On the eve of the Second World War the policies of appeasement and non-involvement, the suspicion encountered by many German refugees abroad, and the pro-fascist sympathies in several Western states helped to radicalize Mann's ideas. Later still, as the truth about Nazi atrocities became known, the emigré intellectuals were caught up in the endless debate about collective guilt and in speculation about whether the Nazi crimes were an inevitable outcome of the character and traditions of the German people. Mann now turned away from an economic explanation of Hitler's power to a study of the German soul.

At the heart of his complex and profound novel *Doktor Faustus* lies the parallelism between Mann's hero, the composer Adrian Leverkühn, and the German nation. The artistic dilemma which prompts Adrian into concluding a pact with the Devil is the failure of true inspiration. What the Devil offers as a substitute for sterile reflectiveness and inhibiting intellectualism is an experience of holy fire that has long been wanting, a rapture, an enthusiasm which God—with his predilection for rationality—can no longer supply; it means freedom from doubt, a compulsive dictation which presents no choices and needs no revision. Modern art seeks inspiration not only for formal or aesthetic reasons. It is also trying to overcome its isolation from the rest of society. Adrian longs for a new innocence, serenity and humility in which art will once again find itself in the service of a whole community or some sort of higher order, a *Verband* or *re-ligio*. The crisis of modern art is paralleled by the decline of bourgeois humanism, the end of a secular, rationalist tradition whose political precipitate was liberal democracy. The loss of creative inspiration is matched by the disappearance of the sense of wholeness in the bourgeois order, by the corrosive scepticism towards its staple values. The charge of mechanical intellectualism here raised against modern art was frequently levelled at Weimar Germany's experiment in liberal democracy; the corresponding fear that pluralism would lead to anarchy, another commonplace of intellectual conservatism, is echoed in Adrian's fear of artistic licence and unbridled subjectivity. In the conversations of the Munich intellectuals of the Weimar era we see Leverkühn's sublime yearnings translated into the base coinage of political slogans. Here the cult of violence, vitalism and myth echoes Adrian's desire for a new *Kultus*, a new barbarism. If the Munich intellectuals show the bizarre degeneration of the Idealist tradition, Adrian embodies the related aesthetic cult of inwardness with its supreme achievements and its terrible human cost. Even the narrator, Adrian's life-long and tragically unrequited friend Serenus Zeitblom, shows the susceptibility and confusion to which contemporary German humanism is prone: as the supreme representative in literature of the 'internal emigration', Zeitblom periodically betrays the ambiguities of his patriotic pride and the insidious influences of the ruling ideology on his thinking. It is not until well into the novel, as the horrors perpetrated by the regime become clear even to an un-worldly scholar, that Zeitblom pronounces his first anathema.

Leverkühn's quest for a way out of his artistic dilemma takes him into a union with the demonic. What the pact with the Devil symbolizes— if indeed it is merely symbolic[6]—is a surrender to monstrous, de-structive forces, to primeval, bloodstained irrationalism, to frenzy and pain, to the dark chthonic powers underlying the phenomenal world. Paradoxically the surrender to the demonic is dictated not by the abandonment of spirituality but by Adrian's determined pursuit of it. In the absoluteness of his commitment, the spirit devours itself in a desperate attempt to achieve self-realization. Adrian Leverkühn succumbs to a blasphemous Messianism which pursues salvation through evil and transgresses in order to redeem. Apostasy becomes a perverse act of faith. For just as the musical tradition has declined into a set of empty formulae; just as the era of bourgeois liberalism is felt to have degenerated into mechanical expediency, so too religious faith is taken so much for granted that it has grown hollow and inconsequential. The mind charged with spiritual yearning cannot find fulfilment in conventional religious forms but must turn to the demonic for succour. So too Germany's 'breakthrough' of 1914, motivated primarily (it is claimed) by the spiritual imperatives of sacrifice, expiation and entry into a higher order of being, justified for Zeitblom all offences against ordinary morality; and Adrian, like his diabolic mentor, accepts that the price of supreme achievement may be what run-of-the-mill ethics would call criminality. This self-appointed redeemer borrows the Superman's licence to transcend the restraints and inhibitions of a cowardly world—and here again forges a link between his proud isola-tion and the national community in which he lives.

The inspiration of Adrian's music is almost always nihilistic and destructive. With his final masterpiece, the Lamentation of Doctor Faustus, Leverkühn sets out to 'take back', to negate or revoke the Ninth Symphony and the Ode to Joy. It is a complete repudiation of the divine in the world, an ultimate confession of spiritual anguish that can be neither healed nor assuaged. Leverkühn's spirituality survives only in the intensity of his blasphemy, in the idea of a 'supreme, self-validating strenuousness' which has been seen as the hallmark of his age.[7] The 'breakthrough' which he ultimately achieves at the cost of his soul drives him forward into nothingness.

And yet a question mark remains. At the conclusion of his Faust oratorio one group of instruments after another falls silent until only a single 'cello note is left to die slowly away. That final note of despair seems (we are told) to become transformed in the listener into a glimmer of hope—the hope that despair may be transcended through a miracle that surpasses all understanding and even the doctrines of faith itself. For by the end, in a state of deepest attrition, Adrian has utterly renounced the demonic alliance, even though he believes repentance can no longer save him. Instead of hazarding everything on the return of inspiration, he tells his audience, one should strive

> klug zu sorgen, was vonnöten auf Erden, damit es dort besser werde, und besonnen dazu zu tun, dass unter den Menschen solche Ordnung sich herstelle, die dem schönen Werk wieder Lebensgrund und ein redlich Hineinpassen bereiten . . .[8]
> (*to attend to what is needful on earth, that things may get better there, and prudently to toil for the establishment of a human order which will prepare a living foundation for the work of beauty and a just place in the affairs of men . . .*)

At the last he repudiates the aestheticism which had led him to value the artistic 'breakthrough' above all else and to divorce his art from humanitarian values. And he appeals in effect for men to work towards a just social order that will provide a proper basis for the work of art, an appropriate setting for the *re-ligio* which he himself had pursued through demonic means. The political corollary is intimated in the contrast between the compassion and charity of Frau Schweigestill, the country woman in whose farmhouse Adrian has sought refuge (did not the Devil concede that he was not one of her kind?) and the indifference, discomfiture, unfeeling curiosity or moral indignation of the bourgeois intellectuals whom Adrian is addressing.

The novel attempts to give the lie once and for all to the notion of a *Geist* that is devoid of sensuality, of an art that inhabits a socio-political vacuum. It offers a critique of the Idealist cult of inwardness at the very point when historical pressures drive it to seek reintegration with the community. It shows that if the values of inwardness and aestheticism are simply transferred to the social dimension, their absolute, uncompromising intensity are fraught with disaster. The condition of 'coldness' which Adrian takes upon himself is a poetic cypher for the inability of the exclusively aesthetic imagination to accommodate the human qualities of love, care and compassion. The temperament which views the world as an aesthetic phenomenon sees life merely as the material of art. That life has its own priorities and its own intrinsic values which may be at odds with the demands of art—this the aesthetic mind cannot comprehend. But its own pretensions are based on an illusion: pure *Geist* is a misconception, for art and life are interdependent. When Adrian concludes a pact with the Devil, he sacrifices his soul and his emotions to the future of his art, a truly aesthetic renunciation. The equivalent in the socio-political sphere is the vision of dreamers, artists and philosophers who seek to shape society to their abstract designs. The sheer intransigence of their unworldly vision overrides all proper considerations, subordinating everything to the realization of the ideal and justifying every means by reference to the spiritual end. Just such an abstract idealism we can observe in the Munich intellectuals and behind them in a host of German writers from the Romantics to Gottfried Benn. In the terrifying ease with which it succumbs to barbarity, aestheticism—one way and another—pronounces sentence on itself.

A central problem remains. Are the two areas of experience, the aesthetic and the political, compatible or commensurate throughout the novel? On one vital issue there exists a radical incongruence which ultimately makes us doubt the wisdom of Mann's choice of an artist figure as his representative hero. Although there is no doubt as to the human cost which Leverkühn inflicts on himself to achieve his purpose, although the moral nihilism of his music is manifest, we are confronted with the equally incontrovertible fact of his aesthetic achievement. Leverkühn does attain the longed-for 'breakthrough' from calculatory coldness into heartfelt expressiveness, and whatever fears and reservations his friend Zeitblom, the narrator, may harbour, he never allows them to invalidate his judgment of the music. The Lamentation of Doctor Faustus is described as the ultimate liberation, and Zeitblom even bases his hope of a religious paradox on the aesthetic paradox mirrored there. As total construction has given birth to authentic expression, so too salvation may yet emerge from the depths of godlessness.

But what social or political 'breakthrough' is comparable to the aesthetic fruits of Leverkühn's union with the demonic? What construction of the Third Reich can offer any matching achievement? What political liberty emerged under the tyranny of National Socialism to match the mystery of artistic freedom which is said to ensue from the formal *Gebundenbeit*, the total order and discipline, of the musical composition? Is there any parallel between Adrian's self-sacrifice for his art—and the hecatomb of Europe? Is the faint hope of redemption with which the novel closes, a prayer dictated by Mann's avowed love for his character, an appropriate response to the political catastrophe that now overshadows Leverkühn's personal fate? By focusing on the aesthetic dimension of the problem Mann ends up trapped by the conflict between moral and aesthetic values which he is trying to resolve. And though on one level Leverkühn's confession repudiates the primacy of art, the experience of his music leaves the problem as open as ever. The ambiguity may be justified in terms of our response to art but is surely inappropriate when transferred to the socio-political sphere where other values predominate. In this exhaustive critique of aestheticism Mann remains tragically enmeshed in the very tradition he is criticizing. His Faust bequeaths to us an *œuvre* which we are bound to judge aesthetically, not just morally or socially. The final conjunction of friend and fatherland is thus possible only in prayer. In symbolic terms—for here again we must judge aesthetically—the two are no longer commensurate.[9]

Conclusion

A generation of German writers who unlike many of their predecessors realized that their art could not ignore the political issues of their day found themselves on the brink of abandoning art altogether. The parties regarded literature at best as serving their ideology and at worst as a frivolous irrelevance. The writers for their part were aware that in seeking even a committed art they were already abstracting from immediate, concrete reality and subordinating it to alien laws, thus depriving themselves of the chance to influence the political situation directly. The dilemma of committed literature is the conflict between didacticism and aesthetic pleasure. The greater the claim of such writing to aesthetic recognition, the more extensively it assimilates historical reality to its own autonomous being. Though the aesthetic experience cannot ever be entirely separated from its historical context (language alone guarantees that link), it remains of a fundamentally different order from our political experience. Art loses the power to effect change in proportion to its transmutation of given historical data into the stuff of aesthetic creation, according to the conventions of its chosen form.[1] In the face of the historical crisis of the inter-war years, the temptation was to abandon literary creation altogether and to sacrifice art to activism, fiction to the documentary. Some writers maintained a productive tension between art and activism by drawing a distinction between their publicistic work and their creative writing, the latter manifesting a far greater degree of reflective detachment and complexity.

At either end of the ideological spectrum the pressure was towards collective art, an art which transcended the bourgeois heritage of individualism and articulated the needs and aspirations of whole social groups. Some of the techniques used and their consequences proved to be disconcertingly similar; the theatrical chorus, the exemplary hero whose private life is totally subordinate to the collective, the degeneration of character into caricature, a 'realism' which confuses the descriptive and the prescriptive, the cult of monumentality and heroicization, a bankruptcy of the imagination in the face of a barbaric reality. The further art progressed towards the collective, the closer it approximated to cultic ritual. Indeed the substitution of ideology for religion is a major feature of both right- and left-wing writing. One prime difference remains. Only Communist or Socialist writers chose to stress the typical by reference to historical, social and economic data, thus appealing to intellectual judgment. The more perceptive left-wing writers even presented their figures with ironic detachment—at least for as long as they were able to avoid the constraints of the Party aesthetic. Fascism, by contrast, uniformly demanded the elimination of the rational faculty and deplored narrative irony.

It was rare for a revolutionary political commitment to go hand in hand with a revolutionary aesthetic. The monolithic parties shared a profound mistrust of artistic innovation and based their own aesthetic canons on conservative premises. Critical thought, linguistic innovations, the very autonomy of the creative imagination were anathema to closed ideological systems designed to manipulate rather than to extend human consciousness. Moreover, the fundamental pessimism of modernist art offended the inherently positive direction of political ideologies. Fascism could accommodate the irrational anti-Enlightenment quality of modernism but not its anarchic destructiveness, its onslaught on traditional values, its subversion of the substance and meaning of the phenomenal world. Communism necessarily repudiated the legacy of irrationalism and equally rejected the modernist emphasis on existential solitude, the agonized isolation of the individual and the irreducible reality of pain and death. If the Communists tolerated the 'revolutionary' modernist,[2] they remained suspicious of his independent judgment and artistic freedom.

Enzensberger has argued that there is an indirect but inevitable connection between the poet's independence and originality in the use of language, and political subversion.[3] If we look at the *language* of poetry as well as at the political *opinions* of the poet, we see that there is no necessary correlation between the two. The conservative can seem revolutionary, the political radical a literary backwoodsman. It is short-sighted or even irrelevant to criticize writers for ignoring political themes—without at the same time considering the nature of their aesthetic achievement, their use of language and their impact on the sensibility of their readers. Viewed in this light, much of the political literature of our period seems overwhelmingly conservative. Paradoxically, the literature of Expressionism and Dada, however 'unpolitical' or historically ingenuous, may have achieved more by its revolutionary grammar than Brecht cared to admit. The real innovators, those writers who decisively rejected the forms and perspectives of the nineteenth century—Rilke, Kafka, Musil, for example—invariably lacked any creative interest in the *données* of the political world or any desire to become actively involved in the political struggle. A text which is committed to the critical elucidation of political issues and which manages to remain aesthetically interesting is relatively rare in the literature we have examined. The history of literary commitment in Germany during this period is all too often one of conflict, compromise, failure or delusion. The insidious corruption of the Lutheran and Idealist legacy is now patent. There were writers whose culpability is a matter of historical record. There were those who kept the memory of decency alive. Few escaped the compulsions of an age whose 'cursed spite' invaded the last sanctuaries of inwardness and finally exploded the myth of the non-political German.

Notes

Introduction

1. Ralf Dahrendorf, *Gesellschaft und Demokratie in Deutschland* (München, 1965), especially 'Der Unpolitische Deutsche'. For a fuller treatment of this subject, see my article 'Writers and Politics: Some Reflections on a German Tradition', *Journal of European Studies*, vol. vi, no. 2 (June 1976).

2. In 'Die Deutsche Literatur [im Ausland seit 1933]. Ein Dialog zwischen Politik and Kunst', now in *Aufsätze zur Literatur* (Olten/Freiburg i.B., 1963).

3. See Reinhold Aris, *History of Political Thought in Germany from 1789 to 1815* (London, 1936); G. P. Gooch, *Germany and the French Revolution*, 2nd Edn. (London, 1965); Hajo Holborn, 'Der deutsche Idealismus in sozialgeschichtlicher Beleuchtung', *Historische Zeitschrift*, vol. CLXXIV (October 1952), pp. 359–85.

4. See the two anthologies edited with excellent introductions by Jost Hermand: *Das Junge Deutschland* and *Der deutsche Vormärz* (Stuttgart, 1966 and 1967).

5. See Fritz Stern, 'The Political Consequences of the Unpolitical German' in *The Failure of Illiberalism. Essays on the Political Culture of Modern Germany* (London, 1972).

6. Roy Pascal, *From Naturalism to Expressionism. German Literature and Society 1880–1918* (London, 1973), p. 11.

7. *Ibid.*, pp. 102–3.

8. *Ibid.*, p. 105 and Friedrich Albrecht, *Deutsche Schriftsteller in der Entscheidung. Wege zur Arbeiterklasse 1918–1933* (Berlin/Weimar, 1970), p. 33.

9. Fritz Stern, *The Politics of Cultural Despair. A Study in the Rise of the Germanic Ideology* (Berkeley and Los Angeles, 1961), p. 208.

10. Max Weber, 'Politik als Beruf' [1918/19] in *Gesammelte Politische Schriften*, J. Winckelmann (ed.), 2nd Edn. (Tübingen, 1958), p. 541 and Heine, *Zur Geschichte der Religion und Philosophie in Deutschland*, C. P. Magill (ed.) (London, 1947), pp. 174–6.

Chapter One

1. See Kurt Sontheimer, *Antidemokratisches Denken in der Weimarer Republik. Die politischen Ideen des deutschen Nationalismus zwischen 1918 und 1933* (München, 1964), Chapter 5, 'Das Kriegserlebnis des Ersten Weltkrieges'; Rolf Geissler, *Dekadenz und Heroismus. Zeitroman und völkisch-nationalsozialistische Literaturkritik* (Stuttgart, 1964), pp. 76–103; Ernst Loewy, *Literatur unterm Hakenkreuz. Das Dritte Reich und seine Dichtung: eine Dokumentation*, Fischer-Bücherei 1042 (Frankfurt/Hamburg, 1969), 'Der militante Nationalismus'; Ernst Keller, *Nationalismus und Literatur* (Bern/München, 1970), esp. 'Langemarck'.

2. See J. P. Stern, 'The Dear Purchase', *The German Quarterly*, vol. XLI, no. 3 (May, 1968), pp. 317–40.

3. For a wider critical assessment of E.J.'s work, see for instance Hans Peter Schwarz, *Der konservative Anarchist: Politik und Zeitkritik Ernst Jüngers* (Freiburg i.B., 1962); J. P. Stern, *Ernst Jünger, a Writer of our Time* (Cambridge, 1953); Helmut Kaiser, *Mythos, Rausch und Reaktion. Der Weg Gottfried Benns und Ernst Jüngers* (Berlin, 1962).

4. For a detailed account of E.J.'s activities and writings during the Weimar years, see H. M. Ridley, *National Socialism and Literature. Five Writers in Search of an Ideology*, Ph.D. Diss. University of Cambridge (1967).

5. So laconic was it that attempts were made to enlist it in the cause of the right-wing heroicization of war. But its nationalist champions were discomfited to learn that Renn, whose real name was Arnold Vieth von Golssenau, had joined the Communist Party a year before. After Renn's arrest in 1933, the Nazis spent several months trying in vain to persuade him to join their ranks, on the strength of the impact made by his war book.

6. A bookseller's statistic indicates the special appeal of Carossa's book. In the first five years after publication, which coincided with the stabilization of the Weimar Republic, the book sold only in moderate numbers. Between 1929 and 1934 the rate at which it sold increased substantially. But from 1934 to 1938 sales accelerated even faster. (Figures in Donald Ray Richards, *The German Bestseller in the 20th Century. A complete Bibliography and Analysis 1915–1940* (Berne, 1968).) In other words it joined with the literature of the '*innere Emigration*' (see pp. 62–9) in offering consolation and vague hope to those who saw themselves at the mercy of forces beyond their control, which they had in fact themselves helped to unleash.

7. See J. P. Stern, *On Realism* (London/Boston, 1973), p. 50 and Stern, *Ernst Jünger, op. cit.*, pp. 31–3.

8. Under the title 'Der grosse Krieg der Weissen Männer' the cycle includes *Die Zeit ist reif* (1957); *Junge Frau von 1914* (1931); *Erziehung vor Verdun* (1935); *Grischa; Die Feuerpause* (1954); *Einsetzung eines Königs* (1937).

Chapter Two

1. For the following I have drawn on John Willett, *Expressionism* (London, 1970); Eberhard Lämmert, 'Das expressionistische Verkündigungsdrama' in *Der deutsche Expressionismus. Formen und Gestalten*, Hans Steffen (ed.) (Göttingen, 1965); Kasimir Edschmid, *Über den Expressionismus in der Literatur und die neue Dichtung* (Berlin, 1920); Walter H. Sokel, *The Writer in Extremis. Expressionism in 20th Century German Literature* (Stanford, 1959); Paul Raabe, 'Das literarische Leben im Expressionismus. Eine historische Skizze' in *Die Zeitschriften und Sammlungen des literarischen Expressionismus* (Stuttgart, 1964); Eva Kolinsky, *Engagierter Expressionismus. Politik und Literatur zwischen Weltkrieg und Weimarer Republik* (Stuttgart, 1970); Jürgen Rühle, *Literatur und Revolution* (Köln/Berlin, 1960); Günther Rühle, *Theater für die Republik 1917–33 im Spiegel der Kritik* (Frankfurt, 1967); Roy Pascal, *From Naturalism to Expressionism, op. cit.*; Friedrich Albrecht, *Deutsche Schriftsteller in der Entscheidung, op. cit.*; Peter Gay, *Weimar Culture. The Outsider as Insider* (London, 1969); Gordon A. Craig, 'Engagement and Neutrality in Weimar Germany', *Journal of Contemporary History*, vol. II, no. 2 (April 1967).

2. Walter Benjamin, 'Karl Kraus', *Illuminationen*, Siegfried Unseld (ed.) (Frankfurt a.M., 1961), p. 404.

3. Walter H. Sokel, 'Brecht und der Expressionismus', in *Die sogenannten Zwanziger Jahre*, Reinhold Grimm and Jost Hermand (eds.) (Bad Homburg/Berlin/Zürich, 1970), p. 48.

4. Peter Szondi, *Theorie des modernen Dramas* (edition suhrkamp 27, Frankfurt, 1966), p. 108.

5. Pascal, *From Naturalism to Expressionism*, p. 196.

6. See Lämmert, *op. cit.*; Keller, *Nationalismus und Literatur, op. cit.*, p. 138 ff. (cp. his analysis of the 'fatal mixture of pietism and patriotism' in Walter Flex's best-selling war book *Der Wanderer zwischen beiden Welten*, p. 48 ff.); and J. P. Stern, *Hitler : the Führer and the People* (London, 1975) esp. 'The Language of Sacrifice', 'The Religious

Expectation and its Ritual' and 'A Society longing for Transcendence'. For a case study of Messianism in the novels of Alfred Döblin, who showed early affinities with Expressionism, see W. G. Sebald, 'Zum Thema Messianismus im Werk Döblins', *Neophilologus*, vol. LIX, no. 3 (1975), pp. 421–34. Some of these links were anticipated in the attack on the Expressionists, above all Johst and Arnolt Bronnen, launched for dubious reasons and with characteristic crudeness by the Muscovite champions of 'socialist realism' in the mid-thirties (cf. n. 14 below).

7. See Wolfgang Rothe (ed.), *Der Aktivismus 1915–1920*, DTV 625 (München, 1969), esp. the introduction and Hiller's policy statements; also Friedrich Albrecht, *op. cit.*, pp. 66–9, pp. 84–6 and pp. 497–501 for the 1918 programme of the 'Rat geistiger Arbeiter'.

8. For biographical details, see John M. Spalek, 'Ernst Toller: the need for a new estimate', *The German Quarterly*, vol. XXXIX, no. 4 (November, 1966) and 'Ernst Tollers Vortragstätigkeit und seine Hilfsaktionen im Exil', *Exil und Innere Emigration II*, Peter Uwe Hohendahl and Egon Schwarz (eds.) (Frankfurt, 1973). I am indebted to Dr Dorothea Klein for allowing me to read her searching, informative and stimulating thesis *Der Wandel der dramatischen Darstellungsform im Werk Ernst Tollers (1919–1930)*, Diss. Bochum (1968). See also Walter H. Sokel, 'Ernst Toller' in *Deutsche Literatur im 20. Jahrhundert. Strukturen und Gestalten*, Otto Mann and Wolfgang Rothe (eds.), 5th Edn. (Bern/München, 1967).

9. Pascal, *From Naturalism to Expressionism*, p. 122.

10. Bertolt Brecht, *Gesammelte Werke 19, Schriften zur Literatur und Kunst 2*, werkausgabe (edition suhrkamp, Frankfurt, 1967), p. 304.

11. For accounts of party policy, critical debates, literary developments and the contribution of individual writers, see e.g., Albrecht, *Deutsche Schriftsteller in der Entscheidung, op. cit.*; *Zur Tradition der sozialistischen Literatur in Deutschland. Eine Auswahl von Dokumenten*, ed. with commentary by the Deutsche Akademie der Künste zu Berlin, Sektion Dichtkunst und Sprachpflege, Abteilung Geschichte der sozialistischen Literatur, 2nd Edn. (Berlin/Weimar, 1967); Alfred Klein, *Im Auftrag ihrer Klasse. Weg und Leistung der deutschen Arbeiterschriftsteller 1918–1933* (Berlin/Weimar, 1972); Walter Fähnders and Martin Rector, *Linksradikalismus und Literatur. Untersuchungen zur Geschichte der sozialistischen Literatur in der Weimarer Republik*, 2 vols. (Reinbek bei Hamburg, 1974); Wolfgang Rothe (ed.), *Die deutsche Literatur in der Weimarer Republik* (Stuttgart, 1974); and above all

Helga Gallas, *Marxistische Literaturtheorie. Kontroversen im Bund proletarisch-revolutionärer Schriftsteller* (Sammlung Luchterhand 19, Neuwied/Berlin, 1971).

12. See J. P. Stern, *On Realism*, p. 53 and § 99.

13. Gallas, *op. cit.*, p. 88.

14. The two debates were separate but revolved around the same issues. Lukács' critique of Expressionism ('Grösse und Verfall des E.') appeared in 1934. He found it 'too imprecise in its idea of "bourgeois" and "revolution", too clamorous in its language, too egocentric in its attitude and altogether too incapable of conveying any but a fragmentary view of the world to live up to its progressive pretensions and admitted achievements in stimulating opposition to the First World War' (Willett, p. 217). The attack was renewed by Kurella in 1937 when he claimed that it was inevitable that a whole-hearted Expressionist should end up on the side of the Nazis. A series of articles for and against Expressionism and the Lukács aesthetic then appeared in the emigré periodical *Das Wort* in Moscow. See Hans Jürgen Schmitt, *Die Expressionismus-Debatte. Zur marxistischen Theorie des Realismus* (Frankfurt, 1973); David R. Bathrick, 'Moderne Kunst und Klassenkampf. Die Expressionismus-Debatte in der Exilzeitschrift *Das Wort*', in *Exil und Innere Emigration*, Reinhold Grimm and Jost Hermand (eds.) (Frankfurt, 1972); Franz Schonauer, 'Expressionismus und Faschismus. Eine Diskussion aus dem Jahre 1938', *Literatur und Kritik*, Band 1, Nr. 7 (1966), pp. 44–54.

For the Lukács-Seghers exchange, see Georg Lukács, *Probleme des Realismus* (Berlin, 1955).

See also Brecht's notes 'Über den Realismus', 'Volkstümlichkeit und Realismus', 'Notizen über realistische Schreibweise' in *Gesammelte Werke 19* (cf. Note 11); and Klaus Völker, 'Brecht und Lukács: Analyse einer Meinungsverschiedenheit', *Kursbuch 7* (1966), pp. 80–101.

15. Spalek, 'Ernst Toller: the need for a new estimate', *loc. cit.*, pp. 594–5.

16. See his somewhat over-generous tribute to it in *Gesammelte Werke 19*, *op. cit.*, p. 330.

17. See C. D. Innes, *Erwin Piscator's Political Theatre* (Cambridge, 1972); Helga Gallas, *op. cit.*, pp. 94–5.

18. For statistics, see Gallas, p. 94; for limitations, see David Caute, *The Illusion. An Essay on Politics, Theatre and the Novel* (London, 1971), p. 68.

19. See Inge Diersen, *Seghers-Studien. Interpretationen von Werken*

aus den Jahren 1926–1935. Ein Beitrag zu Entwicklungsproblemen der modernen deutschen Epik (Berlin, 1965), introduction.

20. Ernst Fischer, *An Opposing Man*, transl. Peter and Betty Ross, with an introduction by John Berger (London, 1974), p. 5.

21. Though even here only by virtue of a solipsistic defence mechanism. See W. A. J. Steer, '*Baal*: A Key to Brecht's Communism', *German Life and Letters*, vol. XIX (1965), pp. 40–51.

22. Most of them between 1932 (65,000) and 1935 (315,000). Even more worryingly, it was still selling a decade ago: by 1965 sales had reached 780,000 (Richards, *The German Bestseller*, p. 4 and Keller, *Nationalismus und Literatur*, p. 260, n. 22).

23. See A. J. Nicholls, *Weimar and the Rise of Hitler* (London, 1968), pp. 94–6.

24. See Ridley, *National Socialism and Literature, op. cit.*, p. 104, 109 n, 115 ff. There too can be found details of Grimm's career, his publicistic writing and his relationship with the Nazis. After 1933 he protested his 'independence' of the regime he had helped to win power. He even instituted an annual *Dichtertreffen* at Lippoldsberg from 1936 onwards, designed to rival the official Nazi literary gatherings at Weimar. It was attended by such writers as Carossa, Dwinger, Kolbenheyer, Von Salomon and R. A. Schröder. On Grimm, see also Keller, *Nationalismus und Literatur, op. cit.*, pp. 122–33 and Francis L. Carsten, '*Volk ohne Raum*. A Note on Hans Grimm', *Journal of Contemporary History*, vol. II, no. 2 (April, 1967), pp. 221–7.

25. Ridley, *op cit.*, p. 105.

26. This was an attempt to combine anti-capitalism and anti-Western feeling with a militant German nationalism in emulation of and in alliance with Soviet Russia. Cf. Kurt Sontheimer, *Antidemokratisches Denken, op. cit.*, and Otto Ernst Schüddekopf, *Linke Leute von rechts. Die national-revolutionären Minderheiten und der Kommunismus in der Weimarer Republik* (Stuttgart, 1960). Jünger was for a time associated with these circles. They were 'neutralized' along with the left wing of the NSDAP in deference to industry and the bourgeoisie.

27. See R. G. L. Waite, *Vanguard of Nazism. The Free Corps Movement in Postwar Germany 1918–1923* (Cambridge Mass., 1952).

Chapter Three

1. I have borrowed this rendering from Helmut Gruber, '*Neue Sachlichkeit* and the World War', *GLL*, vol. XX, no. 2 (January 1967). For the concept itself, see Helmut Lethen, *Neue Sachlichkeit*

1924–1932. Studien zur Literatur des 'Weissen Sozialismus' (Stuttgart, 1970); Horst Denkler, 'Sache und Stil. Die Theorie der "Neuen Sachlichkeit" und ihre Auswirkungen auf Kunst und Dichtung', *Wirkendes Wort*, Jhg. 18, Heft 3 (1968), pp. 167–85; and Wolfgang Rothe (ed.), *Die deutsche Literatur in der Weimarer Republik, op. cit.*

2. Lukács, 'Reportage oder Gestaltung?', a review article concerned with Ottwalt's novel *Denn sie wissen, was sie tun*. Now in *Zur Tradition der sozialistischen Literatur in Deutschland, op. cit.*, together with Ottwalt's rejoinder.

3. *Des Kaisers Kulis. Roman der deutschen Kriegsflotte* (Berlin, 1930). See p. 32.

4. For a list of the changes and a general discussion of their significance, see Dorothea Klein, *op. cit.*, p. 153 ff and pp. 236–7.

5. Jost Hermand, *Unbequeme Literatur. Eine Beispielreihe* (Heidelberg, 1971), p. 163.

6. See J. P. Stern *On Realism, op. cit.*, p. 122 and p. 143.

7. Piscator's new Theater am Nollendorfplatz opened with the premiere of Toller's play. But Piscator found much to criticize in Toller's text: it was too subjective, too emotional and the issues too confused. He thus adapted the text for production, even to the extent of writing in new scenes without Toller's consent. At the end of his version, after a new affirmative last line, the audience spontaneously burst into the Internationale. See Innes, *op. cit.*, p. 128, Klein, p. 118 ff. and Hermand, *Unbequeme Literatur, op. cit.*, pp. 128–49.

8. Both Fritz von Unruh (in *Phaea*, 1930) and Kaiser (in *Nebeneinander*, 1923) likewise depicted the catastrophe of the Expressionist character in a clash with objective reality: cf. Grimm/Hermand, 'Zwischen Expressionismus und Faschismus. Bemerkungen zum Drama der Zwanziger Jahre' in *Die sogenannten Zwanziger Jahre, op. cit.*

9. It seems likely that Reger borrowed his classification from the sociologist Werner Sombart who in *Der Bourgeois* (1913) had distinguished between the heroic adventurer, the patriarch and the calculating dealer, the *Händler*. For details, see Pascal, *From Naturalism to Expressionism*, p. 31.

10. See Walter Bussmann, 'Politische Ideologien zwischen Monarchie und Weimarer Republik. Ein Beitrag zur Ideengeschichte der Weimarer Republik', *Historische Zeitschrift*, Bd. 190, Heft 1 (February 1960), pp. 55–77; for the caveat, see Peter Gay, *Weimar Culture* (London, 1969), pp. 24–5.

11. For an appraisal of Mann's political ideas and attitudes, see Kurt

Sontheimer, *Thomas Mann und die Deutschen* (Fischer-Bücherei 650, Frankfurt/Hamburg, 1965); Erich Heller, *The Ironic German. A Study of Thomas Mann* (London, 1958), esp. 'The Conservative Imagination'; T. J. Reed, *Thomas Mann. The Uses of Tradition* (Oxford, 1974), esp. 'Unpolitics: War thoughts 1914–1918' and 'Republic: Politics 1919–1933'; Ernst Keller, *Der Unpolitische Deutsche. Eine Studie zu den 'Betrachtungen eines Unpolitischen' von Thomas Mann* (Bern/München, 1965); J. P. Stern, *Hitler, op. cit.*, pp. 30–3; Günter Hartung, 'Bertolt Brecht und Thomas Mann. Über Alternativen in Kunst und Politik', *Weimarer Beiträge* 12 (1966).

12. J. P. Stern talks of the 'whole complex relationship between the demagogue and the masses' and of 'the predicament of the European liberal mind in the grip of the demagogue's will'. See his *Thomas Mann* (New York/London, 1967), p. 25.

13. For an even more pessimistic interpretation of Mann's story, see J. P. Stern, *Hitler, op. cit.*, pp. 67–8.

14. Another decade was to elapse before Mann devoted an essay to 'Bruder Hitler'.

15. 'Von deutscher Republik' (Foreword to printed version), *Gesammelte Werke in zwölf Bänden*, Band XI, *Reden und Aufsätze 3*, (Frankfurt, 1960), p. 809.

Chapter Four

1. I have drawn on the following: Ernst Loewy, *Literatur unterm Hakenkreuz, op. cit.*; J. P. Stern, *Hitler : the Führer and the People, op. cit.*; Rolf Geissler, *Dekadenz und Heroismus, op. cit.*; Albrecht Schöne, *Über politische Lyrik im 20. Jahrhundert* (Kleine Vandenhoeck-Reihe 228–9, Göttingen, 1965); Joseph Wulf, *Literatur und Dichtung im Dritten Reich. Eine Dokumentation* (rororo Taschenbuch-Ausgabe, Reinbek bei Hamburg, 1966); Dietrich Strothmann, *Nationalsozialistische Literaturpolitik. Ein Beitrag zur Publizistik im Dritten Reich*, 2nd Edn. (Bonn, 1963); Ernst Keller, *Nationalismus und Literatur, op. cit.*, 'Das letzte Reich'.

The Germanist will find a grotesque sidelight on Nazi literary policy in H. G. Atkins, *German Literature through Nazi Eyes* (London, 1941).

2. 'Der Kunstbericht soll weniger Wertung, als vielmehr Darstellung und damit Würdigung sein', quoted by Geissler, p. 30.

3. Quoted in Walter A. Berendsohn, *Die humanistische Front. Einführung in die deutsche Emigranten-Literatur*, Erster Teil (Zürich, 1946), p. 25.

4. Franz Schonauer, *Deutsche Literatur im Dritten Reich. Versuch einer Darstellung in polemisch-didaktischer Absicht* (Olten/Freiburg, 1961), p. 86.

5. For the following see esp. Schöne, *Über politische Lyrik.*

6. *Ibid.*, p. 20.

7. See Willett, *Expressionism, op. cit.*, p. 198 ff.

8. For accounts of Benn's relationship with National Socialism, see e.g., Walter Lennig, *Gottfried Benn*, Rowohlts-Monographien (Reinbek bei Hamburg, 1962); Helmut Kaiser, *Mythos, Rausch und Reaktion, op. cit.*; Ridley, *National Socialism and Literature, op. cit.*; Peter de Mendelssohn, *Der Geist in der Despotie. Versuche über die moralischen Möglichkeiten des Intellektuellen in der totalitären Gesellschaft* (Berlin-Grunewald, 1953).

9. These included 'Der neue Staat und die Intellektuellen' (April 1933); 'Antwort an die literarischen Emigranten' (May 1933); 'Zucht und Zukunft' (October 1933); 'Expressionismus' (November 1933); 'Rede auf Marinetti' (March 1934); 'Rede auf Stefan George' (April 1934).

10. Many of the most significant works are discussed in Wolfgang Brekle, 'Die antifaschistische Literatur in Deutschland (1933–1945)', *Weimarer Beiträge*, vol. XVI, Heft 6 (1970), pp. 67 ff.

11. My account is based on the following: Reinhold Grimm, 'Innere Emigration als Lebensform' in Grimm/Hermand (eds.), *Exil und Innere Emigration, op. cit.*; Gunter Groll, *De Profundis. Deutsche Lyrik in dieser Zeit. Eine Anthologie aus zwölf Jahren* (München, 1946); W. A. Berendsohn, *Die humanistische Front, op. cit.*; F. Schonauer, *Deutsche Literatur im Dritten Reich, op. cit.*; Charles W. Hoffman, *Opposition Poetry in Nazi Germany* (Berkeley and Los Angeles, 1962); Hoffman, 'Opposition und Innere Emigration. Zwei Aspekte des "anderen Deutschlands"', in *Exil und Innere Emigration II*, Peter Uwe Hohendahl and Egon Schwarz (eds.) (Frankfurt, 1973); H. R. Klieneberger, *The Christian Writers of the Inner Emigration* (The Hague/Paris, 1968); Heinz D. Osterle, 'The Other Germany. Resistance to the Third Reich in German Literature', *The Germany Quarterly*, vol. 41 (1968), p. 1 ff.; Keller, *Nationalismus und Literatur, op. cit.*, 'Das letzte Reich'.

12. For documents and commentary, see J. F. G. Grosser, *Die grosse Kontroverse. Ein Briefwechsel um Deutschland* (Hamburg etc., 1963).

13. The term '*Sklavensprache*' which occurs repeatedly in discussions of the '*innere Emigration*' seems to have been coined by the novelist

Hans Werner Richter in 'Die Gruppe 47', *Moderna Sprak* 58 (1964); cited by Karl Otto Conrady, 'Deutsche Literaturwissenschaft und Drittes Reich' in *Germanistik—eine deutsche Wissenschaft*, 2nd Edn. (edition suhrkamp 204, Frankfurt, 1967), p. 78.

14. Osterle, *loc. cit.*, pp. 5–6, echoing Schonauer, p. 126.

15. R. Grimm, *loc. cit.*, p. 72, and Keller, *Nationalismus und Literatur*, on Jochen Klepper.

16. Theodor Zielkowski, 'Form als Protest' in Grimm/Hermand, *Exil und Innere Emigration, op. cit.*

17. For his relations with the regime, see Sumner Kirschner, 'Some Documents relating to Ernst Wiechert's "Inward Emigration"', *The German Quarterly*, vol. 38 (1965). In his story 'Der weisse Büffel' (read in public in 1937) we are presented with a Schillerian martyrdom, again involving a penitent ruler to ensure the eventual reconciliation with the spiritual principle.

18. Strothmann, *op. cit.*, p. 379. Keller notes that it received a 'positive' evaluation from the Amt Rosenberg and that it fulfilled two major criteria of Nazi fiction, 'Idyllik und Heroismus', *op. cit.*, p. 182.

19. Richards, *The German Bestseller*, *op. cit.*, gives a figure of 23,000; but Strothmann, p. 378, n. 50 cites a much lower figure of 12,000 in the first year of publication.

Chapter Five

1. See Hans-Albert Walter, *Bedrohung und Verfolgung bis 1933*, vol. I of his *Deutsche Exilliteratur 1933–1950* (Sammlung Luchterhand, Neuwied/Berlin, 1972). This work, comprising in all nine volumes of which three have appeared to date, promises to become a standard work of reference on German exile literature.

2. For the following account I am indebted to: Jost Hermand, 'Schreiben in der Fremde' in Grimm/Hermand (eds.), *Exil und Innere Emigration*, *op. cit.*; W. A. Berendsohn, *Die humanistische Front, op. cit.*; Egon Schwarz and Matthias Wegner (eds.), *Verbannung. Aufzeichnungen Deutscher Schriftsteller im Exil* (Hamburg, 1964); Matthias Wegner, *Exil und Literatur. Deutsche Schriftsteller im Ausland 1933–1945* (Frankfurt/Bonn, 1967); Hans-Albert Walter, 'Das Bild Deutschlands im Exilroman', *Neue Rundschau* 1966, pp. 437–58 and 'Deutsche Literatur im Exil', *Merkur* 273 (1971), pp. 71–7; Manfred Durzak (ed.), *Die Deutsche Exilliteratur 1933–1945* (Stuttgart, 1973); Peter Uwe Hohendahl and Egon Schwarz (eds.), *Exil und Innere Emigration II* (Frankfurt, 1973);

and the anthology of documents, memoirs and essays in Heinz Ludwig Arnold (ed.), *Deutsche Literatur im Exil 1933–1945. Dokumente und Materialien*, 2 vols. (Frankfurt a.M., 1974).

3. On the changing image of Germany in the prose fiction of these years, see Walter's article 'Das Bild Deutschlands . . .'

4. See Frank Trommler, 'Emigration und Nachkriegsliteratur' in Grimm/Hermand, *Exil und Innere Emigration*.

5. In conversation with Friedrich Wolf; cited in Hans Mayer, *Bertolt Brecht und die Tradition* (sonderreihe DTV, München, 1965), p. 8. Other useful works from the vast bibliography on Brecht: Reinhold Grimm, *Bertolt Brecht : die Struktur seines Werkes*, 3rd edn. (Nürnberg, 1962); Volker Klotz, *Bertolt Brecht. Versuch über das Werk* (Darmstadt, 1957); *Theaterarbeit. Sechs Aufführungen des Berliner Ensembles* (Dresden, n.d.); Martin Esslin, *Brecht : A Choice of Evils* (London, 1959) and *Bertolt Brecht* (New York, 1969); Walter Hinck, *Die Dramaturgie des späten Brecht*, 3rd edn. (Göttingen, 1962).

6. J. P. Stern has pointed out that, however much we (or the author) suggest rational explanations for Leverkühn's illness, a final doubt remains. See *Thomas Mann, op. cit.*, p. 39.

7. See J. P. Stern, 'History and Allegory in Thomas Mann's *Doktor Faustus*. An inaugural lecture delivered at University College, London on 1 March 1973'.

8. Thomas Mann, *Doktor Faustus. Das Leben des deutschen Tonsetzers Adrian Leverkühn, erzählt von einem Freunde* (Frankfurt a.M., 1960), p. 535.

9. The debate on just this aspect of Mann's novel continues. E. M. Butler in *The Fortunes of Faust* (Cambridge, 1952) was an early critic of the symbolic validity of the composer-hero. Ronald Gray's *The German Tradition in Literature 1871–1945* (Cambridge, 1965) condemned the implications of the ending as 'absurd or horrible'. J. P. Stern takes issue with these arguments in the Inaugural Lecture mentioned above, suggesting 'that on the level of specific events and individual ideas the allegorical parallels are incomplete and intermittent, implying and leaving room for the freedom of the individual from a total determinism'. See also Erich Heller, *The Ironic German, op. cit.*, chapter VIII and 'Faust's Damnation' in *The Artist's Journey into the Interior and other Essays* (London, 1966); Roy Pascal, *The German Novel* (Manchester, 1956), esp. Chapter IX; T. J. Reed, *Thomas Mann, op. cit.*, 'Reckoning'; Erich Kahler, *The Orbit of Thomas Mann* (Princeton, 1969); Gunilla Bergsten, *Thomas Manns 'Doktor Faustus'*:

Untersuchungen zu den Quellen und zur Struktur des Romans (Stockholm, 1963).

Conclusion

1. See Peter Schneider, 'Politische Dichtung. Ihre Grenzen und Möglichkeiten' in Peter Stein (ed.), *Theorie der politischen Dichtung* (München, 1973).

2. Octavia Paz argues that modern (post-symbolist) poetry moves between two poles, the 'magical' and the 'revolutionary'. Both attempt to reconcile the alienated consciousness with the world outside. The 'magical' consists in a desire to return to nature by dissolving the self-consciousness that separates us from it, to lose ourselves in animal innocence and liberate ourselves from history. The 'revolutionary' aspiration demands that the distance between man and nature, word and thing, be abolished through a conquest of the historical world. Quoted in Michael Hamburger, *The Truth of Poetry* (Harmondsworth, 1972), p. 44.

3. Hans Magnus Enzensberger, 'Poesie und Politik' in *Einzelheiten II*, (edition suhrkamp 87, Frankfurt, n.d.). On this point he echoes a Platonic argument, though he stands Plato's political conclusion on its head: 'For the introduction of a new kind of music must be shunned as imperilling the whole state, since styles of music are never disturbed without affecting the most important political institutions.' (*The Republic*, Book IV, §424, translated by Davies and Vaughan.)